CASS LIBRARY OF AFRICAN STUDIES

AFRICANA MODERN LIBRARY
No. 11

General Editor: PROFESSOR E. U. ESSIEN-UDOM
University of Ibadan, Nigeria

GOLD COAST
NATIVE INSTITUTIONS

with

Thoughts upon a Healthy Imperial Policy
for the Gold Coast and Ashanti

BY

J. E. CASELY HAYFORD

 Distributed in the U.S.A. by
Humanities Press, New York

Published by
FRANK CASS AND COMPANY LIMITED
67 Great Russell Street, London WC1

All rights reserved

First edition   1903
New impression   1970

SBN 7146 1754 7

Printed in Great Britain by Clarke, Doble & Brendon Ltd.
Plymouth and London

GOLD COAST NATIVE INSTITUTIONS.

WITH

THOUGHTS UPON A HEALTHY IMPERIAL POLICY FOR THE GOLD COAST AND ASHANTI.

BY

CASELY HAYFORD,

OF THE INNER TEMPLE, ESQUIRE, BARRISTER-AT-LAW, AND OF THE GOLD COAST BAR.

LONDON:
SWEET AND MAXWELL, LIMITED,
3, CHANCERY LANE, W.C.
1903.

DT
511
.H41
cop.2

To

THE *LIVING* INFLUENCE

OF

BEATRICE MADELINE CASELY HAYFORD,

MY LATE WIFE AND DEVOTED FRIEND,

THIS WORK

IS REVERENTLY AND AFFECTIONATELY

INSCRIBED.

TABLE OF CONTENTS.

TABLE OF CASES.

PRELIMINARY.

CHAPTER I.

THE ADMINISTRATIVE PROBLEM.

CHAPTER II.

NATIVE INSTITUTIONS.

1. The Native State—2 (A). The King—2 (B). The King's Paramountcy—3. The Chief—4. The Linguist—5. The Councillors—6. The Headman—7. The People—8. The Company System—9. The Judicial System—10. The Commercial System—11. The Fetish System—12. The Municipal System.

CHAPTER III.

THE CONFLICT OF SYSTEMS.

CHAPTER IV.

THE STATUS OF THE GOLD COAST.

1. The Gold Coast Settlements defined: their Nature and Extent—2. Early Jurisdiction of the King: its Nature and Extent—3. Bearing of Ashanti Affairs upon the British Position on the Gold Coast—4. Bearing of Treaty Relations and Acts of Parliament upon the British Position on the Gold Coast.

CHAPTER V.

LANDMARKS.

1. Early Political Movements, and the Rise and Progress of Journalism—2. The Constitution of the Fanti Confederation—3. The Debate on the Second Reading of the Lands Bill—4. The Concessions Ordinance—5. Native Jurisdiction.

CHAPTER VI.

THE CONFLICT OF SENTIMENTS.

CHAPTER VII.

IMPERIAL GOLD COAST AND ASHANTI.

1. Building the Empire—2. Wrecking the Empire.

APPENDICES.

A.—DECIDED CASES.

1. Oppon v. Ackinie—2. Regina v. Cudjoe Imbrah—3. The Chidda Concession Enquiry—4. The Chidda Certificate of Validity.

B.—COLONY OR PROTECTORATE?

C.—1. THE CONSTITUTION OF THE FANTI CONFEDERATION—2. THE FANTI NATIONAL EDUCATION SCHEME.

D.—OFFICIAL CORRESPONDENCE AND OTHER INFORMATION.

1. Draft of an Order of the Queen in Council—2. Lord Stanley to Lieutenant-Governor Hill—3. The Earl of Carnarvon to Governor Strahan—4. Draft of a Proclamation defining the Nature and Extent of the Jurisdiction of the Queen on the Gold Coast—5. Bond, March 6th, 1844—6. British Charter providing for the Government of Her Majesty's Settlements on the Gold Coast, &c.—7. Palaver held at Government House, Cape Coast, May 10th, 1865.

E.—OTHER MATTER.

1. The Sale of Land at Sekondi—2. List of some principal Native States, with the Names of the Paramount Kings.

TABLE OF CASES.

		PAGE
1.	Homia v. Huma, C. C. Apps.	22
2.	Coffie Yammoah v. Abban Cooma.	33
3.	Opposed Concession Enquiries, Nos. 150 and 343, Axim (Esubankassa and Indumsuasu)	39, 58, 59
4.	Enima v. Pai.	41
5.	Bayaidee v. Mensah	41
6.	The African (West) Exploitation and Development Syndicate, Ltd., v. Sir Alfred Kirby and the Princes River Gold Mines, Ltd.	41, 42, 45, 74
7.	Opposed Concession Enquiries, Nos. 164 and 169, Axim (Impatassi)	49, 50, 58, 59
8.	Appenquah's Case	53
9.	Quamin Dansue v. Tchibu-Darcoon and Cancam	53
10.	Concession Enquiry No. 136, Axim (Essarman)	71
11.	Hima Dicki v. Anansu Mensah	74
12.	Oppon v. Ackinie	94, 208, 273—281
13.	Hutton v. Kutah	202
14.	Bolton v. Madden, L. R. 9 Q. B. 55	205
15.	Regina v. Cudjoe Imbrah	260, 281—288
16.	Concession Enquiry No. 5, Cape Coast (Chidda)	203, 289—310
17.	Le Neve v. Le Neve, White and Tudor's Leading Cases	301
18.	Punchard v. Tomkins, 31 Weekly Reports, 286	301
19.	Yates Bros. and Shattuck v. Garshong.	301

PRELIMINARY.

In the present work I have indicated, or attempted to indicate, the true nature of the problem which Great Britain has to face in her administration of the Gold Coast and her hinterland.

To find out what that problem is, and the way successfully to deal with it, it has been necessary, on the one hand, to examine the aboriginal State System, holding, as I do, that apart from the Natives of the soil any attempt at statesmanlike administration is doomed to failure. On the other hand, I have collected and preserved the most important of the evidence available as to the political relations, past and present, of Great Britain with the Gold Coast. I consider that there can be no greater safeguard to British administration on the Gold Coast than in the free dissemination of the historical facts embodied in this book. Further, I have ventured to suggest a key to the solution of the problem. It is none other than the imperialisation of the Gold Coast and of Ashanti on purely aboriginal lines, leading ultimately to the imperialisation of West Africa.

The propositions in the chapter on Native Institutions have generally been supported by decided cases; and they may be taken, on the whole, as a statement of the law as it exists at present. I have also in this chapter given a sketch of the Native State in Ashanti, as embodying the highest development thereof, since both the Fantis and the Ashantis come from the same stock, and may be regarded as cousins, if not brothers, the difference in character arising merely from their respective local environments.

In the chapter dealing with early British relations with the Gold Coast, and the bearing of Ashanti affairs upon such relations, is embodied a deal of evidence of a highly important character. It forms essentially the Constitutional History of the Gold Coast, and indicates her status.

In the Appendices I have collected a deal of important matter which could not conveniently find room in the body of the work. No earnest student of the Constitutional History of the Gold Coast can afford to pass them by.

The events to which this work relates mostly happened during the reign of Her late Most Gracious Majesty Queen Victoria. Little does the world know how great was her influence in allaying irritation and preserving peace among her dusky subjects and allies on the Gold Coast. Long will be remembered the solicitude which she showed for the good government of this country and the welfare of its people in the dark days of 1898. I take this opportunity, therefore, of recording most respectfully the high regard all Aborigines of the Gold Coast had for her person and character.

It is the desire of the author that the ministers of His Most Gracious Majesty King Edward VII. may have some means of ascertaining the true relations of Great Britain with the Gold Coast, and the nature of the difficulties with which they have to contend; and if this book should be the means of even merely promoting earnest and intelligent inquiry in proper channels for information to guide future conduct, I shall not have laboured in vain.

Now, the sources of information in regard to the Gold Coast are so meagre and, in parts, so unreliable, that the intelligent reader may justifiably enquire how I have come by the facts recorded in this book. I shall satisfy that curiosity; and I do so the more willingly, as I am desirous that the reader should have the opportunity of testing the truths herein stated for himself.

In the fall of 1897, I was requested professionally by the Executive Committee of the Gold Coast Aborigines' Rights Protection Society to prepare a brief for the Western Tribes of the Gold Coast Protectorate, dealing with the new line of legislation then introduced by the Colonial Government, with particular reference to fundamental grounds of objection to the famous "Lands Bill" of 1897.

Early in that year, the public mind of the country had been deeply agitated by reason of the introduction into the Legislative Council of the said Bill, and it was sought to prevent its becoming law by appealing to Her Majesty in Council in the most effective way.

In order to meet the general argument of a claim of right on the part of the Government to legislate away the lands of the Aborigines, I had to examine carefully into the past history of the country, as disclosed, among other materials acknowledged in this work, in tomes of official reports and Government Blue Books, and was in the end able to form a clear, and, I flatter myself, a correct idea—the result of the evidence I had collected—as to the true position of the Gold Coast in her relation to Great Britain.

Some result of my labours was to enable the Executive Committee of the Society to place in the hands of counsel in England, through the Society's solicitors, a clear case for the country, which formed the basis of the petitions to Her Majesty in Council, which were submitted after the same, I believe, had been settled by Mr. Asquith, K.C., M.P. The fate of the "Lands Bill, 1897," is a matter of history. The

Colonial Office yielded to the logic of facts, and the lands of the Aborigines of the Gold Coast were preserved unto them.

It occurred to me, in the course of my critical examination of the issues raised and the evidence necessary to throw light upon them, that ample data existed, if only one would search for them, for a concise statement of the political past and present of the Gold Coast Aborigines, which would be useful in the future, not only to the Aborigines anxious to know the Constitutional History of their country, but also to the official of the Government, seeking for precedents to guide his conduct.

I have endeavoured, therefore, in the present work, to embody the evidence collected by me, which was partly unused in the preparation of the brief; and my object has been to present the facts in the most authentic way in order that the results arrived at may be obvious to the intelligent reader. Nor can a charge of partisanship be levelled at me, since the matters with which the historical parts of this book deal have, by the *imprimatur* of the Colonial Office, passed from the province of controversy to that of history.

It only remains for me to add that the other general propositions of law contained in this work are based upon materials collected by me in the course of over six years' extensive practice at the

Gold Coast Bar, such propositions being generally supportable by decided cases in the Supreme Court.

The following Blue Books have been referred to in the course of this work:—(1) Papers relating to the Gold Coast, 1864 to 1878; (2) Report from the Select Committee on Africa (Western Coast), together with the Proceedings of the Committee, Minutes of Evidence and Appendix, ordered by the House of Commons to be printed 26th June, 1865. With kind permission, reference has also been made to "Fanti Customary Laws," the able work of my learned friend, the Honourable John Mensah Sarbah, and to other works, which will be duly acknowledged in the text.

It is my settled conviction that, unless the administration of the Gold Coast and her hinterland is based upon sound moral principles, it is doomed to failure. It is for this reason that in the last chapter I have ventured to indicate the moral duty of Great Britain to the country and the hinterland.

Now, I know of no more thankless task under the sun than that of criticism. Why a sensible man should criticise at all, it is sometimes difficult to tell.

Surely, it is far more agreeable to take things as they come than to be called a fool by one's friends by assuming the *rôle* of a critic.

Yet, what would become of Government, Politics, and even Religion itself without criticism, fair and fearless?

But as regards criticism on the Gold Coast in public matters, a greater than I has written:—

"English merchants cannot afford to offend the Governor; they may tender for Government contracts, or they may be guilty of some technical violation of the Customs regulations and have to beg for the remission of a penalty. They look on with approval while some more reckless man expresses his and their mind in the press. They may bring their grievances to him to be ventilated, but they carefully abstain from all overt acts of opposition to the powers that be."[1]

If the truth may be told, English merchants on the Gold Coast are by no means singular in a policy of self-preservation.

Personally, I confess, I cannot see any reason why the powers that be should object to fair and open comment upon public matters. There is, on the contrary, good ground for assuming that an enlightened Government would welcome fair and intelligent criticism, however much such criticism may expose administrative weakness.

Be that as it may, no matter what the personal inconvenience to myself may be, I shall be well

[1] Ernest Eiloart, Barrister-at-Law, in "The Land of Death."

satisfied if, by stating the truth and my honest convictions, I am able in some slight degree to promote the successful administration of the Gold Coast and of Ashanti, and to help the cause of the Fatherland!

My acknowledgments are due to Mr. E. Haigh Chalmers, the Editor of *West Africa*, for his courtesy in allowing the reproduction of matter indicated in the Appendix; to the Rev. Attoh Ahuma, formerly Editor of *The Gold Coast Methodist Times*, for kindly giving me leave to use the article, "Colony or Protectorate"; and to the Rev. Dr. Mark Christian Hayford, whose assistance in connection with the correcting of the proof-sheets has been invaluable.

C. H.

THE LIBRARY,
    INNER TEMPLE,
        July, 1903.

GOLD COAST NATIVE INSTITUTIONS.

CHAPTER I.

THE ADMINISTRATIVE PROBLEM.

. . . In dealing with Crown Colonies people at home are apt, on the whole, to take a very narrow and material view indeed, deliberately or unconsciously. And yet these Colonies, even the smaller ones, are countries often as large and as full of people as many a place in Europe which holds a niche of its own in the world's history, and whose movements are watched and recorded by the public press of the world. These latter countries, however small they may be, are deemed important as the homes of a people who are, or have been, factors in the political and social questions of the day. Of imports there may be none beyond those necessary for the civilised wants of a frugal race, and the exports may be equally unnoticeable, because the people are of more importance in the world than the productions they have to dispose of. With the Crown Colonies it is different; they are apt to be written and spoken of as if their productions, actual or potential, were of more importance than the inhabitants; and yet it is a fact that imports and exports, and revenues and debts, may all show an increase, and the condition of the people may not be advanced, or may even have retrograded amidst all this show.

* * * * *

All this is so obvious to those acquainted with these Colonies that it gives rise to a conviction in many minds that the only people fit to judge of internal affairs in any country whatever are the people who inhabit it.—C. S. SALMON, *Ex-Administrator of the Gold Coast, in "The Crown Colonies of Great Britain,"* pp. 1, 2 and 3.

CHAPTER I.

THE ADMINISTRATIVE PROBLEM.

AFRICA, I believe, has been compared somewhere by Dr. Blyden in his writings to the Sphinx of old, which, sitting by the wayside, calmly propounded riddles. Trouble and great confusion to the nation, European or otherwise, which would attempt to read them without her aid. It could only mean disappointment bitterer than Jordan apples.

The analogy holds good with regard to the attempt on the part of Great Britain successfully to administer the Gold Coast and Ashanti without the co-operation of the sons of the soil. Indeed, the very difficulties which beset the path of the British Administrator can be correctly indicated sometimes only by the intelligent ones of the country, and the method, if not the means, of solution must also be with them. I venture here to indicate the problem.

It is desirable, at the outset, to clear our minds of certain impressions which recent writers upon the Gold Coast have sought to create. It has been assiduously inculcated that the only object of Great Britain on the Gold Coast is trade—legitimate trade, if you please. It is then urged that, since trade follows the Flag, and civilisation trade, the Aborigines of the Gold Coast cannot but be benefited by the presence of the British upon their soil. This is true to a certain extent; but let me point out in what way it is not wholly true.

There is a keen pleasure in the sense of possession. *My* land, *my* house, as contradistinguished from *your* land, *your* house, will remain, till the end of time, worthy objects of ambition. As with the individual man, so with the individual nation. That being so, when you come across professions on the part of writers upon the Gold Coast and others that Great Britain is on the Gold Coast for trade and no more, do not take them seriously. You may assent to the proposition, if you please, that her only reasonable ground of occupation is the free expansion of her trade. But that is a different matter. Whether you call them spheres of influence, territories, possessions, protectorates, or colonies, there is hardly a European power which will not fight for their acquisition, even though there is derived from holding them not one farthing's worth of profit, taking the outlay it involves into consideration. I believe Mr. Andrew Carnegie has shown conclusively in an able article[1] how comparatively unprofitable for purposes of trade are some of the colonies and

---

[1] *Nineteenth Century*, May, 1901.

protectorates of Great Britain, let alone the so-called possessions or spheres of influence. There is, in some cases, an insane thirst for territorial acquisition, cost what it may.

To state the proposition broadly, it is simply the primitive instinct of acquisitiveness in man which operates in the case of nations, no matter the extent of their boasted civilisation. Primitive man in primitive society says: "I will have your land, or your hut, if you will give it to me. If not, I will take it. When I have taken it, and you cannot retake it, of course, I will keep it." The civilised nations of the world are to-day like unto primitive man, else international courts of arbitration would more frequently be sitting in one European capital or another, and the weak nations of the earth would have a little peace, if not a little justice.

If you are inclined to deny the foregoing proposition, then I ask you to accept this, that commonly, there are two ethical sanctions to the fact of possession. In the first place, you must come by your possession honestly, and secondly, you must bear manfully its responsibilities; which two sanctions are generally not observed, if recognised at all, by the great nations of the earth.

Since, however, the world is as we know it to be; since the weak must go to the wall, and the fittest survive, irrespective of what is right or wrong, fair or unfair; it is, I confess, but practical philosophy that the weak should side with the strong.

From this point of view, always remember, the Aborigines of the Gold Coast triumph in the wave of imperialism which at present sways the public sentiment of Great Britain. It may overwhelm them, and play havoc with all that is dear to them of law, custom and practice; it may reduce them to the condition of bondsmen and captives in their own fair domains; it may denationalise them and make them a people of no reputation, a by-word and a reproach among men; but, for all these things, they would rather have the ills that they know of than fly to others that they know not of. It is nothing but common sense. What is more, they know what evils there are, are such that they can cope with, and that, truth being on their side, they will triumph in the end.

Now, since we have the British with us, and the object of an enlightened Government should be to promote the healthy national development of the governed by conserving and not destroying the institutions of the people; and since in the past the tendency has been toward disintegration rather than toward conservation—we have the right to say to them: "You have disorganised our institutions, you shall help to reorganise them; you have enriched your homes with the luxury that the

Gold Coast has afforded, you shall help us to rebuild our homes; you have made here princely fortunes, you shall help us to live peaceably in our own vineyards and under our own fig trees"—it is about time, I hold, that the Authorities at Downing Street confined themselves more to external administration, leaving the internal government of the people to develop upon the natural lines of their own institutions. Will the public opinion of Great Britain insist upon this being done, or will it allow the work of spoliation to proceed? This is the problem in its naked form. The people of the Gold Coast observe that for nearly a century you have been trying to mould for them their institutions, and that you have most signally failed. They see in the civilisation you offer much that is fair, but cannot fail to perceive the weak spots and blemishes in the same. They say to you, "We are anxious to take part in the race of nations towards the attainment of higher ideals, if you will only give us a chance to work out our own salvation." But no, you will continue to regard them as innocents, and they, the pigmies, must march with you, the Colossus, whether it is expedient or not. This is not right or fair. It is not even common sense. Therefore, with all earnestness, I humbly urge that henceforth the Aborigines and their Protectors should adjust themselves respectively to their proper spheres of work. Let them do this, and the problem of a century will readily be solved.

But how about this adjustment? you will ask. Permit me to ask you to go to history and to science, and they will teach you what to do. Science will tell you that there can be no healthy growth except from within; and the history of the Gold Coast will disclose to you the facts and circumstances which must guide such internal growth. This has been the stumbling-block all along, this want of adjustment of the proper spheres of work of the parties concerned. It must be removed now. Let us see how.

Truly, the present is a critical moment in the constitutional history of the Gold Coast and her hinterland. He who runs may see that the time has come to determine what policy shall govern the administration of the country by the Colonial Office in the commercial interests of Great Britain and in the practical uplifting of the native tribes in the scale of civilisation.

But unhappy recollections surround the name of the Colonial Office in the mind of the historian. That hoar-headed institution, generally dormant and lethargic, occasionally erratic and irrepressible, if not irresponsible, will have much to answer for in the day when the public intelligence of Great Britain will awaken to the golden opportunities which the

Empire has lost on the Gold Coast and in Ashanti through its blunders.

Let me at once clear this matter, namely, the blunders of the Colonial Office, of all misconceptions. The custom has grown up, within recent years, that the moment the Colonial Office is mentioned the mind of the reader instinctively flies back to the right honourable gentleman who at present presides over that institution. He is at once fixed, rightly or wrongly, with all the blame, past and present, attributable to that office. This is not fair; and I will say this, that the Aborigines of the Gold Coast, in their criticism of the methods of the Colonial Office, disclaim the propriety of attacking any particular Cabinet Minister who, in past, present, or future Administrations, was, is, or will be, Secretary of State for the Colonies.

But, without apportioning blame, one can pretty accurately indicate the line Colonial Office policy has taken under the guiding genius of a particular Colonial Minister. Bear in mind, if you please, that there is a Colonial Office policy, which may be allowed to droop, or pursued to its logical objective, according as the Colonial Minister for the time being is a weak or a strong man. And, remember, the world always admires a strong man who has the courage of his convictions.

If, therefore, you complain of Mr. Chamberlain,

you only complain of the circumstance that the Unionist Government, for once, has done the Colonies the unique honour of placing at the head of their affairs and the direction of their destinies a first-rate man, who has the courage of his convictions, and who presses such convictions home to their logical conclusions. Hence the crisis. Here is a man of nerve, who has schooled himself into the belief that his objective is the right goal. Will he wreck the ship, or will he save it? Men of local experience and knowledge think it looks like ruin; and it becomes necessary to sound the alarm if, haply, the steersman will heed, correct the chart, change the course, and save the ship. For, pray, remember that, whatever the capacity of a Colonial Minister, and with the best of intentions in the world, he cannot be expected to be fully acquainted with local conditions, native peculiarities, and the past constitutional history of the Gold Coast.

Unlike Australia, Canada, and other Colonies of Great Britain rightly so denominated, here, on the Gold Coast, you have to deal with an aboriginal race with distinctive institutions, customs, and laws, which, now and again, European writers may attempt to portray, but which they can never fully interpret to the outside world.

It follows, therefore, that a Colonial Minister has to gather information, as guide for his conduct,

CHAP. I.   THE ADMINISTRATIVE PROBLEM.   11

second-hand. Now, what are the sources of information open to a Colonial Minister? There is principally the Colonial Governor, whose tenure of office is so uncertain, and who, during his administration, be it long, or be it short, is somehow generally surrounded with officials not always the best qualified to inform him accurately concerning the significance and hidden meaning of Native institutions. He, the Colonial Governor, sometimes supplements the erroneous ideas he thus acquires by desultory reading of authors who, in writing, seek not the making of history, but that of their own ephemeral fame. In his despatches he freely makes use of such information; and the Colonial Minister, when pressed for a division in the House of Commons, presses into his service the ill-digested lesson he has learnt from the despatches. Thus, between the Colonial Minister and the local Governor, ignorance at times reigns supreme as to the real merits of a given issue. This adds to the difficulty of the problem under consideration.

What, for example, could have been more pitiable than the excuses put forward by the Colonial Secretary in the "Golden Stool" debate in the House of Commons on the 19th of March, 1901? Speaking of the cause of the rising in Ashanti, the right honourable member for West Birmingham said: "The earlier expedition was so far successful that it was concluded without a single drop of blood having been shed. And when you ask what is the cause of the subsequent disturbance, I have no hesitation in saying that it was the bloodlessness of the previous expedition. The people of Ashanti, in common with every savage tribe, hold it to be a point of honour to fight for their chief, and to fight for their cause. They are ready to accept defeat, but they are not ready to accept the consequences of defeat without being actually defeated."[1] (*Sic.*) Unhappy Ashanti, a nation steeped in grossest barbarism, addicted to human sacrifices, slave-raiding, and the breaking of treaties! You must be thankful for small mercies; for, until the Colonial Secretary spoke, we, your brethren on the Gold Coast, could not believe that you could be guilty of such a thing as a point of honour! But there it is in black and white. Who told Mr. Chamberlain this? Did he read it in books, or in Sir F. M. Hodgson's despatches? I have never seen this in any authentic book on savage tribes, and so it is just possible it was from the despatches.

Or, again, take this bit: " Sir Frederick Hodgson did not ask my permission to go for the golden stool, but, speaking now after the event, I entirely approve of his attempt to secure it. The golden stool is of very great moral and intellectual value (laughter).

[1] *Times* report, March 19th, reproduced in *West Africa*, March 30th, 1901.

It is not loot in the sense the honourable member supposes. It has no great pecuniary value. But in the opinion of the tribe, and according to the custom of the tribe, the possession of the stool gives supremacy. And if, therefore, we should secure this stool, we would be doing more for the peace of Ashanti than, probably, by any armed expedition. Therefore, it was of the greatest importance to get hold of this symbol of sovereignty, if we could possibly do it."[1]

Again, how came the Colonial Secretary by this *ex post facto* explanation? This time I have read somewhere something very similar. Here it is: "The stool appears among the Ashantis and neighbouring peoples to be the emblem of possession, for the expression 'to succeed to the stool' is applied not only to a king on his accession, but also to private persons when they inherit property. Hence a conquered country is not considered to be fully subjugated until the royal stool has passed into the hands of the conqueror. It was for this reason, no doubt, that King Ajiman of Jaman exhibited such eagerness when he spoke to me of his desire to invade Ashanti and recover the Gold Stool, and this is also the probable explanation of the fact that in neither of the British invasions of Ashanti has this stool been allowed to fall into the hands of the invaders."[2]

[1] *Times* report, reproduced in *West Africa*, March 30th, 1901.
[2] Dr. Freeman's "Travels and Life in Ashanti and Jaman," pp. 442—443.

The first point to note in reading these two passages is that, from Dr. Freeman's account of the King of Jaman's eagerness to recover the "gold stool," the said stool must once have been the stool of Jaman, otherwise there could be no need to "recover" it. That being so, the reflection is reasonable that, upon Jaman losing her "gold stool," she did not cease to be a nation, or to possess a stool, "gold," or otherwise, upon which subsequent kings sat, down to the time of Ajiman.

The second point to note is that the Colonial Secretary disclaims having directed Sir Frederick Hodgson to go for the golden stool. It is very unlikely, therefore, that Mr. Chamberlain knew till "after the event" of the great "moral and intellectual value" of the golden stool. But Sir Frederick Hodgson must have known of it, or he would not have, unsolicited, gone in quest of it. I am sure he did not get his information from any of his advisers, for his conduct in this matter has received the severest condemnation alike of officials and the general public of the Gold Coast. It is charitable to assume that the good Governor probably misread Dr. Freeman. Dr. Freeman, like the careful writer that he is, speaks of "appears," "no doubt," "probable explanation." He kept an open mind in the matter. Perhaps later observation and experience might show that, after all, there was no virtue in the "golden stool." But when these tentative propositions pass through the official mill, they come out in a debate in the House of Commons as positive facts.

This sort of thing, or anything like it, is a source of danger, and adds to the difficulty of the problem before us. We want an intelligent and scientific study of Native Institutions, and a right understanding of the nature of the work Great Britain is called upon to do in the Gold Coast and Ashanti, and the limit of her capacity to carry out such work apart from the Aborigines of the country. When once this principle has been fully grasped and an attempt made to work it out, we shall, at last, be on the way to a successful administration of the Gold Coast and Ashanti.

CHAPTER II.

NATIVE INSTITUTIONS.

I had asked him how the more intelligent of the peasantry and workmen regard those constitutional reforms which the educated non-official classes demanded with almost one voice.

"What do you mean by reforms?" he interrupted.

"Western institutions generally—a Parliament, liberty of the press, legal guarantees."

"What on earth have we to do with legal guarantees and Western institutions?" he interrupted, seemingly astonished that any one should ask such a question. "Your mistake is always assuming that Western institutions are a stereotyped model upon which all forms should be based. It is this delusion that is at the bottom of half the wars and predatory aggressions carried on by Europeans against men of other races. If reforms are wanted in Russia, it is not either Western or Eastern reforms, but measures suited for the people, and not other peoples. The assumption that reforms so-called must be constructed upon Western models is a pure product of Western exclusiveness, and is opposed both to Christianity and to common sense."—COUNT TOLSTOY, *Review of Reviews*, May 15th, 1901.

CHAPTER II.

Native Institutions.

1. THE NATIVE STATE.

The Native State, in its highest development, is to be found where a number of considerably important communities combine and own allegiance to one central paramount Authority. Such Authority is the King, properly so called. Thus in Ashanti, before the breaking up of the Court at Kumasi, there were the Manpons, the Juabins, the Kokofus, the Beckwas, the Adansis, and several other large and important communities, owning allegiance to the stool of Kumasi as the paramount stool of all Ashanti. Each of these important communities, when regarded with respect to the entire State, was a sort of *imperium in imperio*—in fact, several distinct native states federated together under the same laws, the same customs, the same faith and worship, the people speaking the same language, and all owning allegiance to a paramount king or president, who represented the sovereignty of the entire Union.

The greater the number of such states in one

great native federal Union, the greater the importance of such Union. Hence the supreme influence which the occupants of the golden stool exerted in the nineteenth century, and the efforts they made, by war or otherwise, to keep the federal States together. This natural process of self-preservation, instinct with high statesmanship, has been, by ill-informed writers, set down for a slave-raiding propensity. You may as well call the war of the North and the South of the United States, or the struggle in the British Isles to preserve the integrity of Great Britain, slave-raiding wars. Having arrived at the zenith of her power about the first quarter of the last century, the central Authority in Ashanti, represented by the occupants of the golden stool, which had its seat at Kumasi, strove steadily to keep the Union together up to the last quarter of the century, when Her Majesty's Government, consciously or unconsciously, set to work to disintegrate the Union. Mr. Fox Bourne seems to think that Great Britain undertook this work consciously, and with a light heart. For he says in a recent pamphlet: "The desire to assert control over natives far away from the seat of government, and for whose conduct the authorities were in no way responsible, had striking exemplification in the treatment of the Ashantis, which, for the time being, culminated in the occupation

THE NATIVE STATE.

of Kumasi in January, 1896. Ever since the Ashanti War of 1873–74, by which the powerful dominion of King Kwofi Kara Kari and his predecessors was broken down, it had been the policy of the British administrators on the Gold Coast to coax away from allegiance to the occupant of the 'golden stool' at Kumasi all its former adherents, and especially those nearest to the coast."[1] This passage is, unfortunately, strikingly in accord with facts. Here we find a civilised Christian Power, the professed Protector of native races, doing unto a people struggling to maintain its national integrity that which she would not be done by. It is as if America should steadily set to work to coax Ireland away from her allegiance to the British Crown. The wrong being clear, will Great Britain make reparation by helping now to restore the integrity of Ashanti, or will she say, it is but a weak, savage nation, and pass by on the other side?

In the Gold Coast proper we have, for example, the native states of Fanti, Ahanta, Insima, Ga, Wassa, and others, having more or less the same laws and customs, and speaking generally the same language, or dialects of the same language.

Each federal State takes rank in the order of its importance in the native States Union, and its composition and constitution is the same as that of the

[1] "Blacks and Whites in West Africa," p. 36.

principal or premier State, which is usually the State of the paramount King.

Next in importance to a federal State is a province of such a State. A province is the district of a Head-Chief. Thus, taking Ahanta as a native State, the district over which Atta, the Head-Chief of Axim, in Ahanta, rules would be a province. A province may be a large or a small one, but every province consists of a number of towns and villages whose principal town or capital is the town of the Head-Chief. The same principles guide the constitution of a province as that of a federal State. Then come the other towns, villages, and hamlets of the province, the government of the smallest hamlet being more or less on the same lines as that of a town.

I may now usefully trace the beginnings of the Native State from the hamlet to its highest development, a union of Native States under one King or President. Let me make use of the facts of a concrete case. In the case of *Homia* v. *Huma*, which went up to appeal, the facts were as follow :[1] A man named Inkertsia, a huntsman, had asked permission to squat near a village called Ankraku for the purpose of hunting elephants, and founded there a hamlet which was called after him Inkertsia Krom, that is, Inkertsia's hamlet. Now, Ankraku, according

[1] *Homia* v. *Huma*, Cape Coast Appeals, November, 1900. *Coram* Griffiths, C.J., and Nicoll, J.

to the evidence, was a village of the district whose chief town was Ayenasi, the district of Ayenasi being in the province of which Attuabu was the capital, which province was the premier province of the State of Appolonia. It was stated that cases arising in Inkertsia Krom, and not disposed of, were first referred to Ankraku, thence to Ayenasi, and thence to Attuabu. Here you have complete the links uniting the lowest to the highest native community.

There is hardly a native of the Gold Coast, where-ever he may roam, who will not tell you, when you ask him, the name of his paramount King. I shall long remember the air of self-satisfaction and pride with which a body of Fanti labourers I once had for clients gave me to understand that they were the subjects of Okra Kwa, King of Mankessim. And well might they, for the King of Mankessim, before the disintegrating influence of the Government upon Native Institutions, was the premier paramount King of the entire Fanti Union.

The authority of the King of the paramount State is no mere shadowy matter. The Head of each province pays him the highest deference. He is the arbiter in cases of dispute between two provinces within his State, and his ruling was always, and even now is, generally obeyed. He never directly interferes in the internal government of a province, but he can bring external pressure to bear in suitable cases.

Thus, with a strong central government, directed by a strong personality, the Native State has all the elements of progress, liberty, and enlightened good government in its composition.[1] How light would have been the task of Great Britain if she had learnt this elementary truth when Governor Maclean sought to press it home by the wise policy which he adopted.[2]

But let me now, in further illustration of the principles which govern the formation of the native state, attempt a sketch of the Native State in Ashanti. It is idle to suppose that the national spirit has been crushed out of existence since the expedition of Sir William Willcocks. You may destroy a nation, but it is another thing to destroy the spirit of nationality.

Without going into the vexed question as to the original habitat of the Ashantis and Fantis, it is enough, for practical purposes, to state that they, in common with other tribes, once lived in the neighbourhood of the Kong Mountains, and were pressed southwards by external conflicts, and, subsequently, by inter-tribal warfare. Nor is any ingenious argument necessary in proof of this. Nature supplies all the argument necessary. They speak the same language with only a difference of accent, such difference being a refinement upon whichever form of speech

---

[1] See Appendix E (2) for a list of the principal Native States with the names of the Paramount Kings, chiefly based upon information given by Mr. Annaman in his book "The Gold Coast Guide."

[2] For Governor Maclean's policy, see pp. 243, 244.

was the original type. It is probable the Ashanti type is the original, since it is reasonable to suppose that the coast tribes were detached from the Ashantis, and not *vice versâ*. There is no tradition showing that the Fantis were ever a distinct and separate people from the Ashantis. On the other hand, there is historical evidence that, at the dawn of European intercourse with the Gold Coast, the Ashanti Union fully recognised the existence and independence of the Fanti Union; and the current of immigration southwards from the north of tribes now dwelling between Ashanti proper and Fanti proper, all of whom have in common the same language with the Ashantis and Fantis, lends weight to this striking fact. At the present moment the guardian to the King Kwamina Enimil, of Eastern Wassaw, in the protectorate, is one Kojo Buaful, an Ashanti man, who is charged with the training of the young and intelligent King. In tracing, then, the Ashanti Native State I am but tracing the Native State of the Gold Coast in its highest development and applicability.

The reader must be prepared to disabuse his mind of all prejudice in this matter. If you once start with the premises that the Ashantis are a barbarous, bloodthirsty people, whose only lot is to be gradually wiped off the face of the earth, you naturally take a different standpoint from the historian, whose object is the ascertainment of truth from facts as they are, and not as they are supposed or wished to be for purposes of argument or invective. Sensible writers are beginning to think that the Ashanti has been greatly misjudged. Let us be fair to him for once, and follow me calmly, if you please, while I attempt to examine his institutions.

The premier State of the Ashanti Union was, before the expedition of Sir Francis Scott, the State of Kumasi, where the King paramount of all Ashanti sat upon the golden stool. In Kumasi proper there were seventy-seven stools, representing seventy-seven public functionaries, as, for example, the Bantuma Chief, or the Chief of the Royal Burial Grove, the Ateni Chief, or the Chief of the Lamplighters.

The King's household was controlled by a number of captains. There were the Captain of the Swordbearers, the Captain of the Stool-bearers, the Captain of the Elephant's Tail-bearers, the Captain of the Court Criers, the Captain of the Royal Butlers, the Captain of the Royal Huntsmen, the Captain of the Royal Farmers, and the Captain of the Royal Physicians.

The local government of Kumasi was in the hands of the Kwaintsirs, a body of men who were the keepers of the golden stool. They formed the Department of War, and the great General Amankwatsia was formerly their Chief. The fact that the Department of War held in its keeping the royal stool illustrates vividly the origin of the kingly office in the Native State, which will be explained later on.

The Akwuamus were the aristocrats of Kumasi, from which body a King was selected to sit upon the stool. Not that the King was selected haphazardly, but the family from which the selection was made belonged, as a matter of course, to the best blood in the land. The Akwuamus were consulted in all internal matters. Assafubuaki was formerly at the head of the Akwuamus. I write in the past tense, not because the Native State idea has been destroyed—for that can never be while there are living any Ashanti women to keep alive in the minds of their sons the ancient traditions of the nation—but because the Native State itself has been disorganised by British aggression and interference.

The King's sons, although they do not succeed to the stool, have a distinct rank in the nobility of Ashanti. They are known by the title of "Sai" or "Osoo." Thus, Sai Bonso, a son of King Kweku Dua, was the father of Osoo Ansah, the father of Prince John Osoo Ansah and Prince Albert Osoo Ansah, whom the Colonial Office, a few years back, attempted to discredit in the eyes of the world, but, happily, without success. The title "Sai" or "Osoo" exactly corresponds to the title "prince." Much ingenuity was used at one time to prove that the Ansahs were not princes.

The Inkidoms or Akempims were the King's bodyguard. Their Chief was Subir.

There were other minor bodies, as the King's scouts, and keepers of the royal arsenals, who properly came under the Department of War.

It is obvious why there should have been a Department of War in the local government of Kumasi, since the premier State of the Union must have been strong in order to command the respect of, and keep together, the several States of the Union.

Every fortieth day the *Adayi* custom fell. It was a time of national festival and general rejoicing. The King on this occasion distributed among his several chiefs, according to their rank, large sums of money. They were not supposed to use the money for their own self-indulgence, but they were expected, like the stewards in the parable, to trade with the money of their master, so that he who had received seven peregwans might add seven peregwans thereto, and render a due account when called upon to do so; though, as a matter of fact, it was seldom that an account was called for. In this way the State naturally encouraged thrift, and in olden days it was quite common to see thousands of Ashantis coming down regularly to the coast and buying goods for their masters, which in turn found their way into the very heart of Africa. Kumasi then was the centre of a state system which directly fostered the trade of the coast and connected it with the trade of the hinterland. It is curious to note that most of the early wars between the Fantis and Ashantis, prior to British advent, were due to the Ashantis wishing to trade directly with the coast, and the Fantis wishing to act as middle-men, and, therefore, sometimes ill-treating the Ashantis when they came down to the coast. There were, besides, actual gifts to different persons in the State by the Sovereign on these State occasions.

Kumasi being the capital of the premier State of the Union, it formed the central convict establishment. Thither, month by month, were brought from the tributary towns persons who had been convicted of different offences and were sentenced to be executed. There was a chief of the executioners, and it was his duty to act as head-gaoler. But the criminals were not executed as soon as they were brought to Kumasi. Some were never killed at all, and, in course of time, were reprieved. On state occasions, when all the people from the tributary provinces would flock to Kumasi, it was usual to execute a large number of those who had been condemned to die. Such public executions would, of course, have a deterrent effect upon the people of the State in general. And when we consider that not only murder but offences like stealing from a farm, rape, swearing an oath upon the King's life, selling a real-born Ashanti, kidnapping, immorality of a certain kind, were all punished with death, it is conceivable the large number of criminals that would be in the convict settlement at a given time. Let the enlightened reader, before moralising on the depravity of the Ashanti, recall to mind the fact that persons were hanged in England for sheep stealing, and witches burnt at Smithfield, not so very long ago. The Ashanti does not boast of being a civilised man in the sense of the European. He is only yet feeling his way out of darkness. But, surely, he is not the savage that he is painted.

Nor is it true that the Ashantis waged war for the sake of securing prisoners to immolate at the fetish customs. They had a better eye to business. They sold the prisoners of war, most of whom, until Europe suddenly turned convert, found their way to European forts and settlements on the coast, and thence to the plantations of the New World. Could not those who participated in the offences of the Ashantis against humanity have had a little patience with them, since they could not help thinking that the work of regeneration in the European was too sudden to be true?

Let me clear this matter of all doubt. The Ashantis waged war among themselves either to preserve the integrity of the Union, or to ward off external attack, where the conflict was with a power outside the Union. The heads of the enemy killed in battle were considered a portion of the trophies of war; but you may be sure that not all the heads that were brought to Kumasi were the heads of executed prisoners. The ghastly practice existed of cutting off the head of a fallen foe, which was brought up to the capital to swell the number of skulls in the public arenas of Kumasi, over which ill-informed writers have waxed eloquent.

Now, I have said that Kumasi was the premier State of the Union. The other principal federal States were Mampon, Beckwa, Insuta, Juabin, Kokofu, Adansi, Akropong Manasu, Asanti Akim, Awiku, and Mamponsu, who were all several thousands strong, with internal governments similar to that of Kumasi, which is, again, simply an elaboration of the Fanti State System, but who were all subject to and owed allegiance to the paramount stool of the Union, namely, the golden stool of Kumasi.

Native Institutions.

2 (a). THE KING.

At the head of the Native State stands prominently the *Ohin* (King), who is the Chief Magistrate and Chief Military Leader of the State. He is first in the councils of the country, and the first Executive Officer. His influence is only measured by the strength of his character. He it is who represents the State in all its dealings with the outside world; and, so long as he keeps within constitutional bounds, he is supreme in his own State.

The term "*Ohin*" is applied to the head of any considerable community of Aborigines, but all kings are not of the same degree. Hence the distinction which is sometimes made of applying the term "king" to the paramount ruler of a state, and the term "chief" to subordinate rulers under the King paramount. Thus the Head of the State of Ahanta is the King Baidoe Bonso, whose capital is Busua, near Dixcove, while the Head of the Province of Axim, in the State of Ahanta, is also known as *Ohin* Atta among all natives. Nor is this in any way strange, since each native community, be it small or be it large, is a composite whole, having its form and method of government the same in all essentials. The entire fabric in either case may be analysed into the same elements.

The term "*Cabboceer*" was at one time employed to mark chiefs of first importance from minor chiefs, but it has fallen into disuse. It will be good policy to revive the title, and generally to enhance the dignity of the native Chiefs, as their influence for good in a well regulated system of government will be simply incalculable.

The office of king is elective. No king, that is to say, is born a king. There are a number of circumstances which may prevent the nearest to the stool from ever sitting thereon. A junior heir to the stool may be selected to sit upon the stool, if a senior heir is a profligate, or otherwise incapable of maintaining the kingly dignity. Nor does a king acquire an indefeasible title to the stool when once he has sat upon it. It is the right of those who placed him thereon to put him off the stool for any just cause. But no other authority can rightly interfere with his position, if his people are satisfied with him. He holds such position for life, and, upon his death, his younger uterine brother, cousin, or eldest nephew, is selected to succeed him. During his life the King often indicates who such successor shall be, and, generally, his wishes are respected.[1]

[1] *Coffie Yammoah* v. *Abban Cooma*, "Fanti Customary Laws," p. 83.
G.C.

In the case of *Hima Diki* v. *Agiman and others*, decided as recently as the 7th of February, 1901, by His Honour Mr. Justice Nicoll, in the Divisional Court at Axim, Hima Diki, the King of Dixcove, had been deposed by the people of Dixcove, and replaced by Anansu Mensah, his uncle. The ex-king sought to recover from the defendants, as representing the Chiefs and Elders of Dixcove, the stool and the paraphernalia thereof. Said His Honour in giving judgment: "I find (1) that the plaintiff was King of Dixcove and duly instooled; (2) that he was deposed according to native custom about a year ago."

Nothing daunted, the ex-King next brought an action to test the legality of his destoolment. It came before the same learned judge on the 21st day of October, 1901, when evidence of a highly important character as to the Customary Law thereto appertaining was given. Kweku Atta, King of Axim, was called as an expert witness.

"*Question:* In the case of a town chief would you tell the procedure in taking him off the stool first when the family complain?

"*Answer:* The family complain to the townspeople, who put me on the stool, and we meet, and I am found to be in the wrong, I ask the townsmen to beg my family. They beg my family to forgive me. I satisfy them. If I do it again a second time, again forgiveness. The third time, you must go, you must have opportunity of defending yourself.

"*Question:* Now when the townspeople complain?

"*Answer:* Your family accompany you to the meeting of the townsmen, and the townsmen put before the family what you have done, and after you have made your defence, and your family found that you are in the wrong the family and yourself beg the town to forgive you. They forgive you, and you pacify them. If you repeat it four times, then, they tell the family they don't want you any more, and that ends it. That is the native law and practice."

The Court in giving judgment in this case said: "I find that the plaintiff was Chief of Dixcove, and that he has never been properly deposed, and is now Chief of Dixcove, sitting on Dixcove stool; and I order the stool to be given up to plaintiff, or some one for him."

The case of Kweku Inkruma, ex-King of Peppissa District, is in point. In April, 1901, the King Kwamina Enimil of Eastern Wassaw being in Axim, the Councillors and Elders of the stool charged Kweku Inkruma with divers acts unbecoming the kingly office, and, the facts being proved to the satisfaction of the King's Court, he was put off the stool.

From the foregoing cases the following principles are clearly deducible as to the destoolment of a king.

Firstly: the authority which, in accordance with the Customary Law, called the King to the stool, is the only authority which can call for his destoolment.

Secondly: To render the destoolment of a king valid, he must have been properly destooled; and before he can be properly destooled, he must have had full opportunity of showing cause why he should not be destooled.

Thirdly: It is not for every petty act of misconduct that a king's destoolment can be called for. He must have been convicted of acts seriously detrimental to the State, or otherwise gravely unbecoming the kingly dignity. The Customary Law herein carries out the spirit of the direction to pardon your brother, if he sins against you seventy times seven.

Fourthly: The proper tribunal, in accordance with the Customary Law, must try the King, and the law is jealous of the procedure on such occasions.

It is obvious why the Customary Law keeps a wakeful eye over the proceedings affecting a king's destoolment. The kingly office is, as we have seen, of the highest importance in the State, and the person of the King is, indeed, sacred. If it were possible for every trifling cause to arraign the first Magistrate of the State before his peers, or to deprive him of power by the merest whim of his people, there would be little or no stability in the State itself. So that, to some extent, it may be said that the people are ever indulgent to their King, and cast around his person a halo of dignity and prerogative which cannot be lightly broken through.

Now, what does it mean when a native king is said to be put on, or off, the stool? What is the idea conveyed by the stool in its concrete sense upon which the King is said to sit? I have said that the King is the First Magistrate of the State, essentially the fountain of justice, and the allusion to him as sitting upon a stool bears out this principle more than anything else. For, you see, in a native state every matter is settled by the "bringing together of stools." When there is a big "palaver" coming on, the people say they are going to bring together stools—*wo ri bobo ingwa*. What actually takes place at the appointed hour of the meeting is, that you observe a number of attendants carrying to the public arena a number of native stools of the pattern generally seen in public pictorial prints after a military expedition in the hinterland of the Gold Coast. Each of these stools represents an ancient house in the community, and the King's stool would, naturally, be the most important and the most ancient stool present. They are now going to hold a "palaver," and the owners of the several stools will be the Councillors, and the occupant of the kingly stool will be the President of the

Council. It is the King's Linguist who will open the proceedings. It is he who will announce to the assembled people the decision of the Council, thus clearly showing the King to be the first Magistrate of the State.

But what is the origin of the native kingly office, and what are the principles which govern the election of a king? The kingly office springs from a period in native history when there was continual warfare among the different tribes inhabiting the country. The choice of a king was most probably determined by the personal valour, intelligence, and capability of the individual to lead the forces of the community in time of war. Such individual was undoubtedly the best man the community could produce. The successful leader would in time of peace be the first man of the community and naturally its head. He would come in for a larger proportion of the lands that had been acquired by the strength of his arms, and when he died, in accordance with the Customary Law, his nephew would succeed him. So also where the community settled in a new country whose virgin forest they cleared, pressed down, probably, after a disastrous war. All the native communities on the Gold Coast proper settled in the country in this way. The old war chiefs came to unoccupied land and settled thereupon, first clearing the virgin forest. The principle of partition would be the same as in the case of settlement after conquest. In all my several years of active practice at the Bar, I have not come across a case where title to land has been based upon a right of conquest. It is perfectly safe to say that it is more the exception than the rule. It is a well-known fact that Kwantabissa, King of Denkira, as late as 1901, claimed the right to lease, and actually did lease, land on the other side of the Offin River from which his ancestors had been driven by the Ashantis in ancient times. The usage of war among the Aborigines would seem to be that after the conclusion of peace the vanquished still retained their lands.[1]

So long as the nephew was a man of character and capacity he would not be disturbed in his leadership of the people, and, gradually, the kingly office would become an institution, and remain in a given family. But still the community would continue to possess the power of veto in case a given member of the royal family was found incapable of performing the kingly functions. They would say, in effect, to the incompetent aspirant, " We appointed your ancestor to the kingly office as a reward for uncommon abilities, and we are prepared to honour his family by seeking election to the kingly office from and by it; but

[1] Opposed Enquiries, Nos. 150 and 343, Axim, July, 1902. *Coram* Nicoll, J.; Williams for Aka Ayima, Hayford for Yamike Kweku and Blay, Ribeiro and Addo for Vanderpuye.

we must object to being ruled by any unfit person. We will, through the family council, decide which member of the family shall govern us, if we are dissatisfied with the family's own selection." And thus we arrive at the principles which govern the election of a king.

Now, how comes it about that there are so many kings in a given native state? The reason is obvious. Before the country was settled in a peaceful way there were many independent chiefs, each a king in his own province. Intertribal strife then began, and, gradually, the weaker kings went to the wall, and the fittest and strongest became the paramount king of a number of provinces in a given state.

Upon the demise of a king, the Councillors meet and demand of the royal family a successor. The royal family then nominates a successor, who may be the uterine brother, the cousin, or nephew of the deceased King. Descent being traced through the female line, such a cousin would be the son of the sister of the deceased King's mother; and such a nephew would be the son of the sister of the late King. The person nominated is next presented to the Councillors, and, upon being approved, is placed by them upon the stool. This is the strict theory of the law; but, as a matter of fact, during the lifetime of the King, there is an heir apparent upon whom both the Councillors and the royal family cast an eye, so that the power of veto is seldom exercised by the Councillors. But that such a power exists is a clearly established principle. In the case of *Enima* v. *Pai*[1] the plaintiff sought, *inter alia*, to be declared the rightful successor to the Assankra Breman or Kwinbontu's stool in the Wassaw district to which the *Werempims*, or Councillors, of Assankra Breman had elected Pai, and upon which they had actually placed him. The plaintiff and the defendant being cousins, the question was as to the right of selection by the *Werempims*, which the Court had no difficulty in upholding.

The King is the Chief Executive Officer of the State, but not the Executive Council of the State. Such a council exists, and any acts done by the King without its concurrence are liable to be set aside.

In the case of *The African (West) Exploitation and Development Syndicate, Ltd.,* v. *Sir Alfred Kirby and the Princes River Gold Mines, Ltd.,*[2] the Head-Chief of Princes had granted a lease of the lands in dispute to the plaintiff company without the concurrence of his Chiefs, and his successor, Kofi Ainibah, had granted the same lands to the defendants with such

---

[1] *Coram* Morgan, J.; Renner and Ribeiro for plaintiff, Sarbah and Hayford for the defendants: Axim Records, April, 1900.
[2] *Coram* Nicoll, J.; Sarbah for plaintiff, Hayford for defendants: Axim Records, July, 1898. Compare the case of *Bayaidee* v. *Mensah*, "Fanti Customary Laws," p. 79.

concurrence. After taking a deal of expert evidence, the Court decided that the subsequent lease should prevail, and judgment was entered for the defendants. Upon appeal[1] the point as to the right of the Councillors to concur in the lease was upheld.

The King is the President of the Legislative Board, but he seldom, if ever, initiates any legislative act. It is the province of the people through their representatives, the Councillors, to introduce legislation, and say what law shall direct their conduct. Hence, when a law is to be promulgated, which is done by the "beating of the gong-gong," the formula, in the mouth of the Linguist is, "The King and his Councillors and Elders say I must inform you——"; then follows the particular command and the words, "PAR HI," an emphatic exclamatory phrase, and a loud rattle of the gong, by way of a general proclamation. Such a law, once thus promulgated, lives from generation to generation, within the memory of the community, and the command is never without its sanction. Any other way of enacting laws for the people is not in accordance with the Customary Law of the people.

The King is the Chief Military Officer of his forces. In time of war, he directs the operations; and if he

---

[1] *Coram* Griffith, C.J., Smith, J., and Richards, J.; Sarbah for appellants, and Hayford for respondents: Axim Appeal Records, February, 1899. See also Sarbah's "Fanti Customary Laws," pp. 75, 96 and 253, where the principle is ably discussed.

is a man of capacity, he has the leading place in the councils of war. There is generally a *Tufu Hin*, or Captain-General, of the forces; but his authority is subordinate to that of the King, and he is, in every essential, an officer of the King.

The King is also, as we have seen, the first Magistrate of his people. In the Native State System the people have not yet arrived at the stage when the King is merely the fountain of justice and appoints officers to dispense it merely in his name. He himself presides over the hearing of all important cases, supported by his principal Chiefs, Councillors, and Linguists. There are other important Chiefs in a state, who are empowered to decide cases; but the courts of such Chiefs are subsidiary to the King's Court, and not independent of it.

Native Institutions.

2 (b). The King's Paramountcy.

To the student of jurisprudence, fresh from the law schools of Great Britain, the doctrines of Paramountcy in the Customary Law must be bewildering and difficult of comprehension. Hence it is that there is so much haziness of view upon the subject. The principles involved are of supreme importance alike to the Administrator and to the occupant of the judicial bench. A mistake here may involve hardships which to the European mind may seem trifling, but which to the Aborigines may affect the very core of Native Institutions.

Now, what are the rights of the King in respect of the lands of a community? The King, *qua* king, does not own all the lands of the State. The limits of his proprietary rights are strictly defined.

There are first of all lands which are the ancestral property of the King. These he can deal with as he pleases, but with the sanction of the members of his family.

Secondly, there are lands attached to the stool

which the King can deal with only with the consent of the Councillors.¹

Thirdly, there are the general lands of the State over which the King exercises paramountcy. It is a sort of sovereign oversight which does not carry with it the ownership of any particular land. It is not even ownership in a general way in respect of which, *per se*, the King can have a *locus standi* in a court of law. To him, indeed, belongs the power of ratifying and confirming what the subject grants, though he may not himself grant that which is given. Such ratification is not even absolutely essential to make the transaction valid, though as being evidence of good faith, such ratification or confirmation is resorted to and is, indeed, becoming quite common in modern grants. Nor is it difficult to see the reason of this. In the early stages of the Native State System, upon the acquisition of lands by conquest or settlement by members of a given community, the lands so acquired or settled upon would be apportioned among those worthy of them in the order of merit. Upon that basis, the Chief Military Commander, who subsequently becomes the King, would have his requisite share, and so would every member of the community down to the lowest ranks of the fighting men. Thus, each man's land would be

[1] *The African (West) Exploitation and Development Syndicate, Ltd., v. Sir Alfred Kirby and the Princes River Gold Mines, Ltd., ante,* pp. 41 and 42.

his own special property and that of his family though the King, as overlord of all, would, undoubtedly, exercise sovereignty over the whole land, every inch of which, however, would have an individual family owning it.

Bearing in mind the foregoing preliminary observations, we may now proceed to discuss the fundamental principles of Paramountcy.

At the outset we must rid our minds of misconceptions. And here we must carefully distinguish between Paramountcy and Ownership. But is Ownership in the Customary Law the same as Ownership in Roman Law? If we examine the incidents thereof in the two systems, we shall find that there is an important difference.

In the time of Justinian, at all events, Roman society had advanced beyond the communistic stage. It was possible even then to speak of the owner's right *to* possess as a right against all the world, a right *in rem*. Indeed, so far had the notion of *exclusive* possession gone, that a person, *sui juris*, could pass his property by will. In the early stage of testamentary disposition, it is true, the appointment of an heir to continue the legal personality of the testator was the primary idea; but later, we come to find the Roman will making the heir a mere trustee for the distribution of property.

But, in the Customary Law, we find no trace of

individual ownership. What the head of a family acquires to-day in his own individual right will, in the next generation, be quite indistinguishable from the general ancestral property of which he was a trustee. Even during his lifetime the person on the stool scarcely makes a difference in his own mind between what he received as family property and what he adds thereto by his exertions. And the law of succession furnishes the best reason for the phenomenon. Both what came to the head of the family and what he has made pass, at his death, to his uterine brother, cousin, or nephew, as the case may be, who being the only possible and legitimate successor to the stool-holder, the latter gladly regards as the trustee in one sense, and one of the beneficiaries in another sense, of *all* after his death.

With this important qualification, namely, that the family in the Customary Law is the unit for the purpose of ownership, we may now proceed to distinguish Ownership from Paramountcy.

The notion is somewhat common that where a chief pays *tribute* to another, the latter is necessarily the paramount Chief of the former. But this is only a loose way of applying the term "paramount." *Tribute* is not only payable to a chief, but to any person holding land in the country, say, as head of a family, by whose leave another person works upon the family lands. It would be absurd to call the licensor in such a case the paramount Chief of the licensee. Take an extreme case, and the absurdity will appear all the clearer. A. has a portion of the family lands allotted her for the purpose of growing ground nuts thereon. A. allows B., her friend, to till a portion of the ground on the understanding that B. will give her one-third share of the ingathering crop. In what possible sense is A. "paramount" to B. ?

It is clear, therefore, that the payment of *abusa*, one-third share, is not the test of Paramountcy: it merely indicates the person having the right *to* possess. Indeed, the custom of the paramount Chief to receive *an occasional contribution*, be it small or be it large, is in respect of *allegiance* due to him by a subordinate chief. Where a paramount chief happens to receive *abusa*, that is, one-third share, of the proceeds of land, then it is by reason of the fact that the right *to* possess is ultimately traceable to his stool. Thus, we have the case where a *person* receives a portion, usually a third, *abusa*, of the proceeds of a sale of land by a licensee of that *person;* and the case where a paramount Chief receives a customary present, the extent of it depending upon circumstances, upon the happening of any event in respect of which the subordinate may suitably mark his allegiance to the superior Chief. The latter may be called the custom of *occasional contribution* to the superior Chief; the former, the right of the owner

THE KING'S PARAMOUNTCY.

or the person having the right *to* possess, to *abusa*, one-third share. Much confusion of ideas would be saved by confining the term "*tribute*" to the case where a licensee is under obligation to make one-third payment to a licensor, and "*allegiance fee*" to the case where a vassal is expected to acknowledge the sovereignty of a paramount chief by the customary present.

In Ashanti, where a stranger kills big game on another's land, the licensee takes to the licensor a portion of the meat, the latter, in turn, taking to the Head-Chief a leg of the animal killed. Again, where a nugget is found in mining, the licensee brings to the licensor a portion of the gold with the nugget, the licensor sending the nugget to the King. In the two cases, the licensor would be the person having the right *to* possess, the Head-Chief or King merely having a claim to the *allegiance* of the licensor. Hence the importance of using "tribute" to denote what is contributed to the licensor, and the phrase "*allegiance fee*" to what the licensee offers to the overlord. *Tribute* would thus be an incident of Ownership, while *allegiance* would be an incident of Paramountcy.

In the *Impatassi* case[1] expert evidence was given

---

[1] Opposed Enquiries, Nos. 164 and 169, Axim. *Coram* Morgan, J.; Renner and Williams for claimants, Hayford for grantors, Ribeiro for opposer: Axim Records, February, 1902.

by Atta, King of Axim. The question was asked: "Was tribute ever instituted in respect of the sovereignty of one stool over the other?"

Answer: "The person on whose land you have settled, although his stool may be small, can claim tribute. Tribute is paid in respect of ownership."

In giving judgment, the learned judge remarked: "Now, from the evidence of the King of Axim, it appears that the right to demand and receive tribute on land is based on ownership, and I am of opinion that on ownership also must be based the right to give or withhold consent to dealings with land. It may possibly be that by custom in some cases a chief can claim tribute from his sub-chiefs in respect of their lands apart from the question of ownership of such land, but in such cases I do not think that his consent would be necessary to render valid dealings with land the right to hold and occupy which was not derived from his family or town stool."

This case went up to the Court of Appeal which sat at Cape Coast in October, 1902,[1] which affirmed the judgment of the Court below, declaring the concessions, the subject of the enquiries, to be invalid on the ground that the consent of the opposer had neither been asked for nor obtained, the right of

---

[1] *Coram* Sir Brandford Griffith, C.J., Smith, J., and Nicoll, J.; Hayford for grantors, Renner and Williams for claimants, Savage for opposer: Cape Coast Appeal Records, October, 1902.

the grantors of the concessions, the subject of the enquiries, to hold and occupy the lands comprised therein being derived through and from the stool on which the opposer was now sitting, and that the opposer's consent was necessary for the valid leasing of the said lands.

On the 6th of October, 1902, counsel for the claimants moved *ex parte* " for leave to appeal from judgment of the Full Court, dated 1st October, 1902, refusing to grant special leave to appeal from the judgment of the Divisional Court of 28th April, 1902, at Axim," and the Full Court, in ruling upon the motion, took opportunity to emphasise the point that in its opinion the judgment of the Court below "is right," and "is supported by the evidence."

The Full Court, therefore, clearly supported the proposition that "the right to demand and receive tribute on land is based on ownership . . . and that on ownership also must be based the right to give or withhold consent to dealings with land."

Having shown that *tribute* pure and simple is really an incident of Ownership in the Customary Law, and that the obligation of a vassal to render *allegiance fee* to his superior lord is erroneously termed *tribute*, it will be interesting now to discuss "*allegiance*," the bond which unites the superior chief, usually a king, to his vassal.

Allegiance, then, is that *personal* relationship

between the occupants of two stools whereby the inferior acknowledges the authority of the superior over him. Such acknowledgment may take the form of military or other service, and occasionally an *allegiance fee*. Such relationship has nothing to do with the lands of the vassal. It may happen that the superior lord is at the same time the licensor of the vassal in respect of his holding, but that will be merely accidental.

That *allegiance* is personal and not territorial is seen from a number of instances in the history of certain communities of the country. Take for example the case of the *Akataki* people, known as the Commendas. Now, it is an historical fact that the people of *Akataki* originally came from *Akatakiwa* in the Inkusukum district, the present Head being the well-known King Essandor. Now, if you trace the etymology of the two words *Akataki* and *Akatakiwa*, you will find that the one is the feminine form of the other. Whether it be that *Akataki*, the masculine form of the word, was chosen by the people of Commenda to indicate their origin, or whether *Akataki*, the brother of *Akatakiwa*, founded the present town of Commenda, matters little; but there can be no doubt about it that the two branches of the *Inkusukum* people have always recognised the same origin, the *Akataki* people owning allegiance to the paramount King,

Essandor. Such relation is personal, and has no territorial significance; but it is, nevertheless, as vital in the conceptions of Native Institutions as *Succession* is to property in the Customary Law.

The case of Apenquah[1] is in point. It came before His Excellency Governor E. B. Andrews in Council at Cape Coast, on the 7th of February, 1861. The main point in the case was whether or not Apenquah, being a subject of the stool of King Chibbo of Assin, could rid himself of his *allegiance* to the stool or transfer his *allegiance* to another stool. Said the Court: "It has been decided long since that Apenquah was not a private slave to any person, but that he was a subject of the stool of Assin Chibboo, and at this day is consequently a subject of Amba Danquah, Regent of Southern Assin, and, according to strict law, he cannot rid himself of the allegiance to the stool.

"The Court has taken into its serious consideration the importance of this case. There are grave questions involved; the most important, and that which in this peculiar country might be practised with the most serious consequences to the well-being and tranquillity of the protectorate, is a proceeding similar to that which the Court is now called upon to decide as to its legality, it being

---

[1] See Sarbah's "Fanti Customary Laws," p. 203; also, *idem*, the case of *Quamin Dansue* v. *Tchibu-Darcoon and Cancan*, p. 130.

whether a man occupying a considerable position, as does Apenquah, can suddenly march off with a number of his prince's lawful subjects, and deliver himself and them to a rival chief.

"The Court is of opinion that Apenquah does not possess the right to leave his sovereign Amba Danquah, with all his people, and place himself under Inkee, and that he has not been able to show any grounds on which he could complain of bad treatment towards him by his sovereign. . . .

"For the future, it is to be distinctly laid down that a headman, captain, or chief shall not be suffered to transfer his allegiance with his followers to the chief or prince of another country. Neither shall he be allowed to domicile in another country as a captain with his followers, though he may not have removed his allegiance to his former prince.

"To act thus shall be held to be treason, the punishment being the loss of all property and degradation of rank within the protectorate, such headman, captain, or chief to be given up with his followers, it being a high crime, the prince harbouring them to be deposed from his stool. But where a headman, captain, or chief is of full age, and wishes to domicile in another country, and is a free man, he shall be permitted to do so, taking with him his one wife and children by that wife; at the same time he shall not transfer his allegiance to the prince of his adopted country as a captain, but retire to live under that prince as a private man, leaving all his possessions, which become forfeited to the sovereign whose country he has quitted."

Our early Administrators and the Judicial Assessors somehow always managed to get to the core of Native Institutions. It may be because they took the precaution not to decide a given point without collecting the opinions of native Councillors, competent to advise upon the point in issue. Thus, it happens that Apenquah's case states the doctrines of *Allegiance* in a form at once intelligible and scientific.

We gather the essential features of *Allegiance*, then, to be :—

1. That it is a personal relationship which has nothing to do with property rights.

2. That a subject holding any public position in a country cannot transfer his *allegiance* at will without forfeiting his rank and "all his possessions to the sovereign whose country he has quitted."

And the doctrines of *Allegiance* have the sanction of sound common sense.

But what happens where the subjects of a native king found a colony in another district with the sanction of such king, as in the case of the *Akatakiwa* colonists settling at *Akataki*, Commenda ? It would follow, as a matter of course, that they would carry with them the protection of their King, and, consequently, they would remain loyal to him and owe him *allegiance*. Here they would pay *tribute* for the land they have settled upon to the owner of that land; while they would repair occasionally to their ancient and mother country with suitable presents to the paramount King, and which we have called " *allegiance fee.*" If the paramount King went to war, he would call for the services of his children over sea or over country. Hence you have the phenomenon in a given war of seeing the people of even a small town dividing themselves under the banners of contesting paramount Kings.

When the reason of things begins to dawn upon one, one is moved to pity the helplessness of present-day Administrators of the country, who are in the dark as to why, for example, Essandor, King of all the *Inkusukums*, should tenaciously cling to the tie of *allegiance* which unites *Akataki* with *Akatakiwa*; or why people in the far west end of the country should wish to preserve their *allegiance* to one paramount King instead of to another.

In further illustration of the principles we are discussing, take the case of the community of Esiama, in the state of Elmina, who, nevertheless, own *allegiance* to the state of Anamaboe. In the *Gold Coast Leader* of September 13, 1902, the Anamaboe

Correspondent, writing on the "stool festival" of King Amonoo V., says: "The arrival of the *Klanamonoos* and other vassals in full force from Amonoo Ekroful, Eshroa, Mpredwi, Fomina, Abonu, and other villages on the evening of the 1st announced the beginning of the festival. . . . Chief Kofi Nyam, of Esiam (Elmina district), whose distance was rather long, arrived in the nick of time with his retinue to offer presents and participate in the ceremony."

Now, note carefully the colonist, Chief Kofi Nyam, of Esiama,[1] coming all the way from the state of Elmina to "offer presents," but not to "pay *tribute*," to his paramount King. If you enquire to whom he pays *tribute*, the answer, of course, is to the person who gave his ancestors leave to settle upon Esiama lands—in other words, the person having the right *to* possess the colonial lands.

Other instances of colonists maintaining allegiance to the paramount stool are found in the *Imperegus* of Abura, who acknowledge the stool of Anamaboe, and the King of Agimaku's vassals in the Akem country.

We may now usefully and satisfactorily address ourselves to the question, whether the paramount King's *consent* is necessary to the validity of a grant of land? If you confine the term "paramount" to

---

[1] The name of the town is Esiama and not Esiam, and the dropping of the final " a " was probably a typographical omission.

its legitimate and appropriate use in the way I have above explained, we can answer the question only in the negative. It is clear that by no stretch of imagination could Amonoo V. claim *tribute*, *qua tribute*, from his vassal at Esiama, the relation between him and his vassal being purely personal and not territorial. And it is equally certain that Amonoo V.'s *consent* would not be necessary before Kofi Nyam could deal with Esiama lands. The only authority whose *consent* is necessary is that of the stool having the right *to* possess Esiama lands, the stool, that is, whose occupant originally allowed the Esiamas to live on Esiama lands. "I am of opinion that on ownership also must be based the rights to give or withhold consent to dealings with land."[1]

In the Esubankassa and Indumsuasu Opposed Enquiries,[2] which raised the important issue of Paramountcy, expert evidence as to *consent* was given. The Court examined Quamina Annobil, the principal Linguist of the King of Lower Wassaw. Said he: "The under chief can sell his land without the head-chief's consent; he only gives him a share of the money." This evidence coming from the Linguist of the King of Lower Wassaw, where almost

[1] Per Morgan, J. *Impatassi* Opposed Enquiry, *ante*, p. 49.
[2] Opposed Enquiries, Nos. 150 and 343. *Coram* Nicoll, J.; Williams for Aka Ayima, Hayford for Yamike Kweku and Blay; Ribeiro and Addo for Vanderpuye: Axim Records, June, 1902.

every chief pays tribute to the King, or, in substitution thereof, has handed to the King a portion of his lands, is remarkable. But it denotes clearly the general rule of which the particular tenure of lands in the Wassaw country is, perhaps, the sole exception.

The Court, in its judgment, found " that the King of Beyin is not the owner of any of these lands. The owners of these lands must, however, report to the King *before* they dispose thereof." The italics are mine. This case also went up to the Court of Appeal,[1] which sat at Cape Coast on the 6th October, 1902, the same Court which decided the *Impatassi* case; and the judgment of the Court below was upheld. Let us now recall the express words of the judgment of the Court below in the *Impatassi*[2] case. They are: " I am of opinion that on ownership also must be based the right to give or withhold consent to dealings with land," from which proposition the Full Court did not dissent. Clearly, the two judgments are in conflict with one another. Assuming that the owner of land only has the right to give or withhold *consent*, why must a person who is not such owner be informed *before* the owner of land disposes

---

[1] Opposed Enquiries, Nos. 150 and 343. *Coram* Sir Brandford Griffith, C.J., Smith, J., and Nicoll, J.; Hayford for appellants, Yamike Kweku and Blay; Renner and Williams for respondent, Aka Ayima: Cape Coast Appeal Records, October, 1902.

[2] *Ante*, p. 49.

thereof ? One can only come to the conclusion that the Full Court failed to draw the distinction between "*tribute*," payable to a landowner, and a customary present, "*allegiance fee*," rendered to a paramount chief *after* the owner, it may be, has disposed of his land, and not necessarily in respect of such disposal. The point is an important one, and it is to be hoped that some day the Appeal Court will patiently hear it argued out, and the full weight of its learning and authority be brought to bear upon a vital point in Native Institutions.

The learned author of " Fanti Customary Laws " has remarked upon this matter thus :—

" Where the concession is made by a subordinate chief, enquiries should be made to find out whether the concurrence of his paramount chief is necessary or no, for whatever lawful grant or permission is so given by a person *de facto* chief with the concurrence of men *de facto* members of the village council or stool, is good and valid according to Customary Law, and the grantee by taking possession of the land and working thereon becomes a tenant of the stool, village council, or family, as the case may be, and not of a specific individual." [1]

Here we find one of the best authorities on the subject making it clear that the " concurrence " of the paramount Chief may or may not be necessary.

As I have before shown, the only possible case in which the paramount Chief's "concurrence" or *consent* will be necessary is where such paramount Chief's stool is the root of the licensee's title, while, at the same time, the licensee owes *allegiance* to the stool of the licensor. If care is taken, as suggested, to use the terms "*tribute*" and "*allegiance fee*" in their proper connections, there need be no confusion of ideas.

Ownership, then, must be carefully distinguished from Paramountcy. The principles involved in the foregoing discussion may be embodied in a few simple rules :—

1. A. gives permission to B. to settle on Daman Land. The permissee becomes a tenant at will, who, so long as he does not claim adversely to the permissor, will be supported by the permissor in his holding. But the moment the permissee sets up adverse title to the land, the permissor's ownership or right *to* possess revives as against the permissee's right *of* possession.

2. While the permission subsists, the permissee would be liable to contribute one-third, *abusa*, of the proceeds of the land to the permissor, whose consent would be absolutely necessary before the permissee could validly deal with the land.

3. A. is B.'s paramount King. B. holds lands, the title to which is not derived from A.'s stool.

A. has only a right to B.'s *allegiance;* and the customary present (which I have called *"allegiance fee"*) which B. brings to A. from time to time is certainly not *tribute* in the sense that A. can exact it as of right. Such personal relation between A. and B. is Paramountcy pure and simple, which has nothing to do with property rights.

4. The paramount King, as such, has no right to exact *tribute,* nor is his *consent* necessary to make a grant valid.

5. *Tribute* is an incident of Ownership, in other words, of the relationship subsisting between landlord and tenant.

6. *Allegiance* is an incident of Paramountcy, indicated sometimes by the rendering of *"allegiance fee."*

Native Institutions.

3. THE CHIEF.

The term "chief" is in the present day used indiscriminately to represent a king, a chief, or even a headman of a village. It is a careless use of the word. The foreigner, unable or lacking the patience to discern between one native authority and another, groups them all under the designation "chief." Let me try to bring order out of chaos.

The Chief properly so called is that important personage next to a king in the Native State. When he is a principal chief of a king, he is properly called a head-chief.

In a township, a province, or a state there may be several chiefs, who will rank among themselves in the order of their importance and influence.

Chieftainships in the country spring from the same circumstances which originate the office of a king. In early times, when the King led his men to battle, the most valiant and intelligent among his men would be selected to carry out his orders, and to lead portions of the army. In times of peace, naturally, the king's lieutenants in the field would be rewarded with portions of the lands of the vanquished, and when internal civil disputes arose the King would, of course, call in the war Chiefs to settle them. Hence it happens that we have the same term *sarfuhim*, primarily meaning a war chief, used as a designation for both a captain or a war chief as well as for a civil chief. The term *brempon* is sometimes used to designate a civil chief, but it is by no means general. It appears to be confined to chiefs who have been so created by reason of their immense wealth or civic services.

A chief is generally a captain of a company. In fact, every male member of the community is liable to military service in time of war, and during peace he has to drill every year with his company. *A fortiori*, a chief is the natural leader of the men of his company. There are cases known, however, where civil chiefs hold no military command in their companies.

It is the duty and privilege of a chief to hold court and decide cases arising in the community according to his influence, character, and importance. Whether his court will be regularly resorted to by the entire community, or only by his immediate dependents and the people of his ward, is purely a question as to what extent his court commands respect in the community. In fact, it may be stated generally and broadly that the judicial function appertains to the head of every ward and every family in the country.

But the Chief whose position entitles him beyond all question or doubt to the full exercise of the judicial function after the King is the *Tufu Hin*, who is next in rank to the King. He holds regular courts, and is entitled to receive court fees and fines, which form to him a source of revenue. There is a right of appeal from a minor chief's court to the court of the *Tufu Hin*, and from the latter to the King's Court, although there may be a direct appeal from the court of a minor chief to the King's Court.

The important position of the *Tufu Hin*, or the Captain-General, in the community arises from the same circumstances as I have described in the case of a chief. Being the King's right-hand man in time of war, it is only natural he should hold rank next after the King when the community has settled down to peaceful pursuits.

The *Tufu Hin* is at the head of the Military System of the community. He it is who regulates the affairs of the seven companies of the community. He is present at their annual general drill to inspect the men, and to satisfy himself how far the Head-Captains of the several companies have done their work during the year. In time of war he leads the van of the army, the King in person bringing up the rear. He is, in brief, the King's principal military Councillor and executive officer.

The *Tufu Hin* is, *ex officio*, also the principal civil Councillor of the King. All the Chiefs of the community have a right to sit in the King's Council.

The same order of chiefs we shall find in a community whose head is a king or a head-chief. It is only a matter of degree as to the importance of the respective chiefs of the two communities.

Where the paramount King of a state summons the Head-Chiefs of provinces and chiefs of minor communities to attend a State Council, it is the privilege of the Councillors of the several communities composing the State, according to their rank and importance, to accompany their several Heads to the capital and to join in the "palaver," or discussion, that will take place, the King in person presiding over the deliberations, supported by his own Councillors and principal Linguists. This is the full Parliament of the people, who are thus fully and duly represented in every way from the highest to the lowest. The commands which go forth from this assembly are binding upon every individual family of the entire State, from the most important province to the most insignificant hamlet, and the sanction operates equally upon all.

In time of war, the Chiefs share in the deliberations of the King as to the means of defence or offence as the case may be, and the terms of peace are discussed with them before being submitted to the enemy.

To put it generally, the Chief is the right-hand man of the King. By the oath of allegiance which he swears to the King upon his enstoolment he undertakes to be always loyal to the King, to attend to the latter's summons by night or by day, *ana fo-o, awia-o,* as the native expression runs; and, supported by a religious sanction, it is remarkable how faithful he is to the King, and how harmoniously the Native State System works together in its different parts.

The succession to a chief's stool is regulated by the same principles which govern the succession to a king's stool, and the like statement is true in the case of his destoolment.

Native Institutions.

4. THE LINGUIST.

The Linguist is a most important personage in the Native State. He is in some cases more influential than the Chief. But he must not be taken literally. He is not a person skilled in the tongues of men; he generally speaks but one language. He was called a linguist first by a half-educated native interpreter, tasked to explain his position to the white man, and as "linguist" he has been known ever since in the language of law and politics on the Gold Coast. We might correct the term and substitute "spokesman" for it, but it will be going dead against all precedent, so I shall content myself with the explanation that the so-called "linguist" is the spokesman of his lord and master. But he is more than a spokesman. He is by no means a mere figurehead: he is one of the main props in the Native State System. Both the King and the Head-chief have their Linguists, and so have the *Tufu Hin* and even subordinate Chiefs. He is a sort of confidential officer, who is always about the person of the King or Chief, and is his mouthpiece in every public function, as well as in judicial proceedings. He is, generally speaking, an intelligent, bright, and witty individual, skilled in the use of language, smoothing down an angry word of his master, or putting a keen edge to a retort, when the occasion demands it. If he is a right down capable man, he often attains to a position of great influence in the community.

The Linguist's place is not filled by his successor to the ancestral stool. It is filled by his son if he follows in the steps of his father, and has his capabilities. The son, living in his father's house, and often carrying his stool to the public meetings and to the King's Court, would, if he were intelligent, pick up the knowledge which would qualify him to become a linguist after his father.

The Linguist is generally the repository, or, if you like, a walking encyclopædia, of all traditional knowledge and information in connection with the stool under which he serves. He is supposed to be acquainted with the etiquette of the Court, and, in case of a new succession, it will be his duty to instruct the new monarch in the functions of the Crown. As a reward for valuable services, he may occasionally be promoted to the King's Council, in which capacity he will practically be the ruling voice, warranted by his great experience.

The Linguist, as we have seen, comes by his knowledge from his very early acquaintance with Court functions, history, and tradition, continuing his education or training throughout the greater portion of his life, and often extending the field of his enquiries till his knowledge embraces the political history of the whole State, as well as of sister States. When he speaks, therefore, he does so as one having authority, and is listened to with the greatest respect.

When the Linguist rises up to speak in public, he leans upon the King's gold cane, or a subordinate linguist holds it in front of him. He is going to make a speech now, and it is sure to be a happy effort. It will sparkle with wit and humour. He will make use freely of parables to illustrate points in his speech. He will indulge in epigrams, and all the while he will seem not to possess any nerves—so cool, so collected, so self-complacent! He comes of a stock used to public speaking and public functions.

The art of "linguistic" oratory is at its best in Ashanti, where, coupled with acuteness of a high order, it makes the members of the linguistic body about the most enlightened men of the kingdom. Boatsin, the Linguist of the King of Ashanti, being once pressed with questions about the indemnity in a "palaver" between the Governor and some Ashanti ambassadors, calmly said : "*Se yeri bo inkoro, na se yansa na yeri dzi kaä asem dzia, inke ma ka bi.*

Na iyi dië waba itumi asem;" meaning, "If this were a regular 'palaver,' and we were discussing matters with wisdom, I could hold my own. But this is a matter of might."

Moreover, the Linguist often represents his master in matters where he cannot be present. Now and again the rule of best evidence is relaxed, and a linguist is allowed to give evidence on behalf of his master where the former has been sent down to represent the latter in an enquiry before the Court. This is quite correct. For in strict customary practice the King or Chief is not supposed in public functions to speak save through his Linguist.

In Enquiry number 136 (Essarman),[1] Kwamina Annobil, sworn, stated: "I am Linguist to King Enimil of Wassaw. The King is a minor and his guardian is Chief Buaful, and as such guardian he sent me and the other Linguists to this Court." The distinguished Linguist then proceeded to give expert evidence.

In the days of the Judicial Assessors, when Sir David Chalmers of honoured memory was Chief Magistrate of the Gold Coast, the Kings and Chiefs, when required to assist the Court with points in the Customary Law, sat on the Bench with the Magistrate, and the latter lost none of his dignity thereby.

[1] Axim Concession Records: *Coram* Nicoll, J.; October 30th, 1901.

There will be no harm in going back to the old practice, particularly now that the stools of the Gold Coast are gradually being filled by men with English education. It will inspire yet greater confidence in the hearts of native litigants in purely native cases.

Native Institutions.

5. THE COUNCILLORS.

The Councillors in a native community are those intelligent men who, by reason of their experience in matters political and judicial, are selected by the Head of the community to assist him with their counsel in the affairs of the community.

The Chiefs of the community are, *ex officio*, members of the Council; and the King may include such other men, being captains, headmen, or otherwise, who by general consent are competent to help in the public deliberations of the community.

The Councillor holds his office for life. So long as he behaves himself, it is not customary to remove him. When he dies, in the case of an *ex officio* member, his heir, if of mature age and experience, succeeds him. If not, the infant's guardian takes his place in the Council until he becomes competent to act for himself. Where the Councillor has been selected by the King with the concurrence of the other Councillors, the office does not go from uncle to nephew, or from father to son, though it is not unusual, as a matter of courtesy, if the nephew or son is a man of intelligence and experience, to appoint him to take the place of the deceased Councillor.

The Council, when duly constituted, is the ruling voice in all matters political as well as judicial in the community. The head of the community can do no legal act affecting the interests of the community without the knowledge, approval, and concurrence of the Councillors.[1] They represent the sovereignty of the people, the King being their Head and the embodiment of the sovereign idea. As such, they pay him every homage and respect, but he must in turn respect their time-honoured laws, customs, traditions, and sentiments. If he goes contrary to any of their well-cherished ideas of proper government, they can call him to account, and, in serious cases, may in due course demand his deposition. But the Councillors cannot exercise their right capriciously. Every step they take must be legalised by tradition and custom.[2] As a matter of fact, it is very rare that the Councillors of a community have occasion to resort to extreme measures with the Head thereof. For the person of their King is as sacred to them as the person of the High Priest of the community.

[1] *The African (West) Exploitation and Development Syndicate, Ltd.*, v. *Sir Alfred Kirby and others.* *Coram* Nicoll, J.; Sarbah for plaintiffs, Hayford for defendants: Axim Reports, June, 1898.

[2] *Hima Dicki* v. *Anansu Mensah:* Axim Reports, October, 1901.

The Councillors are entitled to a portion of the public revenues of the community. What comes to them they again subdivide among subordinate head-men of their wards, and they in turn among their dependents, until it becomes true to say that every male adult member of each ward has at least "drunk" his portion of the distribution. It is communism of a very high type. Is it to be wondered at that the average Native is so contented and satisfied with his surroundings? The careless foreign critic puts down the nonchalance of the Native to ingrained laziness. Whenever I come across such critics I smile at their simplicity. As a matter of fact, the "lazy Fanti" is capable of putting forth effort amidst his own surroundings which men of no other race on earth can. Who, in truth, have been the pioneers and developers of the mahogany, gold, and rubber industries of the Gold Coast but the "lazy Fanti"? Moreover, I make bold to say that the future work of the country will be done by him, but not in the foreign critic's way.

Native Institutions.

6. The Headman.

The Headman, as his name implies, is the Head of a village community, a ward in a township, or of a family. His position is important, inasmuch as he has directly to deal with the composite elements of the general bulk of the people.

It is the duty of the Head of a family to bring up the members thereof in the way they should go; and by "family" you must understand the entire lineal descendants of a head *materfamilias*, if I may coin a convenient phrase. It is expected of him by the State to bring up his charge in the knowledge of matters political and traditional. It is his work to train up his wards in the ways of loyalty and obedience to the powers that be. He is held responsible for the freaks of recalcitrant members of his family, and he is looked to to keep them within bounds, and to insist upon conformity on their part with the customs, laws, and traditional observances of the community. In early times he could send off to exile by sale a troublesome relative who would not observe the laws of the community.

It is a difficult task that he is set to, but in this matter he has all-powerful helpers in the female members of the family, who will be either the aunts, or the sisters, or the cousins, or the nieces of the Headman; and as their interests are identical with his in every particular, the good women spontaneously train up their children to implicit obedience to the Headman, whose rule in the family thus becomes a simple and an easy matter. "The hand that rocks the cradle rules the world." What a power for good in the Native State System would the mothers of the Gold Coast and Ashanti become by judicious training upon native lines!

The Headman is *par excellence* the judge of his family or ward. Not only is he called upon to settle domestic squabbles, but frequently he sits as judge over more serious matters arising between one member of the ward and another; and where he is a man of ability and influence, men from other wards bring him their disputes to settle. When he so settles disputes, he is entitled to a hearing fee, which, however, is not so much as would be payable in the regular Court of the King or the Chief.

The Headman is naturally an important member of his "company," and often is a captain thereof. When he combines the two offices of Headman and Captain, he renders to the community a very important service. For, in times of war, where the members of the ward would not serve cordially under a stranger, they would in all cases face any danger with their own kinsman as their leader.

The Headman is always succeeded by his uterine brother, cousin, or nephew—the line of succession, that is to say, following the Customary Law.

Native Institutions.

7. THE PEOPLE.

We now come to the general bulk of the people whose system, representatives, and officers of state I have discussed in the foregoing parts of this chapter. They are, generally speaking, intelligent, and take great interest in all political movements around them. This is not to be wondered at since every Gold Coast and Ashanti mother takes a pride in educating her sons in the traditional history of the country. If the son is intelligent, he will have graphically portrayed to him in a way that a native mother only can the causes of the political situation of the day, and he will retain every scrap of information thus imparted to his dying day—such wonderful memory the average native has. I have often been surprised at the accuracy with which a Gold Coast illiterate witness has described in Court his genealogical line from the remote *materfamilias* down to himself. When he has exhausted the list and his counsel can breathe more freely, to the question, "Who told you your family history?" the answer is often returned, "My grandmother told me," the probability being that he first learnt the story at his mother's knees.

And they are a people with no mean history. Driven southwards by their more powerful brothers, the Ashantis, they have shown, in the struggle for existence, some of the finest traits of manly character. Cautious, slow, and diplomatic, the Gold Coast man is sometimes by the ignorant foreigner labelled "stupid," but when this stupid piece of human mechanism is examined with a calm and impartial judgment, it is found to possess those high qualities which make it easily, in the race for existence amidst its own environment, the survival of the fittest.

Moreover, they are conscious of their destiny, and they are working steadily towards its attainment. Where so-called stronger and more intelligent races have gone under under British rule or protection, losing all they hold dear of liberty and political rights, these people have from the first held tenaciously to their ancient rights, political and otherwise, with the force of a logic which no decent British Cabinet can withstand; and, to-day, their position is unique in the history of British Dependencies and of political conceptions, as far as they relate to so-called subject races. And yet certain wiseacres dub them "stupid," and find no epithet strong enough to express their contempt of this coming people of the African continent.

And they are a progressive people, but they add a grain of salt to such progressive tendencies which they affect in the way of a sort of natural conservatism. It is not quite thirty years since a High School was opened at Cape Coast, which did not go on regularly working for more than eight years. With such meagre advantages the sons of the soil have since competed successfully for the highest honours in arts, law, medicine, and divinity. In every industry and in the practice of every profession they are to the fore, and if they only had a Government which went to work on scientific lines, what could not these people do? Whatever the Gold Coast man becomes in the struggle for existence, whatever position he attains, he generally remains a Gold Coast man who loves his country dearly. He may adopt European culture, European tastes, European comforts and amenities; but, take him for all in all, he remains at heart a Gold Coast man, ready to serve his country at any moment with all the resourcefulness, tact, and practical common sense of his nature.

Before the "Emancipation Ordinance" of 1874, the people of the Gold Coast might be roughly divided into two classes, freemen and slaves or pawns.

The freeman, or *dihi*, is he whose ancestors were

Aborigines of the country, and who can trace the line of such ancestors up to a remote *materfamilias*. He is a free man in every sense of the word. He is eligible for any important office in the body politic, and he can always hold up his head among his fellows, however poor his condition. So dearly does the freeman prize his condition that, if by any act of folly on your part you call him a slave, he will bring you before a native tribunal, prove that he is no slave, and get you mulcted in heavy damages. The freemen formed the bulk of the people.

There were next the class of people known as slaves. But Gold Coast slavery was neither the slavery of ancient Rome, nor that of Afro-American history. The Gold Coast master was always humane and considerate. He actually went so far as to consider the slave a member of his family, and to adopt him as such. When his line of descent failed, he promptly named the slave his heir. There is no form of slavery, ancient or modern, to compare with what Gold Coast slavery was. But, for all that, the dividing line between the two classes of people was always clearly defined. The slave never forgot, however highly he might rise in favour with his master, that he was a slave. Hence arose the saying : " *Akwa onyi ni wura ba rigura, na nakwa owo ni tsirim* ; " meaning, " When a slave is playing with his master's son, he remembers his condition of being a slave." It is remarkable, even in post-emancipation days, with educational and civilising influences all around in the country, how true and loyal the descendants of slaves remain to the ancient houses which afforded their progenitors in times past food, shelter, and protection. It speaks volumes for the humanity of Gold Coast masters in the days that are gone.

The system of pawns was a form of servitude practised among persons of the same community when they were sore pressed and wanted aid. The uncle pledged his nephew, or his niece, for a sum of money, with a proviso for redemption upon the first opportunity. He invariably took steps to redeem his kith and kin at the earliest moment, an everlasting disgrace becoming attached to the family if he, or any member thereof, did not perform this sacred duty.

People generally pawned their relatives with persons they knew well, and who, they felt sure, would be kind and considerate to the pawns. In some cases it took the form of a training for the boy or girl, and instances are known where pawns have, after redemption, elected to remain with their guardians.

In an age when no member of the community could read or write, it was found convenient by the system of pawns to register and evidence a loan. In the hands of the pawnee, the pawn served as a charge upon the loan advanced. Thus the system originated, not in a barbarous spirit of enslaving people of the same community, but as a guarantee of good faith to return a *quid pro quo* for help rendered in the hour of need.

Native Institutions.

8. THE COMPANY SYSTEM.

We have seen that every adult member of the community belongs to a ward, and that each ward constitutes a company, with its captains and subordinate military officers. The Captain-General of all the companies, usually seven in number, is the *Tufu Hin*. It is his duty to supervise the military training of the different Companies, and he is present once a year at the general review, when all the Companies turn out with their flags and banners and full accoutrements.

The annual review takes place about the time of the yam festival, known as *Ahuba* in the Fanti States, and as *Kuntum* in the Wassaw and Ahanta countries. *Ahuba Kakraba*, or Small *Ahuba*, takes place about May of each year. The crops are not yet gathered in; they are even now maturing. So this is not the yam festival proper. What is it, then? It is a season of mourning—a time when the deeply religious native mind remembers the dead, and mourns them accordingly. At four in the morning of the day *Ahuba Kakraba* falls, you would hear a general wailing all over the town, or village, as if a great calamity had suddenly overtaken the community. The whole State is similarly in mourning. Here and there, in some ancient ruins, you would see women weeping as if their hearts would break, and the menfolk offering libations to the spirits of the departed. It is a solemn act of faith in the unseen world around us, which, renewed every year, and from one generation unto another, tends to deepen the highly religious sense of the Aborigines.

Nine weeks after *Ahuba Kakraba* comes the festival known as the "Stool Celebration." The King is now about to remember his dead, in the same way that his subjects had done nine weeks previously. But that is only a part of the ceremonial. He is about to inaugurate at the same time the harvest rejoicings, for the crops are nearly matured by this time, and the king will taste of the first fruits of the earth. For the purpose of this ceremonial, he has caused to be gathered into his capital all his vassals from the four corners of the State, who have all arrived in fine style, with their big drums, big silk umbrellas, and sweet-sounding horns, the several Head-Chiefs riding in their palanquins, and all assuming great pomp, with the women in holiday attire, for this great festival. Each Head-Chief has brought the picked men of his Companies, who will range themselves in their respective regiments at the capital. The *Tuafus* of each province will have joined the *Tuafus* of the capital, and the *Inkidoms* will have joined the *Inkidoms*, and all under the orders of the King's *Tufu Hin*, before the great ceremonial takes place. These regiments will take an important part in the ceremonial that is about to take place. And wherefore has the King gathered all his vassals together on this special occasion ? It is but to receive the allegiance of all, from the least even unto the greatest.

But let us now come to the actual functions of the day, in the course of which we shall perceive clearly the working of the Company System. The King, if he has any regard for his memory, will have caused to be manufactured for him a stool by which to mark his reign. This is not *the* stool upon which he sits. It is only a symbol that he has come to the stool of his ancestors, the great Stool of the State. The first function of the day is a religious one. There will be a procession of all the small stools of the State, followed by the great Stool, and the King, in semi-state, will mount his palanquin, with the horn-blowers, sword-bearers, and other functionaries after him. His praises, and the praises and glory of his ancient house, will be proclaimed by the minstrels, and slowly the procession will wend its way in a particular direction, first through the town and then out of it. Whither is it bound? you will begin to wonder. Follow it, if you please, and you will soon know. First through the plantain farms of the capital; then through the yam-fields, whose vines are fast shedding off the leaves which crowned them with virgin glory, a sign that Nature's work for man is nearly done; then an abrupt turn, which leads first up a hill, and then down dale, till gradually you come to where the primeval forests unite their myriad foliage in one everlasting shade, away from the warm embraces of the mid-day sun. Here the procession suddenly halts, the music ceases, and the King dismounts. The fact is, the people have arrived at the sacred stream of the capital. Its clear, pellucid water, through which you can discern the white, clean sand, is very tempting, and you would fain quench your thirst at this nectar of the gods, but that the ceremony which immediately follows the halt is one that is awe-inspiring. This stream is probably the first from which the hero-warriors of the ancient royal house drank, when they settled in the neighbourhood, and which has been made sacred since the little community grew and expanded into a state. The Priest now proceeds to offer up a sacrifice, sprinkling the royal stools with the blood of the slain. Next follows an act of purification, which consists in sprinkling the stools with the sacred water of the stream, the Priest the while going through the necessary incantations. The procession then re-files, and returns to the capital.

And now begins the festive part of the functions of this unique anniversary. After a short interval of rest, the King, in full state, takes his seat at the public open square of the capital, surrounded by the court functionaries, the big horns and drums playing the while. The several Head-Chiefs and minor Chiefs from the provinces and districts have also assembled, and the moment of rejoicing has arrived. The women, adorned in rich silks and gold ornaments, are dancing before the King, and palm wine flows like water. It is a season that comes once a year, and all are invited to help themselves freely to the good things which the King has provided.

Meanwhile the different regiments, under their several Head-Captains, and all commanded by the Captain-General, are preparing to go through their manœuvres. To avoid disputes, the several regiments parade through the town one after the other, pouring forth thunderous volleys from their long flint Dane guns. After the parade each regiment presents to the King its flags and emblems, new and old, as an act of homage, which the King returns with suitable words. The several Head-Chiefs next renew their allegiance to the King; and, after more dancing and popular rejoicing, the King retires to his "compound," where his vassals subsequently take leave of him, each vassal receiving a suitable present. The King has now sacrificed to his Stool—*Ohin watu nay-gwa du*—all his people having turned out in their best to pay their homage, and all hearts having warmed to show attachment to the ancient royal house of the State. The corresponding function in Ashanti is the *Apafram* festival, when all the provincial Kings and Head-Chiefs, such as the King of Mampon, the King of Juabin, the King of Kokofu, and other Kings, met at Kumassi to pay their homage to the King paramount of all Ashanti. Three weeks pass, and we come to the time for *Ahuba Kesi*, or *Great Ahuba*, the real harvest festival of the year, which is celebrated separately by each province.

It occasionally happened that at the annual turn-out of the regiments, one regiment tried to outshine the other in smartness and skilful manœuvring, and war songs in praise of past exploits were indulged in. This at times led to friction between one regiment and another, ending in a free fight. Deplorable as these conflicts were before the display was regulated by ordinance and practically put an end to, the annual military review was a means of familiarising the young men with the use of firearms and preparing them for national defence in time of war. It was, moreover, an important adjunct to an imposing ceremonial. It ought to be possible to allow the annual displays under suitable control and regulations. In former times every male adult of the community understood fully the use of a gun, and made a point of possessing one with the first money he earned, or could coax from his uncle or father. Such are present governmental restrictions that hardly ten per cent. of the young men of the country either possess, or can use, a gun ; and as for powder and shot it is extremely difficult for the Natives to obtain any even for ordinary sport.

In time of war the King and Head-Chiefs supplied the Companies with powder and shot. When they marched to battle the *Tufu Hin* led the van and the King the rear-guard. The King, *Tufu Hin*, Head-Captains, and principal Chiefs formed themselves into a council of war; and the King held supreme command throughout the struggle, though the *Tufu Hin* would practically be the Commander-in-Chief.

The flags of the Company are of immense importance to the Company, whose members guard them as a sacred trust. They generally have worked in them emblems with symbolical meanings. There is a guard of honour attached to each company, whose duty is to guard the flag. They are known as *Assikamba*, being the picked men of the Company.

The women of the wards form a sort of commissariat department to the Company. They may be seen at the front in time of active war, carrying refreshments to their husbands, brothers, fathers, or uncles. They are full of the praises of their Company, and to hear them chant their beautiful war-songs is to nerve one for the severest struggle. It is moreover the privilege of the women of the wards to propitiate the gods, and ask for blessing upon the arms of their country. They do this at home while the Priests busy themselves at the front, attending to the wounded among other things. The women-folk may be seen in the interval between one supply of victuals to the men in the field and the getting ready of the next, bedaubed with white clay and dressed in white calico, singing solemn dirges through the streets of the town. So fervent is their belief in spiritual forces influencing mundane affairs.

The military spirit is not dead in the people. It deserves to be encouraged on scientific lines as an element of strength in Gold Coast manhood. It is absurd to practically destroy martial spirit in a people, and then turn round and call them cowards in a given emergency.

It is an historical fact worth placing on record that the people of the Gold Coast steadily held their own against Ashanti incursions, until by diplomatic weakness and mistakes the British Government forced inglorious war upon the people in the first quarter of the nineteenth century.

Native Institutions.

9. THE JUDICIAL SYSTEM.

The King is the Chief Magistrate of the community, and, as I have shown, there are minor courts exercising concurrent, but not co-ordinate, jurisdiction with the King's Court.

You have first the Courts of Headmen, then Chiefs' Courts, and, finally, the King's Court, which is both a court of first instance and a court of appeal. In suitable cases, the King's Court can require a matter before a minor court to be brought up before it for adjudication.

At a "palaver," which is the word for a suit before the Court, the King sits with his Councillors; and the Court is an open one, which any member of the community may attend. There is no secrecy about the proceedings.

The complainant states his case as fully as he can, and he is given a patient hearing. In the course of his statement questions are freely asked him by the Councillors, and doubtful points elucidated. The same process is gone through with the defendant, and with the witnesses called by either party. The Council then retires to deliberate upon the facts, and its verdict is given by the King's Linguist, leaning over the cane of state, or the same being held before him by a sub-linguist, who cries out "*Wontsey, wontsey,*" meaning, "Hear, hear," while the Linguist proceeds with his delivery.

Where there is a strong conflict of evidence, and the Court is unable to arrive at a decision, the ordeal is resorted to, which consists of drinking a large quantity of a herbal preparation known as *edum*. If the party drinking returns the stuff, he is declared free, or not guilty. If he retains the *edum*, he is found guilty. In some parts of West Africa the suspected person, in criminal matters, is made to chew a handful of rice. If he is unable to do so, he is declared guilty. I have heard this explained on physiological grounds as being highly scientific, and possibly there may be some physiological reason why a guilty person attempts in vain to return the *edum*.

The Gold Coast Ordinances recognise the jurisdiction of the Kings and Chiefs of the country in matters judicial, such jurisdiction being regulated by Ordinance No. 5, of 1883, and sanctioned by the opinion of the Full Court,[1] consisting of Mr. Justice Macleod, C.J., Mr. Justice Smallman Smith, J., and Mr. Justice Francis Smith, J.—an abler appellate trio the most critical mind could not desire.

[1] *Oppon* v. *Ackinie*: Cape Coast Appeals, October 24th, 1887; reported in Sarbah's "Fanti Customary Laws," pp. 207—212.

Native Institutions.

10. THE COMMERCIAL SYSTEM.

In the olden times a most active trade was carried on between this country and the hinterland through Ashanti. There were merchant princes in those days, when such men as the Hon. Samuel Collins Brew, the Hon. George Blankson, the Hon. James Bannerman, Samuel Ferguson, Esq., the Smiths, the Hansens, and others flourished. Those were grand times. The run of Europeans who came out to the Gold Coast were quite a superior class of men. They mixed freely with the intelligent sons of the soil, and helped to lay the foundations of a new civilisation.

The King of Ashanti knew most of these merchant princes, and His Majesty, at stated times in the commercial year, sent some of his head tradesmen with gold dust, ivory, and other products to the coast to his merchant friends in exchange for Manchester goods and other articles of European manufacture. In one visit the caravan cleared off several hundred bales of cotton goods, which found their way into the uttermost parts of Soudan.

It was a part of the State System of Ashanti to

encourage trade. The King once in every forty days, at the *Adai* custom, distributed among a number of chiefs various sums of gold dust with a charge to turn the same to good account. These chiefs then sent down to the coast caravans of tradesmen, some of whom would be their slaves, sometimes some two to three hundred strong, to barter ivory for European goods, or buy such goods with gold dust, which the King obtained from the royal alluvial workings. Down to 1873 a constant stream of Ashanti traders might be seen daily wending their way to the coast and back again, yielding more certain wealth and prosperity to the merchants of the Gold Coast and Great Britain than may be expected for some time yet to come from the mining industry and railway development put together. The trade Chiefs would, in due course, render a faithful account to the King's stewards, being allowed to retain a fair portion of the profit. In the King's household, too, he would have special men who directly traded for him. Important Chiefs carried on the same system of trading with the coast as did the King. Thus every member of the State, from the King downwards, took an active interest in the promotion of trade and in the keeping open of the trade routes into the interior.

Nor was the Fanti petty trader left in the lurch; for, while the merchant princes drove magnificent trade with the caravans from Ashanti, the native petty trader hawked his goods to great advantage in the intermediate towns and villages, his customers being private speculators from the interior.

Often the men in the coast towns acted as middlemen between men of the interior tribes coming down to trade and the merchant houses, and gained an honest means of livelihood in that way.

Some of the Chiefs in the intermediate districts would sometimes prove obstreperous to the caravans coming down, which became a cause of grievance to His Majesty the King of Ashanti, whose ruffled temper would often be smoothed down by diplomatic messages and an exchange of presents. Thus all went merrily, and the country prospered, until the dawn of that evil day when its Protectors, instead of letting well alone, began to meddle with unscientific hands in the working of its State System.

The commercial prosperity of the Gold Coast was affected by the "Emancipation Ordinance" of 1874. Soon after that enactment the traders who came down with their men, some of whom were slaves, found they could not take back the merchandise they had bought, as some of these men were induced to run away from their masters and join themselves to the band of freedmen, in the case of Cape Coast, at Freetown, most of whom eventually perished from disease and want. As the traders could not afford to hire men to go back with them, they in most cases left their goods behind—cursing the system which caused them such grievous losses—never to return again. After the first shock, some of those traders generally made their way to Assinee and to French and German ports, thus laying the foundation for, and subsequently establishing, the French and German trade on the Guinea Coast.

Let it be distinctly understood that the bulk of the trade done at the present moment is but the remnant of the great trade which sprang up in the thirties, and was at its meridian in the sixties, between Ashanti and the Gold Coast, the Gold Coast then being the source of supply, and the Ashantis the middlemen who distributed it among the most distant peoples of the Great Desert and elsewhere.

It was a trade based on good-will and mutual confidence between merchants on the Gold Coast and their friends, the middlemen, in Ashanti.

That confidence, by slow degrees, has been completely shattered by British diplomacy and aggrandisement; and it is doubtful whether a system of railways will materially affect the situation. The fact is, that Downing Street policy has killed the goose—the Ashanti middleman, that is—which laid the golden egg; and the man at the helm has not even yet discovered the mistake. What a miserable counterfeit is the opening of Government stores in the hinterland in the vain hope of inducing trade! Whoever heard of Government stores anywhere in the land even as far back as the first half of the old century? As if the Aborigines of the Gold Coast, Ashanti, and the hinterland were not born traders, and accustomed to European goods, even while the old century was young. The truth of the matter is that the people must believe in and trust the Administration before they will build towns and villages along the railway route. You may lead a horse to a brook, but you cannot compel it to drink. What if, as fast as the Government extended the line, the native village communities trekked further north, east, or west, until they threw themselves into the ready arms of the French or Germans? The matter requires neither argument, figures, nor official assurances. It is one to be approached with ordinary common sense, which dictates that the open sore of Ashanti must be healed as quickly as possible. The Ashantis will remain restless while their institutions lie crumbling in the dust; and a state of restlessness in a people is not one calculated to promote trade and the arts of peace. It is important for British merchants and tradesmen to open their eyes to the situation, if the trade of the Gold Coast is not to be ruined.

The fact of the case is, when you strike at Native

Institutions and those ideas that are dear to the aboriginal mind, you strike at native trade and native co-operation. The only way to remedy the past is to undo what wrong to the Ashanti middleman has already been done; and the way to do so is by restoring his Native State System as nearly as may be, and his exiled princes. I do not say you are wrong in every particular of your policy, but this I do say, that you will never be able to convince the native mind that you are right from the historical facts as he knows them, and how he is affected by them.

And, after all, you cannot do without the Native.

Native Institutions.

11. THE FETISH SYSTEM.

Overshading and permeating the political, judicial, and social economy of the Aborigines is that system of faith and worship known as Fetishism. In no department of his life is the Gold Coast Native more faithful to the traditions of his forefathers than in matters of faith and worship. Here and there you find so-called converts to Christianity, but it seems difficult for an uncultured Native ever absolutely to forsake the gods of his fathers.

And why should he? When he comes to examine the teaching of the missionary, he finds there is a good deal in it that is unsuitable to his condition, and that he is required to give up practices which to the unscientific mind seem barbarous, but which, when critically examined, cover a mine of truth and inspiration.

The Native of the Gold Coast profoundly believes in the world of spirits. He believes that the spirit in man never dies. So vivid is his faith that he holds open and direct communion with his dead friends, not through a medium, but, as it were, face to face. You should watch him as he takes offerings of food and drink to the grave-side. There he carefully sets a chair for the dear one gone before, then places the meal in order, and pours out a libation, addressing the spirit of the departed the while. He earnestly believes that the spirit of the departed relative hovers around him by day as well as by night, and he has both the physical and the spiritual sense to perceive its presence. He sees in the mammiferous bat, winging its flight from room to room at night in the home once dear to the loved one, who is supposed to dominate it, a kindly providence which does not leave him all forlorn in his grief, but sends the spirit of the departed back occasionally to watch and to protect. He even speaks to it in endearing terms at times, and would fain believe that it understands and is in full sympathy with him. You may sneer at the seeming simplicity of the native mind, but the Aborigines believe that there are mysteries in this world yet unrevealed to man. He, the Native, implicitly believes in ghosts, and has many an authentic story to tell of some strange visitation which he has experienced. Nay, more, his sense of smell detects the presence of a ghost in a house.

If there is aught that is invigorating in absolute faith in things beyond while man struggles here below, surely you find it in its simplest and truest type in the heart of the Native of the Gold Coast. Mark you, he does not look to communion with the gross, material matter that lies mouldering in the grave; but he looks to that indefinable something beyond which has defied the reason of mankind for all time. He looks beyond his present squalid surroundings to a world hereafter where he will meet every member of his family, and particularly those whom he has dearly loved, and where he will dwell with them in joyous intercourse as he has done in this world. It matters not what happens to-day, since to-morrow may find him in the grave and at rest with his forefathers. In this happy frame of mind he goes through life contentedly, free from carking care, and wonders sometimes at all the excitement and ado of men of another race. And as for a material hell, the scarecrow of the missionaries, he merely smiles at such a suggestion. Is there not trouble enough in this world? God knows there is. Why should God add trouble to trouble? Thus he reasons with philosophy.

I shall not soon forget a scene I witnessed in a grave-yard on the Gold Coast not long ago. A widow had just lost her only son, whom I knew. He had belonged to a friendly society, and at his burial the "brethren" had brought flowers for the bier. A few days afterwards I noticed this woman come to the grave of her son, who had belonged to the Church, with the usual food and drink for the dead. But she had brought something else—a bunch of flowers. Surely her son would want the flowers—would like them. I saw her—a simple native woman, who, probably, in all her life, had never loitered by the wayside to wonder at God's simple daisy—amidst her tears, gently place the flowers upon her son's grave.

On another occasion I was lingering in the same grave-yard by the side of a figure of "Hope," my thoughts far away from the immediate surroundings. Suddenly a woman's voice addressed me: "*Ye wura ahaö : awuraba su ahaö ;*" meaning, "Master, good day; and you too, mistress, good day!" I was startled at the strangeness of the salutation; and, before I could recover my senses, she had slowly walked away. So fervent is their belief in the hereafter. To them man never dies.

Now, when the missionary comes along, simple soul that he is, and gives the would-be converted Native the comprehensive command to give up all fetish as a thing abominable in the sight of God, his reason reels, and the foundations of his faith are, for the first time, shaken. But he soon finds himself on *terra firma :* and when he remembers the lessons of his youth and considers that, after all, the missionary may be wrong in a matter that affects the vital interests of the life beyond, he remains for ever afterwards only a Christian worshipper in form, if he does not openly revolt. Where he remains a formal worshipper, it does not necessarily follow that he is a hypocrite. The fact is that he likes the music and the ceremonials of the Christian Church, and would fain continue to enjoy them, while at heart he remains true to the faith of his fathers.

Yet, what a different state of things would prevail if the missionary had first studied the Religious System of the Native before trying to improve it, or, which is worse, before introducing a new one! Why, for example, should not the native convert sing his own native songs, and play his native airs in church? Why should he not attune his horns, his *adziwa*, his *gomey*, or for that matter, his *adankum*, to the praise of God, much as the Israelites of old praised Jehovah upon the cymbal and the harp? Again, why should not the native be invited to church by the call of the big drum, as he is generally called to any public meeting in the country? Why, in the name of reason and common sense, should not the Native bear his own name and wear his own native garments? Why, indeed, except that the simple missionary has, from the beginning, ruled that all these things are against the letter, if not the spirit, of the Gospel? There will never be anything like genuine Christianity on the Gold Coast and in the hinterland till the missionaries have begun from the beginning to build up a national Church on scientific lines—a Church wherein the Spirit of Christ will be all in all, and the letter a dead thing.

The King, in the Native State System, is the Spiritual Head of his people. But the actual working of the System is in the hands of the Priests, who combine with their office the cure of disease. Some of them are very good doctors and pull through cases where European skill has failed. They are skilled in the use of herbal remedies, and it might repay European medical men to study native therapeutics in its application to the treatment of diseases peculiar to the Gold Coast.

The Priest generally invests his practice with a certain amount of secrecy. He pretends to hold communion, not in a spiritual sense, but in a matter-of-fact way, with the spirits of the dead, and he will often bring you back a message from a dead friend, if desired. When a priest is called in from a distance to attend a case, he will generally tell the friends of the patient much about the family history, and indicate that a deceased relative is troubling the patient for some act of disobedience. The deceased relative must accordingly be propitiated. How does he come to know the history of the family to which he is a stranger ? There is a Guild of Priests in the country to which all Priests belong, whose members are absolutely faithful to one another. Upon the arrival of the Priest in the town where his attendance is required, he immediately goes to meet his brother Priest, or some student of the Priest, if he is out of town, who gives him all the information he requires, and which he subsequently puts to such effective use. The people understand the deception, but they never expose it; for the Priest's office is a sacred one, and they philosophically look to the spiritual side of things and not to the letter.

A Priest's training begins early in his life. He is generally sent away to another district to a seminary, where he serves out his apprenticeship, which may cover a period of three years. During that time he learns the use of herbs and their application to the cure of disease, at which he becomes very proficient in the course of after practice. When he returns from his apprenticeship to his own town, he generally gives a show, which takes place when his "company" folk hold a "company" dance. He, on this occasion, performs various feats in clever dancing to the beating of his favourite airs on the *tom tom*, and he generally succeeds in working himself into a frenzy of excitement, when the "fetish" is said to have come upon him—"*Suman aba nu du.*"

In time of war the Priest goes forth with the army, and he generally can tell, or is supposed to be able to tell, what the result of the conflict will be. He is supposed to be bullet-proof, and he generally gives such rude aid as he can to the wounded. He would now and again be called in consultation with the Council of War.

Native Institutions.

12. THE MUNICIPAL SYSTEM.

The principle of municipal government, in so far as this country is concerned, is as old as the hills. Without asserting that at any time in the history of the country the genius of the people had developed the idea to the same extent as may be found in civilised countries at present; yet the fact that the Aborigines of this country have always in their townships and districts had a system of municipal government, independently of the central government of a given province, may be distinctly traced by the careful student of their history.

To note this the more clearly, the observer has only to travel a few miles up country, and there he will find that each important township has its Sanitary Board, arrangements for the carrying out of public works, and other necessary provisions for the due and proper regulation of the internal government of the little community. These arrangements may not be on a grand scale, but the idea is distinctly there, and there cannot be the slightest doubt that, in the hands of an intelligent civilised central government, the different embryo municipal corporations of the country may be developed and adapted to the local peculiarities of the people without coming into conflict with any of their cherished ideas.

I have indicated in the preceding parts of this chapter the functions of the Headman of the ward. It is his duty also to supervise the sanitary arrangements of the ward. He would ordinarily cause the womenfolk at regular and stated periods to sweep out the whole ward, the women of each family doing the cleaning up of their portion of the ward. This would include the brushing up of weeds and all waste vegetable matter and other noxious substances, which would be burnt.

The menfolk of the ward would be turned out in a company to clean up certain portions of the main road leading from the township to the next township up to such a point as the two townships would agree upon. They would also provide places of public convenience both for themselves and the womenfolk. When such places of convenience were out of repair, they would be burnt down and fresh ones provided. In erecting places of convenience and lavatories, care would be taken to place them where the township would suffer least from bad odours.

In advanced communities the head of the ward

THE MUNICIPAL SYSTEM.

would see to the regulation of the buildings of the ward, so that when you arrived in a township, it would present broad streets and avenues, hardly to be expected in the heart of Africa.

The effect of intercourse with Europeans on the part of the people of the coast towns has been to disorganise their own former municipal arrangements, and to throw them back upon such haphazard provisions as the Government has felt inclined to make. It is like the case of the dog in the manger. The Government will do nothing effective, and they neutralise the influence of the native Chiefs who would otherwise carry out necessary sanitary arrangements.

It is true that there is in existence a "Town Councils Ordinance" on the Gold Coast which has been applied to Accra. But it does not work, and it is because it is not on a sound basis. The people of Cape Coast have steadily refused to form a corporation under the Ordinance, feeling as they do that no system of municipal government on the Gold Coast will succeed which is not based on popular and representative lines.

The idea of rates and taxes without the people having an effective voice in the expenditure thereof is obnoxious to the average aboriginal mind. The Native resents an imposition of this kind upon the same principle involved in his protest against the "Lands Bill" of 1897. He considers that the land upon which stands his family house is his own peculiar lot and portion, much in the same way as he regards his gold, rubber, and timber lands. He will spend his uttermost farthing in defending his rights to the one or the other when the occasion arises. Therefore, when you ask him to pay rates and taxes upon his house, giving him no adequate control over the funds, he imagines you are simply introducing the thin end of the wedge, and sees no difference in the claim put forward and one which would oust him altogether from his tenement. To him the principle is the same.

Nor does the working of the Ordinance appeal even to the sober sense of the average educated native. The Government element prevails to an alarming extent. There is too much eagerness to collect every available penny, and there is want of tact in the practical working of the scheme.

Take at random a report of a meeting of the Accra Town Council, held at the Municipal Offices on Tuesday, the 12th day of April, 1898, at 4.50 p.m. First, as to the *personnel*: of the five members present two were Government officials, Mr. J. K. Holmes, the District Commissioner of Accra, being the President.

THE MUNICIPAL SYSTEM.

Secondly, as to the business discussed. *Inter alia*, under the heading Finance Committee, the following resolution appears: "That notices for the issue of summonses for non-payment of rates be placarded throughout the municipal area, and that the Town Clerk institute proceedings against King Tackie for the recovery of the rates due by him on his two houses."

If you have a little imagination it will occur to you how this resolution, put into action, would appear to the King of Accra, referred to in the said resolution. " Has it come to this," he would say to his courtiers, "that I, to whose ancestors ground-rent was paid for the very land upon which stands the forts of Accra, must pay tolls for occupying my own houses, about the only possession left to me now?" He will but see in the situation a travesty upon human affairs. The irony of it all! It is like the Lord of the Manor being subjected to fines and forfeitures because forsooth he would not pay rates for the tenements, his own, standing upon his ancient domains. Your matter-of-fact Englishman is too prosaic for the average native intelligence. The French do these things differently, and succeed where the English fail. Common sense and tact are their forte. They work through the native Chief wherever they can, and generally effect what they seek in the end.

To restore, then, the original municipal institutions of the people is the surest way to popularise

G.C.

the principle of municipal government on the Gold Coast. And you cannot do this unless you give full sway to the working of the Native State System by candidly recognising the authority of the Kings and Chiefs, strengthening their influence, and working through them. Barring cases of gross injustice, there should be as little interference as possible in the internal native government of the Provinces. When once you have adopted this policy, under the direction of a well-informed central government, firm but conciliatory, you have gone a great way in solving the problem of Gold Coast administration. For you will easily perceive that in this question of municipal government, unless the native Authorities have the power to enforce the necessary regulations, backed by their ancient prestige, there can be no progress possible.

I believe that when once it has been impressed upon intelligent native municipal councils that the destiny of their towns is in their hands, free from unnecessary interference on the part of the central government, funds will be forthcoming to meet the requirements of the municipalities. Where works of public utility for the township are being undertaken, there will be, in my view, no difficulty in raising money from the different wards in the customary way.

But before calling upon the people to contribute, the Government must have redeemed their pledges.

in the past. When the *ad valorem* duties of ten per cent. were imposed during the Administration of the late Sir William Brandford Griffith, it was proclaimed from the housetops by the Government that works of public utility would be undertaken; but the sums thus collected were spent largely in fruitless expeditions, the same thing occurring in subsequent Administrations. It is true a railway is being built, the cost of which is being met by loans upon the country's credit ; but where are the wharves, the harbours, the pierheads, and the waterworks which have been promised over and over again in the Budget speeches of succeeding Administrations ? They simply do not exist, and there is no apparent hope of their ever doing so. Progressive people in the country, European and otherwise, are burning to transform the Gold Coast into a fairly decent country; but the Authorities do not seem to be in touch with the times somehow.

Again, I suggest, get a well-informed central government, with a Science Department, directing but not interfering with internal native government and institutions; encourage foreign capital to open up the country, licensing syndicates to light up the towns and to introduce modern conveniences; and you have gone a great way in setting this country on the path of progress, which will lead to the fulfilment of her destiny.

CHAPTER III.

THE CONFLICT OF SYSTEMS.

Where the power of legislation is so loosely conferred on such a variety of persons, it is certain there will be great confusion of laws, and there is also great danger of the worst of all evils, namely, of doubts being raised as to whether the legislative authority of some of the subordinate bodies has not been exceeded.

For the supreme sovereign authority is always obliged to allow the authority of its subordinates to be questioned, in some form or other, by judicial authority, in order to keep up a check on their usurpation of power; though sometimes it resorts to that highly unsatisfactory expedient for getting out of the difficulty—an *ex post facto* ratification of acts which are admittedly illegal.—MARKBY, *Elements of Law.*

* * * * *

With respect to the public opinion of the Crown Colonies, it is undeniably a power which in recent times is making itself more and more felt. The press in many of them has organs conducted with ability, and in some of them with singular power and conspicuous fairness; the proprietors and editors are not confined to any one race, and no one could proclaim from internal evidence the nationality of a writer. But the wants and rights of the majority of the people are not always represented in the columns of the public press in a Crown Colony, and this makes it the more necessary for the people and Parliament of the United Kingdom to pay some attention to what is passing, for they are undoubtedly responsible for the laws and systems upheld in such dependencies.—C. S. SALMON, *Ex-Administrator of the Gold Coast, in " The Crown Colonies of Great Britain," p.* 5.

CHAPTER III.

THE CONFLICT OF SYSTEMS.

The Gold Coast, whose institutions we have been considering, is at present legislated for by the Governor in Council. Such Council is composed of five Heads of Departments, with the Governor as the President thereof, namely, the Chief Justice, the Colonial Secretary, the Attorney-General, the Treasurer, and the Officer Commanding the Troops, formerly known as the Inspector-General. If, therefore, you reckon the Governor's " original vote in common with the other members of Council, as also a casting vote, if upon any question the votes shall be equal,"[1] you have six distinct official votes in the Council.

There are generally four unofficial members of Council, who are Government nominees, and who hold their appointments for five years, subject to renewal for a further period of five years, upon the recommendation of the Governor. They take their leave of absence from the country in the same way, and with the same sanction, as ordinary officials in

[1] Standing rules and orders of the Legislative Council.

the Government service. They keep their seats during the pleasure of the Government. A recalcitrant member may never cross the threshold of the Council chamber again after his first term of office. It is a system altogether peculiar to Crown Colonies. At the present moment, I believe, the number of unofficial members has been increased to five.

Of the five unofficial members of the Council, three are Europeans, one of whom is a solicitor[1] in local practice, the other two representing, as we may take it, the mining and the mercantile interests respectively of the country.

The two native non-official members of the Council may be said to represent the Eastern and Western Provinces of the Gold Coast.

The official members of the Council are bound to vote with the Government. At a meeting of the Legislative Council held at Government House, Christianborg Castle, on Wednesday, the 26th day of June, 1889, there were present : His Excellency the Governor, Sir W. Brandford Griffith, K.C.M.G.; His Honour the Chief Justice, J. T. Hutchinson, Esq.; the Honourable the Colonial Secretary, F. M. Hodgson, Esq.; the Honourable the Queen's Advocate, E. Bruce Hindle, Esq.; the Honourable the Treasurer, Charles Pike, Esq., C.M.G.; the

---

[1] This chapter was written before the Honourable Member was made the Attorney-General of the Gold Coast.

Honourable Major Bingham, 2nd Batt. W. I. Regiment, Commanding the troops on the Gold Coast; and the Honourable Charles W. Burnett, Esq., unofficial member. The Honourable John Sarbah, Esq., unofficial member, was absent.[1]

At this meeting, " Mr. Burnett asked the question, of which he had given previous notice, as to whether official members are bound to vote with the Government."

" The Colonial Secretary replied that the officers of the Government, being part and lot of the Executive Government, are bound to obey the Queen's commands, conveyed by the Secretary of State, in their legislative as well as their executive capacities, whether or not the course presented accord with their personal views and opinions. In questions of religion, and other questions of high moral import in respect of which officers of the Crown may happen to have conscientious scruples, which, after being explained to the Governor, His Excellency is unable to remove, they may reasonably expect to be excused from taking part in measures to which they object on these grounds. At the same time an officer, whose seat in the legislature is by law inseparable from his office, could not be continued in his office and his seat if his conscience

[1] See the report of the meeting published in the *Gold Coast Echo*, August 15th, 1889, reproduced from the Government Gazette.

should not permit him to give the Crown such a measure of support as might be necessary to enable the Governor to carry on the business of government in the legislature in accordance with the Queen's instructions."

In whichever way you view this diplomatic answer to a simple question, one must see how awkwardly a Chief Justice, for instance, may find himself placed in the Legislative Council. Being an officer of the Government, he is "part and lot of the Government," and, as such, bound to support the policy of the Government, or, in plain English, take the alternative of being sent about his business. If he is a strong man, he will hold out occasionally, and may even go so far as to sit a silent member in the Council, holding that his function is not to make, but to dispense, the law; not to administer, but to judge between person and person, if even one of the parties should happen to be the Executive branch of the Administration. In a country teeming with political issues, where a judicial officer may at any moment be called upon to decide upon the legality of an administrative act, the Chief Justice will perceive the incongruity of "supporting" a governmental policy, and the possibility of afterwards sitting as judge to decide issues arising out of such a policy, and would, therefore, wish himself out of an ambiguous position. But it is a peculiarity of the Crown Colony System that it insists upon this unsatisfactory arrangement. A way out of the difficulty, while the System lasts, would be to place the control of judicial appointments in the hands of the Lord Chancellor of England, and remove a judge of the Supreme Court from a seat in the Legislative Council of the Gold Coast, substituting the Solicitor-General.

But to come back to Mr. Burnett's question. The honourable member, in a matter before the Council, was hard pressed for support. The odds were six to one, and he was obliged to put the question point-blank. The difficulty which confronted Mr. Burnett as to the permanent non-official minority still confronts us. The non-official members are men of business. Occasionally you have one or two of them away on leave. If even they are in the country, it is not always that they can be present in their places; and if they could all be present, still their minority would be none the less a minority.

But all this is on the assumption that from the non-official members is expected free criticism. That is not so. They are supposed to support the Government. Their province is not so much to criticise as to advise. When they do advise, they must do it in such a way as to fall in with the view for the moment entertained by the Government. If you want to know the truth of the matter, they are put there as an apology for the denial of proper representation to the country. They never initiate legislation. How can they? It would be a presumption on their part to attempt it. For that matter, the Governor himself does not initiate legislation: he merely suggests. Legislation proper comes from Downing Street, and the Governor and his Council are merely the obedient servants of the Colonial Secretary. To see the matter in its proper light, even after a given measure has passed the Legislative Council, it is subject to revision by the Authority at Downing Street, who may or may not advise His Majesty to exercise his power of veto.

If you want further light upon the matter, you have it in the perfunctory way in which Bills are passed into Ordinances in the Council. It is a matter of course where a Bill has received the official *imprimatur*. There cannot, in the circumstances, be any such thing as a regular debate when raised by a recalcitrant member.

It so happens, therefore, that when the people think themselves seriously affected by the provisions of a given Bill, they resort to the expediency of getting themselves represented by counsel in the Council Chamber. For the rest, they allow legislation to pass over their heads by default. The right of the people to present petitions is admitted in theory, but in practice, if the petition is ever attended

CHAP. III.   THE CONFLICT OF SYSTEMS.   125

to by the Council, the attention is given after the evil prayed against has become an accomplished fact. If you want to have an idea as to how this sort of thing works, let me refer you to an interesting correspondence between the Axim branch of the local Aborigines Society and the Government anent the sale of lands at Sekondi, which, with the kind permission of the Editor, I have reproduced from *West Africa* of July 5th,. 1902, in the appendix.[1]

What system is this which places in the hands of the Governor, as the obedient servant of the Colonial Secretary, a power beyond that exercised by the Sovereign, Emperor-King of the British Dominions? A curious arrangement this, surely, by which the Governor is not responsible to the taxpayers, who keep the machine going, and who do really know what is good for them, but to an overtasked official, some 3,000 miles away, who may or may not be a capable man, and who gleans his information as to the local conditions from his obedient servant, the Governor! How long will public opinion tolerate a system which makes against true imperialism and the expansion of British influence and prestige in the dark corners of the earth—which throws a damper, in several directions, upon British capital and enterprise?

The laws passed by the Legislative Council are put

[1] See Appendix, pp. 382—396.

in force by the Executive Council, which consists of the official members of the Legislative Council, save one, with the Governor, again, as its president.

Sometimes the only information that an ignorant Native has of the passing of a given law is when he has to pay the penalty. A typical case is that of the Criminal Code, which penalises a good many acts which are not offences by the general principles of the Criminal Law of England, or by the Customary Law of the Gold Coast.

We have seen from the discussion of Native Institutions how widely diffused among the people is the idea of representative government. It is the very essence of the Native State System. In that System, the right of every adult member of the community to be represented in the State Councils is fully recognised and guaranteed. What conflict of ideas must there be in the mind of the Native when he contemplates the farcical pretext in respect of the representation of the country in the presence of the non-official members of Council in the Council Chamber!

The trend of progress the whole world over is toward free institutions—a state of society whose members are free to govern and regulate their own affairs. It is the keynote of healthy imperialism. It is this very principle, recognised by Great Britain in her relations with the Dominions over the Seas, which is strengthening and consolidating Greater

Britain. But I shall possibly be met with the criticism that self-government is reserved by Great Britain for those English-speaking Colonies whose populations are nearly or wholly white. That may be. But what is the essence of the matter? I am inclined to think that it is not so much a question of the particular people inhabiting a particular Dependency, as a yielding to the logic of facts in the given circumstances. Statesmen, in time, have come to learn the hidden meaning of the bitter lesson which cost Great Britain the loss of the American Colonies, and the world one of the greatest opportunities of conserving universal peace, progress, and goodwill among men. In the case of the Gold Coast we shall appeal to the logic of facts, and shall not appeal in vain.

I believe, therefore, that whenever a strong case has been made, showing the capability and the right of any given community in free alliance and friendship with Great Britain, call such connection by what name soever you please, to manage its own internal affairs, Great Britain will not be backward in extending to such a community the blessing of free institutions, feeling certain that therein lies the fastest bond with the Mother-Country. In the case of the Gold Coast, we simply say, " Allow us to make use of our own Native Institutions, which we understand, and which from experience are adapted to us." We shall ask once, twice, and ask again, and, if this generation is not listened to, we shall hand on the legacy of legitimate and constitutional request to the next generation.

But where are your facts, you will rightly ask, making it logically proper to ask for the revival of representative government, on native lines, on the Gold Coast? To a fair question allow me to return a fair answer. I have endeavoured to show that, on the Gold Coast, you are not dealing with a savage people without a past, who are merely striving to copy or imitate foreign Institutions. I can understand why, for example, you will rightly or wrongly refuse full representative government, say, to Jamaica or Trinidad. There you are not dealing with an indigenous people. You are face to face with the problem of trying to train up a people who have lost touch with their past, and whose immediate past dates from the time when Europe went into sackcloth and ashes over her grievous sin against the African race. You may seriously or not assume that they are not ripe for self-government, and postpone the time till the Greek calends. But here you are confronted with no such difficulty. On the contrary, you are stimulated by the circumstances of the case. If you are free to admit it, you will see that you find here already a system of self-government as perfect and efficient as the most forward nations of the earth to-day can possibly conceive. A people who could, indigenously, and without a literature, evolve the orderly representative government which obtained in Ashanti and the Gold Coast before the advent of the foreign interloper, are a people to be respected and shown consideration when they proceed to discuss questions of self-government.

Nor in discussing this matter must we lose sight of the fact that the position of the Gold Coast is perfectly unique among all the other so-called Dependencies of Great Britain. Without anticipating the discussion in the next chapter, I may broadly state that the relations between Great Britain and the Gold Coast originated in friendship, mutual trust, and commercial alliance. It will be seen, therefore, that the people have a right to mould their institutions upon their own lines, Great Britain being merely a Protecting Power, and only properly concerned with their relations with the outside world. It will be also seen that at no time have the people divested themselves of their right to legislate for themselves. Before the spread of education in the land, they did these things for themselves, sometimes in co-operation with their Friends and Protectors. Why not now?

It is sad to reflect in this connection that the policy of the British Government has been retrogressive rather than progressive. It is as if the

G.C.

Colonial Office had resolutely set to work to discourage national spirit, and to destroy every vestige of it, in the breasts of the people. But this kind of thing will not do. Hence the humble appeal to-day that Great Britain should fully and seriously consider this question of free institutions for the Gold Coast, upon which so much of the future progress of the country depends.

It is conceded, I believe, on all sides that the Crown Colony System of administering the affairs of the Gold Coast has failed, hopelessly failed. What then? Is the country to be left to go to rack and ruin? It may mean nothing to the Colonists, but to the Aborigines it means everything that is dear to them of country, home, and fatherland.

If the Gold Coast were a country with free institutions, free from the trammels of Downing Street red-tapism, we should soon have good wharves and harbours, gas works, water works, and railway communication all over the country. Prosperous cities would grow up, and knowledge would spread among all classes of the people, producing a willing and an efficient body of workmen for the material development of the vast wealth and resources of the country.

In a well-regulated system the whites would find they could not do without the blacks, and *vice versâ*, and soon would grow up a spirit of forbearance, tolerance, and mutual respect, each race doing its allotted work upon natural lines in a prosperous and contented federal Gold Coast and Ashanti.

All this may be a dream. At least, so you may think. But if a dream, it is one worth attempting to realise, instead of sitting bound hand and foot in the face of ugly facts.

CHAPTER IV.

THE STATUS OF THE GOLD COAST.

It is difficult for a civilised Government to deal justly with primitive communities, because they have not the courage to restrain their subjects from taking those unfair advantages which even the commonest and dullest of civilised men have over the shrewdest of savages. There are not wanting those who look on the extermination of savage races as a benefit. But experience, scientific research, and history all prove, every day more and more, that such conclusions are mistaken. Civilised people know something, but not much, about their own intelligence, and they know something of their own history, but they know nothing whatever about those people they condemn to extinction simply because they do not understand them.

  * * * * *

It is to be hoped many races will survive in the world, were it only to avoid too much monotony.—C. S. SALMON, *Ex-Administrator of the Gold Coast, in " The Crown Colonies of Great Britain," p.* 85.

CHAPTER IV.

The Status of the Gold Coast.

1. THE GOLD COAST SETTLEMENTS DEFINED : THEIR NATURE AND EXTENT.

ALL writers are agreed that the British Settlements on the Gold Coast consist of a number of forts, studded along the coast, which, in one way or another, have fallen into the hands of Great Britain since the seventeenth century, with the exception of three or four, which were actually built by the English.

In the " Gold Coast Guide," 1895—1896, the Rev. Jacob B. Anaman, F.R.G.S., gives the forts in the following order :—

French fort at Elmina, built in 1383.

Fort St. George del Mina (Portuguese), built in 1481.

Fort Fredensborg, or Ningo Fort (Danes), built in 1620.

Fort Cabo Corsa, or Cape Coast Castle (Portuguese), built in 1624.

Fort Nassau, or Mori Fort (Dutch), built in 1637.

Fort Conradsburg, or Fort St. Jago, at Elmina (Dutch), built in 1640.

Kramantine Fort (English), built in 1640.
James Fort, at Accra (English), built in 1662.
Fort Vanderpurgh, at Commenda, built in 1688.
Dixcove Fort (English), built in 1691.
Anamaboe Fort (English), built in 1753.

For further particulars, and an account of a few unimportant forts not included in the list above given, the reader is referred to the pages of Bosman.

Now, the objects for which the several forts were built are obvious. They were mostly built in the seventeenth century, when the Portuguese, the French, the English, the Dutch, and the Danes were alike engaged in the abominable slave trade, and they were, of course, intended to serve as barracoons, or temporary depôts, for the human cargo before it was shipped to the plantations in the New World. The different companies, incorporated by the Governments of the several European nations, were keen competitors in the slave market, and jealous of one another; while the Aborigines, slowly awakening to the horrors of the traffic in human flesh, hated them all equally. Hence arose the necessity of building these forts for protection.

It is also clear that ground-rents were paid to the local Magnates, or Chiefs, for the grounds upon which these forts stood and still stand, and for them only, since the state of unrest in which was the country in those unhappy times rendered it unsafe for the

European traders to acquire holdings outside their forts, which were never free from the dangers of outside attack.

Accordingly, when in later times we read in official reports, despatches, and Blue Books of "Her Majesty's Settlements on the Gold Coast," and "Her Majesty's Forts and Possessions on the Gold Coast," it must be understood that these self-same forts are meant which served as temporary resting-places for the kidnapped Aborigines, groaning in chains, and subsequently exiled to foreign labour.

But by-and-by slavery was abolished, the day of legitimate trade dawned upon the Gold Coast, and the Aborigines began to have confidence in the white man, and to recognise and appreciate the advantages of having him in their country. Thenceforth, the Englishman was the honoured guest, who must be entertained and humoured; and, so long as he knew his place and did not assume airs or bully the people, he was welcome to have his full share in the good things of the land for all time, the Aborigines being conciliatory above all things.

These are the main fundamental propositions of British tenure on the Gold Coast: and it will be interesting to mark the march of events in the course of this work—how the honoured guest gradually worked his way into importance and influence, a logical result scarcely contemplated by the Aborigines, when they offered their white visitor a place at their hearth.

We have the propositions. Where are the proofs? We find them scattered here and there. Let us hasten to collect and preserve them.

The first work I shall refer to is the work of Mr. Lucas, of Balliol College, Oxford, and of the Colonial Office, being the third volume of his "Historical Geography of the British Colonies." I may premise that Mr. Lucas, in his Preface, mentions the name of the late Sir William Brandford Griffith, K.C.M.G., then Governor of the Gold Coast, as having been among many others who had given him assistance in the preparation of his work. The information we derive from him, therefore, may be taken as distinctly bearing the official hall-mark.

On page 3 of his work Mr. Lucas refers to the Gold Coast as a Settlement, dating from the year 1618; and when we come to page 199 he refers to it in these words:—

"To judge from the old maps a row of isolated forts and factories lined the water's edge, but they had no territory or territorial rights attached to them."

Referring to this same matter, Captains Brackenbury and Huyshe say, on page 3 of their work[1]:—

"It appears that all the European companies on the Coast, Dutch and Danish as well as English, had paid ground rent to the Coast tribes for the land on which their forts were built."

[1] "Fanti and Ashanti."

THE STATUS OF THE GOLD COAST.

Now, these writers must have gathered their information from official documents extant, and it will, therefore, be satisfactory to confirm them from those official sources.

It appears that in the sixties Her Majesty's Government was desirous of ascertaining the true relation of the Gold Coast to Great Britain. For this purpose a Select Committee was appointed, and a deal of valuable evidence was taken.

On page 287 of the Report of the Committee[1] we find that Richard Pine, Esquire, Governor of the Gold Coast, was called in and examined. He was asked:—

"What did you consider your Governorship to be at the Gold Coast? Was it simply a number of military posts or forts without any territory round each of them?"

To which he replied:—

"I consider that I was technically the Governor of the forts and settlements, but I also supposed myself to have jurisdiction to a certain extent over what is called the Protectorate."

Colonel Ord, R.E., was also called and examined. He was asked the specific question:—

"You are not prepared, are you, to recommend any exact area of land which ought to be declared British territory around the forts at the Gold Coast?"

To which he replied:—

"With regard to the Gold Coast, I would declare nothing

---

[1] See preliminary chapter, p. x.

British territory but the land on which the forts or buildings which were occupied by our civil officers were situated."

Please note carefully the next question, which follows, and the answer to the same:—

"We have had evidence that there was some disadvantage there (Gold Coast) from the uncertainty: one or two witnesses seem to suppose that it was British land within a gun shot; do you not think that there is a disadvantage in the actual British territory not being defined?"

"It is thought by some a disadvantage in the present state of our relations with the people at the Gold Coast, but I think it is somewhat advantageous that our exact position cannot be too closely defined."

In the year 1865, William Hackett, Esq., was Her Britannic Majesty's Lieutenant-Governor at the Gold Coast. The indefinite position of Her Majesty's Government in the country troubled him, and he wished to give concessions of land in Cape Coast in the name of the Queen, to be probably followed by acquisitions in other parts of the country. I have published the whole palaver, held at Government House, Cape Coast, on the 10th of May, 1865, in the Appendix. It is interesting reading, but the substance is this:—

The Governor wanted the illiterate Aborigines to sign a paper, making the Queen a grant of land. They respectfully declined to do so, remarking that the signing of a paper was doubtful to them.

Eight long years passed away, and then followed the Ashanti Expedition of 1873—1874. It is well

CHAP. IV.   THE STATUS OF THE GOLD COAST.   141

known that Lord Wolseley, then Sir Garnet, was given the military command of the expedition, while at the same time he acted as Civil Administrator of the Gold Coast Settlements. Let us see how he describes himself in his letter written at the camp at Prahsue, on the 2nd of January, 1874, to His Majesty Koffee Kalkalli, King of Ashanti. He describes himself as "Administrator of Her Majesty's Forts and Possessions on the Gold Coast, and Commander of Her Majesty's Forces in the West African Settlements."

Nor have the facts altered since 1874. In the speech of His Excellency Governor Hodgson, in introducing the estimates of revenue and expenditure for the year 1899, reported in the Gold Coast Government Gazette for October, 1898, at page 409, occur these words:—

"I do not, I may state, regard Ashanti as being in the same position to the Government as other districts which together form the colony and protected territories of the Gold Coast. Ashanti is a conquered country—a country upon which blood and treasure have been spent—and the kings and chiefs know that in accordance with native custom they must pay tribute to the paramount authority."

Sir F. M. Hodgson in these two sentences throws the whole question of British relations with the Aborigines of the Gold Coast into a nutshell, and shows greater appreciation of historical facts than did his late lamented predecessor, the brilliant and versatile Sir William Edward Maxwell, K.C.M.G.

And we have already seen how these "Forts," "Possessions," or "Settlements" were acquired, and the local limits of them.

The Status of the Gold Coast.

2. EARLY JURISDICTION OF THE KING: ITS NATURE AND EXTENT.

We may now usefully direct our attention to the enquiry as to the nature and extent of the early jurisdiction of the King of England, consequent upon the acquisition of certain Forts or Settlements on the Gold Coast by Great Britain.

It is a matter of general history that, before the close of the eighteenth century, the public conscience of Great Britain had been fully aroused by the efforts of the Abolitionists to the evils of the slave trade. The philanthropic movement, which began in much feebleness, had, as time went on, increased in importance and influence, and had, moreover, created in its favour a public sentiment of a highly moral character, destined not merely to influence British policy for all time, but likewise to form a bulwark for the liberties of the race whom civilised Europe had so long wronged.

But how did this result come about? It happened this way. The reaction in public opinion against the slave trade made the British conscience for a long time afterwards tender in pursuing any policy which might happen to work injustice to the Aborigines of this country. The Colonial Ministers kept a firm hold on the Lieutenant-Governors of the Forts and Settlements in those earlier times, and would not countenance any unlawful extension of jurisdiction, however convenient to the local government.

On the other hand, the Aborigines of the Gold Coast were for ever wary. They knew fully well that they had come in contact with powerful neighbours, who might, at any moment, show themselves inconveniently aggressive; and so, with remarkable tact, they gave in where they could do so without injury to the fundamental basis of the relationship between them and their white visitors, mildly remonstrating, but always with effect, where they felt firmness was necessary.

There were, besides, operating in the country other influences at the same time which had the effect of bringing about a good understanding between the Aborigines and the British Government. In the year 1818, the principle of abolition had been accepted by all the European Powers; but it left undisturbed the internal labour system of the Aborigines, and the active trade which depended upon it. It would not have been wise to attempt any interference with domestic slavery as it then existed, and, besides, Great Britain had only so recently turned convert that she could not with any grace preach at the very tribes some thousands of whom she had kidnapped in the days of her unregeneration.

It happened, therefore, that when the day of legitimate trade dawned in these parts, the transport service was in the hands of well-to-do Aborigines, who kept slaves for the purpose. There was, thus, immediate gain to the Aborigines, and gain indirectly to the European trader in the new order of things. And it is not possible to see how otherwise the country could have been opened up to trade and civilisation in those earlier times.

Trade, then, it is to be distinctly understood, was the primary, though not the only object of Great Britain in settling in the country, and whether in the hands of the Directors of the African Company of Merchants, or the Administrators of the United West Africa Settlements, the primary purpose of the Administration was the same, namely, the encouragement and protection of trade. But, pray, remember that it was only the primary purpose. For, as we shall see in the course of this work, now and again an aggressive policy asserted itself, giving way almost immediately afterwards to the main and primary policy. The intelligent reader, who gets a firm grasp of this central idea, has a key to the whole political history of the Gold Coast people.

G.C.

From this starting point, it becomes easy to form a clear idea of the nature of British tenure, and the extent of the jurisdiction in those earlier times.

On page 287 of the Report of the Select Committee, the opinion of Governor Pine was asked upon this question of British jurisdiction on the Gold Coast. His reply was this : " I had heard so long that I can recollect Africa that the question of jurisdiction was a doubtful point."

The opinion of Colonel Ord, R.E., is given on page 337. To the question, " You are not prepared, are you, to recommend any exact area of land which ought to be declared British territory around the forts at the Gold Coast?" he replied : " With regard to the Gold Coast, I would declare nothing British territory but the land on which the forts or buildings which were occupied by our civil officers were situated."

In the year 1836, as Mr. Sarbah tells us on page 15 of the " Fanti Customary Laws," the President in Cape Coast Castle assumed power and tried Adoasi and Ammah for wilful murder. Upon the report of the trial reaching England, the Committee of the African Merchants, then administering the Forts and Settlements under the Crown, in a letter bearing date the 20th of October, 1836, observed :

" Your proceedings in Council, April 6th, in reference to the trials of Adoasi and Ammah for wilful murder, we observe, were

CHAP. IV. THE STATUS OF THE GOLD COAST.   147

conducted in the Public Hall of Cape Coast Castle in your presence and that of Cabboceers and Peynins, and, found guilty upon their own confession, these men were executed. It seems from your information to us, that there has been a very important departure from the proceedings of our Criminal Courts, inasmuch as the confession of the prisoners was the chief evidence against them, but of the justice of the sentence there can be no doubt. These remarks lead us to remark to you, which we feel bound to do, that *we have been instructed expressly by Lord Gleneg* 'that the British Government pretends neither to territorial possession, nor to jurisdiction over any portion of the Gold Coast, excepting the actual site of the several forts and castles.' It is, therefore, necessary that your authority should be exercised with very great caution."

In the year 1865, Colonel Conran was the Lieutenant-Governor of the Gold Coast. He believed in an aggressive policy, as did his illustrious but ill-starred predecessor, Sir Charles Macarthy. He sought to prevail upon Her Majesty's then principal Secretary of State, namely, the Right Honourable Edward Cardwell, to sanction the extension of the Queen's jurisdiction on the Gold Coast. The Secretary of State wrote from Downing Street, under date the 23rd of November, 1865, as follows :—

"Sir,—I have to acknowledge your despatch No. 144 of 17th October, enclosing the copy of a notice which you have issued, in which you define the limits of Her Majesty's possessions on the Gold Coast. I am unable to approve the step which you have taken in declaring the territory within five miles of eight separate British forts to be British territory, and I have to instruct you to recall the notices in which this is done. Whatever influence you may be able to exert in discouraging or repressing barbarous customs leading to loss of life will be very proper, and I shall be happy to approve your exercise of it, but the extension of British territory is a different matter and cannot receive my sanction."

Again on the 22nd of December of the same year, the Secretary writes to the Lieutenant-Governor " to avoid introducing any expressions which bear the appearance of extending jurisdiction over territory at the Gold Coast"; and on the 23rd of December he once more urges upon him " to avoid any new step which may have that appearance."

One can easily discover the underlying reason which prompted the emphatic disavowal of the Lieutenant-Governor's aggressive policy by the Colonial Secretary. There was clearly no ground for the assumption that Her Majesty owned any territory in the country outside the forts, and the Colonial Minister had the courage to tell Colonel Conran so.

Again, if we turn to " Fanti and Ashanti," page 17, we have it there stated that a Select Committee of the House of Commons was appointed to consider the state of the British possessions on the West Coast of Africa. It reported in the year 1842, *inter alia*, " that all jurisdiction over the native tribes beyond the immediate radius of the forts should be the subject of distinct agreement with them; not the allegiance of subjects, but the deference of weaker powers to a stronger and more enlightened neighbour."

Another Select Committee sat, as we know, in the sixties, and this question of jurisdiction was then left indefinite. Colonel Ord in his report, quoted on page 356, refers to this matter in the following terms:

"After enquiry it was admitted that although we possess no legal jurisdiction in the country, it was possible that we might exercise with a great advantage to the people a species of irregular authority, partly tolerated from a conviction of its usefulness and partly compulsory from the nature of our position."

As showing that there was no mistake at all about the merely friendly relations between Great Britain and this country in the minds of the Natives, we find that, early in the seventies of the last century, there was an attempt made by the people to form a confederation of the various Fanti tribes, and a constitution was actually drawn up, known as the Mankessim Constitution.

To clinch the matter, once more, in 1887, Mr. R. H. Meade, writing for Lord Knutsford, then Sir H. Holland, to Mr. A. McArthy, M.P., respecting the question of jurisdiction, said: "The term annexation used by Mr. S. is also incorrect, inasmuch as the greater portion of the Gold Coast Colony still remains a protectorate, the soil being in the hands of the natives and under the jurisdiction of the chiefs."

The intelligent reader, with these facts before him, will rise from a perusal of the article, "Colony or Protectorate," reproduced in the Appendix, strengthened with the conviction that the position therein taken is in every way warranted.

The Status of the Gold Coast.

3. BEARING OF ASHANTI AFFAIRS UPON THE BRITISH POSITION ON THE GOLD COAST.

It is of importance to the student of history, seeking to know the truth as to the status of the Gold Coast in her relation to Great Britain, to have clear ideas as to the bearing of Ashanti affairs with respect to British position on the Gold Coast.

The impression seems to prevail in the minds of those unacquainted with the facts that Great Britain, having in the course of her intercourse with the Gold Coast, come into conflict with Ashanti on certain occasions, she has thereby acquired certain prerogatives, rights, and jurisdiction in the Gold Coast which she otherwise would not have. The following passage in the late Governor Maxwell's message to the Legislative Council on March 10th, 1897, shows how widespread is the misconception. Said he : "The occupation of Kumasi, and the conclusion of treaties of protection with all the Ashanti States, has enlarged the field within which traders and miners may safely and profitably carry on commerce and industry. These events have also contributed to the urgency which now exists for some settled understanding in regard to rights arising out of land, the manner in which rights of various kinds may be created, the authority which is necessary, and the terms and conditions upon which such rights may be enjoyed. In the House of Commons, on July, 1896, the Secretary of State for the Colonies stated that he had sanctioned the policy under which it would be made impossible for native chiefs to make any concession of land without the sanction of the Governor." It is worth noting that in this message the Governor justifies the adoption of the drastic policy proposed by events which took place outside the Gold Coast. There is thus an ever-present danger of the affairs of Ashanti being confused with those of the Gold Coast even by those who may be supposed to be able to differentiate them. Hence arises the need for the examination of what evidence there is in the matter, and for a clear statement of the exact part which Ashanti affairs have played in the political history of the Gold Coast.

I propose, therefore, briefly to refer to the causes which brought about troubles with Ashanti, and the exact part, if any, that the people of the Gold Coast took in such troubles. For this purpose I must go back to the work of Captains Brackenbury and Huyshe, who, as military writers, were seeking to instruct the troops engaged in the Ashanti campaign

CHAP. IV. THE STATUS OF THE GOLD COAST. 153

of 1873 and 1874 on the real causes of the war. It will be enough for my purpose to take the authors from the year 1852.

Now, on page 20 of the book before us, it is made clear that as far back as 1852 a certain Assin chief, to wit, Cudjoe Chibbo, had received bribes from the King of Ashanti to bring his people under the authority of that monarch, and, having defied the authority of the Governor, he had been apprehended, tried, convicted, and sentenced to imprisonment for life. The gallant writers add immediately: "We gain here from the Governor's despatch an insight into the spring moving the Ashantees at this time towards war." Accordingly we are told on page 22 of this work that on March 22nd, 1853, the Ashantis crossed the frontier in force to take away Chibbo.

Now note, please, that from 1853 to 1863 there was peace; but in December of 1862 the restoration of a runaway slave boy was demanded by the King of Ashanti, and rightly refused by Governor Pine. There was at the same time a demand for the return to Ashanti of an old chief who was charged with appropriating gold belonging to the King. This demand was also refused.[1] Accordingly, when our authors came to summarise the causes of the war of 1873 and 1874, they warn us on page 45 that there had been no peace with the Ashantis since 1863.

[1] "Fanti and Ashanti," p. 26.

Let us now study carefully some of the most direct causes of the war of 1873 and 1874.

Early in the seventies of the old century, negotiations were in progress between Her Majesty's Government and the King of the Netherlands for the transfer of certain forts on the Gold Coast. According to the arrangement, "the boundary between the possessions of Her Britannic Majesty and those of His Majesty the King of the Netherlands was to be a line drawn true north from the centre of the mouth of the Sweet River as far as the boundary of the present Ashanti kingdom." By this treaty Appolonia, Dixcove, Sekondi, and Commenda were handed to the Dutch, and there were many circumstances, in the view of Captains Brackenbury and Huyshe, leading them to the belief that it was effected without any consultation with the tribes affected by the treaty. As it was, the Commendas refused to accept the Dutch protectorate, and were punished by the Dutch. The Commendas being Fantis, the Fantis retaliated upon Elmina, which was Dutch.[1]

Now, the Elminas were friendly with the Ashantis, and about this time there was an Ashanti force, under Akempon, actually in Elmina, who claimed a right to an annual tribute from the Dutch,

---

[1] If the authorities took the trouble to study Gold Coast history, they would see the incongruity of any attempt on the part of the Commendas to throw off their allegiance to the King of Inkusukum.

THE STATUS OF THE GOLD COAST.

and therefore objected to the transfer. The claim was, of course, denied by the Dutch. In the result the transfer took place, and it formed a standing grievance on the part of His Majesty the King of Ashanti, which is couched in these words in a letter by the King to the Governor[1] :—

" I beg to bring before your Excellency's kind consideration regarding the Elmina, if it is included in the change. The fort of that place have from time immemorial paid annual tribute to my ancestors to the present time by right of arms, when we conquered Tutim Gackidi, King of Denkara. Tutim Gackidi having purchased goods to the amount of nine thousand pounds (£9,000) from the Dutch, and not paying for them before we conquered Tutim Gackidi, the Dutch demanded of my father, Osai Tutu I., for the payment, who (Osai Tutu) paid it full the nine thousand pounds (£9,000), and the Dutch delivered Elmina to him as his own, and from that time tribute has been paid to us to this present time. I hope, therefore, your Excellency will not include Elmina in the change, for it is mine by right."

Subsequently, the Dutch Government opened negotiations with the King of Ashanti through an agent, who succeeded in eliciting a letter of withdrawal from the King from his former position.

Accordingly, we read on page 59 of this work: "On the 1st of September, 1871, only a few days after his positive renunciation of the claim to rights over Elmina, as already stated, the King of Ashanti had written making several complaints to Mr. Salmon, who was now administering the Gold Coast Government."

[1] "Fanti and Ashanti," p. 48.

The King was informed that the affair as regards the Elminas was a Dutch affair, and that until peace was made, the King could not be allowed access to Elmina through the Protectorate. Mr. Salmon then proposed peace and arbitration, the preliminary condition being that certain German and French captives were to be sent back.

After some delay on the part of the King of Ashanti, Mr. Salmon decided to close the road to Ashanti traders. On this point the following observation occurs on page 62 : " I fear it cannot be doubted that this step, however righteous the motive which prompted it, would scarcely be viewed by the King of Ashanti as another proof of friendship." And on page 70 a letter written by the captive missionaries is quoted in which they state:—" The shutting of the roads they consider, as we yesterday could understand, as a declaration of war."

In an official despatch, quoted on page 73, the then Fanti King of Abra, in the Gold Coast, reported on the causes of the invasion as follows :—

" I respectfully beg leave to bring to your notice that the causes and purposes of these inroads of the Ashantis are the cession of the Elmina Fort, and the Elminas having become British subjects ; because (from what we have repeatedly heard) the King of Ashanti says, that from the time immemorial his ancestors ate and drank at Elmina, *i.e.*, he gets all his wants from there, and that the fort is theirs ; therefore he will come and take it by force of arms. The chief of Anamaboe also agreed with me in this statement."

Now, it will have become abundantly clear that from the year 1853 to 1873 the people of the Gold Coast Protectorate, as such, had in no way been concerned in the transactions which brought about friction with the Ashantis; and that the immediate cause of the war of 1873 and 1874 was the transfer of territories between the English and the Dutch. The expeditions of Sir Francis Scott and Sir James Wilcocks are within recent memory, and require no explanation as to their being entirely Government affairs in pursuance of a given Government policy. When we come, therefore, to determine the status of the Gold Coast and the true nature of her relations with Great Britain, it will be with the conviction that, whatever the motives be which have prompted British policy with respect to Ashanti in the past, such policy can possibly have no bearing upon the legal status of the Gold Coast.

The Status of the Gold Coast.

4. BEARING OF TREATY RELATIONS AND ACTS OF PARLIAMENT UPON THE BRITISH POSITION ON THE GOLD COAST.

The nature and limits of the King of England's jurisdiction in the Gold Coast having been seen in the foregoing examination of evidence, it may be asked whether there are not in existence any treaties between His Majesty's Government and the Gold Coast, defining the position of His Majesty's Government.

Captains Brackenbury and Huyshe in their able work assure us that "the Treaty of 1831, construed together with the unsigned treaty of 1827 and the Bond of 1844, formed, up to 1852, the only documents which defined the position of the British Government, Ashanti and the Fanti tribes."[1] Let me, therefore, for a moment, collect together what evidence there is regarding this treaty of 1831.

On page 42 of the Report of the Select Committee, Colonel Ord is asked the question: "Can you state to the Committee summarily the main points in the Treaty of 1831, which is now the ruling treaty

[1] "Fanti and Ashanti," p. 19.

between the British Government and the King of Ashanti?" To which he replies: "It was agreed between the King of England and the King of Ashanti and the chiefs of what is now the protected territory, that in order to prevent quarrels in future and for the protection of lawful commerce, the ports should be open to all persons engaged in lawful traffic, and any person molesting them in any way should be liable to punishment."

It will be seen, therefore, that this was a tripartite agreement in which the main object was the encouragement of lawful trade, and the protection of traders. Later on Colonel Ord tells us that the Treaty of 1831 and the "Terms" of 1827, being the unsigned treaty before referred to, must be construed as one document. I am, therefore, saved the task of examining intimately the "Terms" of 1827.

I must now deal with the Bond of 1844, which, for convenience of reference, I have had printed in the Appendix to this work. It refers to power and jurisdiction having been exercised within divers places and countries adjacent to Her Majesty's Forts and Settlements, and acknowledges the same on the part of the signatories; declares human sacrifices and other barbarous customs contrary to law; and provides for the trial of offences by the Queen's judicial officers and the chiefs of the districts, "moulding the customs of the country to the general principles of the English law."

Now, a careful reading of this Bond makes it clearly evident that its main object was to enable Her Majesty to exercise jurisdiction in suppressing heinous offences committed within districts adjacent to the forts. In the exercise of such jurisdiction, the Queen's judicial officers were to act conjointly with the Chiefs of the districts.

The Bond had no reference to territorial acquisition; it did not extend the Queen's Possessions beyond their former limits. In brief, such jurisdiction as it conferred was restricted to criminal matters.

But Colonel Ord refers to a fresh engagement that was entered into in 1852. I will quote his own words. Says he: "In the year 1852 a fresh engagement was entered into by the Governor of the Gold Coast at a general meeting of the chiefs and headmen of the towns and districts in the Gold Coast under British protection; and it was resolved that this meeting constituted itself into a legislative assembly with power to enact laws for the better government of those countries. And in the third paragraph of this document (the Poll Tax Ordnance) it is stated: 'The legislative assembly, having taken into consideration the advantages which the chiefs and natives derive from the protection afforded them by

Her Majesty's Government, consider it reasonable that the natives should contribute to the support of the Government.' "[1]

In the next paragraph he is asked the pregnant question, " In what sense is this agreement a legal Ordinance ? " To which he replies : " It was made so probably to give it additional validity."

We have an idea as to how the Natives regarded these several transactions in the answer of Colonel Ord on page 43, where he says : " The support which the tribes may be disposed to give to the British Government will generally be found to depend on the feelings they entertain for the local administration at the time." Further on, he is asked : " Is the general understanding of the native tribes the same now as that which I see was given in evidence in 1842, namely, that they understand the forts to belong to the English and the country to belong to them ? " To which he replies : " That is the general understanding, although it appears at Cape Coast the local government has exercised from time to time within the last forty-five years a power of granting to persons portions of unappropriated lands in the town of Cape Coast, and this right is now acknowledged by the chiefs; but they object to its being understood to carry with it any right to exercise jurisdiction." As to this, on the authority of

[1] See p. 52 of the Report.

Captains Brackenbury and Huyshe, we learn that in 1865 Aggery, the King of Cape Coast, claimed jurisdiction upon ground actually within a few yards of the forts, and, upon Governor Pine resisting the claim, the King became insolent and offensive, and the Governor refused to recognise him as King.[1] Thus, the student of history will see that the practice of refusing to recognise native Kings as Kings by an authority practically deriving its existence from such Kings is nothing new. The only question is what effect such *brutum fulmen* has upon the position of the King not so recognised.

Next follows the pregnant questions : " Are there towns around the forts ? " *Answer:* " There are." " And is the same right claimed by the British Government over these towns ? " *Answer:* " No ! nor has it been exercised."

On page 53 Colonel Ord is again asked : " You have said that there is no definition of our boundaries at all on the Gold Coast. I suppose that all those protected states know perfectly well their own boundaries ? " " I imagine," he replied, " that the natives know their own boundaries perfectly, but we have so little acquaintance with the interior that we are in ignorance on these points." Again he is asked : " But still the native tribes know distinctly their own boundaries ? "—" No doubt they do, as

[1] " Fanti and Ashanti," p. 34.

they attach considerable importance to that point." He is then asked: "Is it not a fact that by certain Colonial Office instructions it is understood that the British territory reaches to the extent of a gun range round all the forts?" *Answer:* "It has been so said, but those instructions have not been acted upon." Of course, it takes two to make a bargain.

A reference has been made in the foregoing examination of evidence on the question of treaty relations between His Majesty's Government and this country to the imposition of a poll tax, and it may be said to carry with it an acknowledgment on the part of this country of a distinct jurisdiction. I will, therefore, go a little into the evidence on this point.

The question is asked on page 44: "The poll tax which was the first attempt at direct taxation by Lord Grey appears to have rapidly fallen off, and I believe has finally ceased?"—"Yes, since 1861." "Has not Governor Pine recently attempted the imposition of a similar tax, though not a poll tax?" *Answer:* "An Ordinance has been recently passed by the local government, which has not yet been confirmed by the Government at home, prohibiting the sale of wines or spirits, wholesale or retail, until a license has been taken out." "Was the opposition to this license on the ground that the natives considered themselves, as not being subjects, free from taxation?" *Answer:* "The natives at first made great objections on the plea that its operation extended to a distance of two miles inland from the sea-board—in fact, over a country in which we had no right to impose taxation." The earnest student will seek in vain for evidence that the right to tax the people of the Protectorate has since been acquired by His Majesty's Government.

On page 47 we have a further light thrown upon the engagement of 1852. Colonel Ord is asked: "Of course the imposition of such a tax tends, as far as it goes, to convert our protectorate into a direct dominion?" *Answer:* "As originally devised, it does not appear that this was intended; he [the Governor] called the chiefs together, and constituted with them a Legislative Assembly which should enact laws for the government of the country. This was the origin of the poll tax, and if any tax on the people be ever carried out, I conceive that it can only be effected in that manner, namely, with the consent and the direct co-operation of the chiefs themselves."

You have the solution of the problem of the difficulty of Gold Coast Administration indirectly in this important answer. Legislation, to be effectual, must be with the Chiefs in a representative legislative assembly. Any important measure affecting the people must be passed with "the consent and the direct co-operation of the

CHAP. IV.   THE STATUS OF THE GOLD COAST.   165

Chiefs themselves." If the policy of the Government had been based upon this sound principle, there would be no need to-day for this work. What the country requires, and requires most urgently, to-day, is a national assembly wherein all sections of the community will be adequately represented. That is the fundamental element of progress —the reform at which all right-thinking men must directly aim.

This important principle is fully recognised by Lord Stanley, Colonial Secretary, in his letter to Lieutenant-Governor Hill on the "Assessor's Jurisdiction," dated at Downing Street, November 22nd, 1844, which is published by Mr. Sarbah, with other official documents, in the appendix to "Fanti Customary Laws," and which, for convenience sake, with his kind permission, I have reproduced in this work. The particular letter runs thus:—

" You will bear in mind that the power of the assessor in his judicial capacity is not derived from either the Acts of Parliament above referred to or from the order in Council. . . . It must be founded on the assent and concurrence of the *sovereign* power of the state within which it is exercised, either expressed, as in the case of the Treaty transmitted by you in your private and confidential despatch of the 6th of March last, or implied from long usage, as in the case of the long and general acquiescence, which can be shown in many districts, in the authority hitherto exercised by Mr. Maclean."

His lordship here fully recognises the sovereign power inherent in each of the Native States which must be invoked in sanction of the exercise of the power of the Judicial Assessor. It is interesting to note how, in the course of years, the admitted "sovereign power of the state" comes to dwindle in the eyes of the British Government. Conveniently, it is forgotten the necessity of "assent and concurrence" on the part of the "sovereign power of the state" even in legislative acts, affecting such "sovereign power." Gradually, the native Authorities come to be regarded as having no recognised jurisdiction save such as is guaranteed them by the British Government; and you have introduced a "Native Jurisdiction Ordinance" with ambiguous clauses, which make it possible for the British Authorities to remove a native sovereign from his stool. Such are the sweets of British protection! Where this kind of thing will end, surely, the Native can see for himself. He does not require his "credulity to be played upon"; for he has long ago discovered that when the white man puts in the thin end of the wedge, you never know how far it may go—"*Brofu woye amangaydua.*"

But, after all, what are the odds? We have no quarrel with the goal of British policy, but with the methods adopted in attaining that goal. For I take it that no British Minister would willingly go against the spirit of fair play shown in much of the evidence I have examined in this chapter. We quarrel with the methods of British policy, because, we know, they are conceived in feebleness, and without reference to the facts.

From my long experience of the people of this country, from my intimate acquaintance with their grievances and wants, I can conscientiously say that there is no Native of the country who would not vote for the supremacy of British authority on the Gold Coast, if put to the choice between Great Britain and any other European power. But though he would gladly see the consolidation of British power in the country, he must emphatically protest against the ignoring of his well-tried institutions, and any attempt to deal with him as belonging to a people of no past.

Whatever authority, by usage, Great Britain may be able to exercise in these parts, we naturally expect will be exercised with fairness, and in full recognition of the historical facts relating to British relations with the Gold Coast. Having come to the people as Friends and Protectors, is it too much to ask that they might be protected, not so much from outside attack, as from those internal, insidious assaults which leave their ramparts bare and their institutions crumbling in the dust?

CHAPTER V.

LANDMARKS.

"And it is our further will and pleasure that you do to the utmost of your power promote religion and education among the native inhabitants of our said forts and settlements and their dependencies, and of the lands thereto adjoining, and that you do especially take care to protect them in their persons, and in the free enjoyment of their possessions, and that you do by all lawful means prevent and restrain all violence and injustice, which may in any manner be practised or attempted against them, and that you take such measures as may appear to you to be necessary for their conversion to the Christian Faith, and for their advancement in civilisation."—*The Queen's Instructions to Governor Stephen John Hill,* 1857.

CHAPTER V.

Landmarks.

1. EARLY POLITICAL MOVEMENTS AND THE RISE AND PROGRESS OF JOURNALISM.

A MORE splendid victory in the annals of Gold Coast Constitutional History could not have been scored than that which marked the labours of the Gold Coast Aborigines' Rights Protection Society in the fall of 1898. Early in that year, the Society had despatched to England a deputation consisting of the President, the late Mr. Jacob Wilson Sey, and Messrs. T. F. E. Jones and George Hughes, two other prominent members of the executive committee of the Society. The members of the Deputation were received at Downing Street on Friday, the 5th day of August, 1898, by the Right Hon. Joseph Chamberlain, Colonial Secretary, when they were introduced by Mr. E. F. Hunt (Messrs. Ashurst, Morris, Crisp & Co.), Mr. Corrie Grant, barrister-at-law, also being present to represent the Deputation. Mr. Chamberlain was supported by Lord Selborne, Mr. Wingfield, Mr. Atrobus, and the Hon. J. Cochrane, M.P.

At this historic meeting the discussion had particular reference to the land legislation of 1897. In the "Lands Bill" of that year, the Gold Coast legislature had practically enunciated the proposition that Her Majesty's Government had the right to administer the lands of the country as public lands. The principle involved in the proposition, as might naturally have been expected, was stoutly opposed by the whole country, but particularly so by the Kings and Chiefs of the Western Province thereof, who sent their representatives to London to enter a protest against it. In the result, the Colonial Office withdrew from the position of having the right to administer the lands of the Gold Coast as public lands. As I have said elsewhere, the logic of facts was too strong for the Colonial Office.

But how came this sudden outburst of patriotism and political spirit on the part of the people of the Western Province at a critical juncture in the history of the country? If you wish to understand the political movement of 1897 and 1898, you must at the least go back twenty-seven years in the political history of the Gold Coast.

In the early seventies of the last century, and before the expedition under Lord Wolseley (then Sir Garnet Wolseley) against Calicali, King of Ashanti, the policy of the Government in native affairs was at times of a most vacillating nature. The "solvent influence" of British administration was already fast disorganising native rule and authority, and making the people of the Gold Coast less able to cope with external foes. The native Kings and Chiefs were alive to what the dog-in-the-manger policy pursued by the British Government would mean to their institutions in the near future; and, stirred by a patriotic impulse, they formed themselves into a confederation, historically known as the "Fanti Confederation," and drew up the "Mankessim Constitution," which was intended to form the basis of one general government for all Fantiland in a States Union. King Ghartey of Winnebah was chosen as the first President of the Confederation; but when His Excellency Charles Spencer Salmon, the acting Administrator, had knowledge of this movement, he promptly had some of the prominent members arrested, among whom were Prince Brew, J. D. Hayford, and the late James F. Amissah, on a charge of "conspiracy to subvert the rule of Her Majesty on the Gold Coast."

Considering the evidence given before the Parliamentary Committee before referred to, it is difficult to see the exact nature of the rule that Prince Brew, and Messrs. Hayford, Amissah, and others were charged with conspiring to subvert. However that may be, it does not appear that these worthy sons of the soil were ever put on their trial. They were soon released; but the movement had received a severe check.

Considering the well-known views of Mr. Charles Spencer Salmon expressed in his able work, "The Crown Colonies of Great Britain," a curious psychological question here arises. Did Mr. Salmon at the time that he, in his official capacity, put a damper upon the Confederation movement, feel in his heart of hearts that British administration on the Gold Coast was exercising a "solvent influence" over native rule (which circumstance he reprobated), and did he, nevertheless, because he was an official, restrain the movement intended to counteract such influence? I prefer to believe that at the time of the Confederation movement the matter had not struck him as it did when he was penning "The Crown Colonies of Great Britain."[1] If the reader differs from me, then, he has a fair example of the strange, and yet not strange, conflict of sentiments in official circles in West Africa.

The late Mr. Fitzgerald of the *African Times* fame warmly took up the matter of the policy of the Government in suppressing the movement in the able columns of his paper; and the good seed sown germinated in the following years in the free discussion of Gold Coast political matters in local journals.

[1] See "The Crown Colonies of Great Britain" (Cassell & Co., Ltd., London), pp. 89—92.

One of the first newspapers of the country to attract attention was the *West African Herald*, which was edited by the gifted and lamented Charles Bannerman, of Accra, lawyer, wit, and publicist. It appears this remarkable man had no press, and he took the extraordinary pains of first composing his articles, and then making out several copies of a given issue in his own handwriting. There are some copies of the *West African Herald* in the editor's handwriting extant. Other able writers, hailing from the Eastern Province, of the period and after, were Edmund Bannerman, younger brother of Charles, and the late Robert Hansen, known among his friends in his day as the "Hermit." I had the pleasure of meeting this gentleman in 1893 when I was sub-editing the *Gold Coast Chronicle* at Accra; and seldom had I come across a man with such ardent love for the welfare of his fatherland. He was true as steel, and knew no fear or favour when espousing the public cause.

To come back to the Western Province, young Brew's political ardour was not quenched by the hard knocks he had received in connection with the Confederation movement. Receiving a liberal education in early youth, and associating afterwards with such brilliant men as George Blankson of Anamaboe, (by far the cleverest man of his day from all accounts), Charles Bannerman, Edmund Bannerman, and others, not to speak of a successful career at the Gold Coast Bar, he developed, in the eighties of the last century, into the most brilliant journalist the Gold Coast has ever known. The columns of the *Western Echo*, which he edited, were for a number of years a source of inspiration to the rising youth of the country in matters relating to the political enfranchisement of the fatherland. I had just left school, and but a youth, when I was offered the post of assistant-editor on the *Western Echo*, with Mr. T. Laing—subsequently Town Clerk to the Town Council, Accra—as manager. They were glorious days, those days of early inspiration in the offices of the *Western Echo*. With all his ability, I never knew a humbler man than Prince Brew. Never did he pass an article to the head printer without first reading it aloud to us, and inviting our free criticism. The "Owl" column of the *Western Echo* is spoken of to this day. Officials in high places dreaded from week to week the literal vivisection carried on by the "Owl," spectacled and sapient; so cleverly and so neatly was it done. Moreover, it was the *Western Echo* which first mooted a Deputation to England to lay before the British public the political evils from which the Gold Coast was suffering. Under its auspices, the seven companies of Cape Coast appointed educated gentlemen of the community to represent them in matters between them and the Government, which became the prototype of the Gold Coast Aborigines' Rights Protection Society.

In 1888 the brilliant editor of the *Western Echo* left for England, and the writer was charged with the production of a new paper, the *Gold Coast Echo*, which he edited for two years. It fell to the lot of the *Gold Coast Echo* to expose the atrocities which were perpetrated upon the Tavievies, a small tribe in the Krepi district, in 1888, by the Colonial troops. "No like instance," writes Mr. Fox Bourne, in "Blacks and Whites in West Africa," on page 36, "has since been recorded of what in a local newspaper were spoken of as the 'beauties of English civilisation as reflected in the Gold Coast,'" quoting from the *Gold Coast Echo* of November 5th, 1888. It was the privilege of the *Gold Coast Echo* to have espoused the right of the community of Cape Coast to elect and enstool Cudjo Imbrah as their King, with or without official recognition, and to advocate a scheme of municipal government for Cape Coast on native lines.

The next paper which attracted public attention was the *Gold Coast People*, which was owned and edited by a native gentleman of sterling qualities, who kept his identity unknown to the public, and whose silence upon the matter I am bound to respect. The quaint pages of Bosman's great work on the Gold Coast were reproduced in the pages of G.C.

the *People;* and it formed the medium of instruction to the people in matters political for a considerable length of time.

The efforts of the Eastern Province in the line of journalism, meanwhile, had led to the production of the *Gold Coast Chronicle* and the *Gold Coast Independent,* papers which, according to their light, sought to excite interest, though in a spasmodic way, in matters political in that part of the country.

I now come to the greatest effort in journalism on the Gold Coast in recent times—during the closing years, that is to say, of the last decade of the last century. I refer, of course, to the *Gold Coast Methodist Times,* which was organised, edited, and managed by that able young man, the Rev. Attoh Ahuma, then in the active ministry of the Wesleyan body on the Gold Coast. The paper was the property of that body, and Attoh Ahuma was but their servant. But the intrepid editor did not think it right to confine the columns of the paper to church news and religious controversy. He saw no reason why the grievances of the people should not be ventilated, and their temporal amelioration enhanced in as far as it lay within the power of that spiritual organ.

At the time the young editor thus made up his mind, Governor Maxwell was preparing to bring before the Legislative Council the now famous

"Lands Bill." The *Gold Coast Methodist* at once took up the gauntlet, and fought like a veritable Achilles; and right loyally was it supported by the best intellect of the land. It fought and won. It lived to report the very able speeches of counsel in the Legislative Council upon the second reading of the Bill. It barely saw the despatch of the Deputation to England; for the Wesleyan Synod had suddenly awakened to a sense of an alleged incongruity in the discussion of political issues in a spiritual organ, and with the awakening Ahuma gave up the editorship, and the paper died from sheer inanition.

Closely connected, but in another way, with the political movement from 1886 to 1898 were Messrs. J. P. Brown and J. W. de Graft Johnson of Cape Coast. In every upward movement in a given community there are always one or two ardent souls to whom it is given to lead or to inspire. It was pre-eminently the work of these two gentlemen to infuse life and vigour into the clustering units of patriotic sons of the soil. Honour to whom honour is due. It is only fair that I should hand the names of Messrs. Brown and Johnson down to posterity. Mr. Brown, as I write, has attained the proud position of President of the Gold Coast Aborigines' Rights Protection Society, a mark of the confidence reposed in him by his countrymen.

I have given the above recital with the view of placing down in a connected form for the benefit of the rising generation a record of the political movements of the most pregnant period of our national history, and to impress upon our young men the important part good, fearless journalism has played in the political history of the country in the past, and is yet likely to play in the future.

If I had not gone to the Bar, and were editing a paper on the Gold Coast, I would strive to make it as perfect as it could be as to literary matter, get up, and finish. I would adopt a firm, bold, and unswerving policy, courteous in tone and fearless in criticism. In other words, that is, I should set before myself a worthy objective, some material good of the fatherland, and work steadily up to it. I would not for support depend upon public contributions; for that would not be business. I would promote a small syndicate of independent men of means with patriotic fire in their hearts, and would endeavour to deserve the confidence and support of the community. I would assiduously inculcate the study among Aborigines of vernacular literature with a view to instructing them in matters political in their mother tongue. I would, then, once a month, bring out a vernacular edition of my paper in which I would summarise for the bulk of the people the leading thoughts in the weekly editions of the paper.

Above all things, I would study to make the people feel that they had in the columns of the journal a mouth-piece, and in the editor a ready friend, one who sympathised with them in all their troubles and who would give his very life's blood to ameliorate their condition. In brief, I would say with that distinguished journalist, Mr. W. T. Stead: "The people are silent. I will be the advocate of this silence. I will speak for the dumb. I will speak of the small to the great, and of the feeble to the strong. I will speak for all the despairing silent ones. I will interpret the stammering, I will interpret the grumbling, the mourning, the tumults of crowds, the complaints ill-pronounced and these cries of beasts that through ignorance and other suffering man is forced to utter. I will be the word of the people. I will be the bleeding mouth whence the gag is snatched out. I will say everything."

I venture to make a present of these thoughts to enterprising journalists of the present day.

LANDMARKS.

2. THE CONSTITUTION OF THE FANTI CONFEDERATION.

The Constitution of the Fanti Confederation, otherwise known as the "Mankessim Constitution," deserves more than a passing notice in the political annals of the Gold Coast. A careful study of the provisions thereof leaves the impression upon the mind how harmful, and yet how useless, it is at any time for a Government to attempt to set back the onward tide in the progress of a nation under its protection. It is harmful, because it entails waste of national energy; it is useless, because you may as well expect the spider not to weave anew its web after a wanton child has destroyed it once, twice, and yet again.

The preamble of the remarkable document before us states that the signatory Kings and Chiefs, having taken into consideration the deplorable state of their peoples and subjects in the interior, and they being of opinion that unity and concord among themselves would conduce to their mutual well-being, and promote and advance the social and political condition of their peoples and subjects, who were in a state of degradation, and without the means of education and of carrying on proper industry, they, the said kings and chiefs, had unanimously resolved upon certain Articles following, the same having been previously discussed and considered at meetings held at Mankessim on the 16th day of October, 1871, and following days.

It will be only necessary for the purposes of this sketch to deal with the leading Articles of importance in the Constitution.

Articles 1, 2, and 3 deal with the due constitution of the Confederation, stating that the "compact body" thus formed shall be recognised under the title and designation of the "Fanti Confederation."

Articles 4—7 merely deal with the election of officers, and it is when we come to Article 8 that we find the object of the Confederation to be:—

FIRST OBJECT.—" To promote friendly intercourse between all the kings and chiefs of Fanti, and to unite them for offensive and defensive purposes against their common enemy."

The history of this section is interesting. It appears that in the Ashanti War of 1863 Her Majesty's Government had suffered the full brunt of the struggle to fall upon the Fantis, and Mr. Richard Pine, the then Administrator, had let out that he had received instructions from Her Majesty's Government not to interfere with any disturbances in the interior, nor in the quarrels of the King of

Ashanti and the natives of the Protectorate. Subsequently Governor Ussher had also practically endorsed Mr. Pine's statement.

As to this, Mr. Ussher, in a letter to the Administrator-in-chief on the situation, under date the 4th of May, 1872, states, in paragraph 4 thereof: [1]

"There can be no doubt that since the termination of that war, Her Majesty's Government has given the Fantis to understand that they must in future in a great measure protect themselves under certain modifications. Doubtless Governor Pine appreciated the difficulties of the future for the native tribes, and was wishful to consolidate them, and put them in some kind of united attitude for purposes of self-defence."

The allusion to Governor Pine in the above quotation was intended for a commentary on a statement appearing in an interesting document, being a scheme[2] anent the Fanti Confederation, submitted to His Excellency Mr. J. Pope Hennessy for the approval of the home Government, which is in these words: "Mr. Pine further informed them (the kings and chiefs) that he had received instructions to return to Europe, but that he was determined to wait until he had formed a compact between them (the kings and chiefs) before he would leave Cape Coast."

It appears that, subsequently, such a compact body, even before the so-called promulgation of the

[1] Parliamentary Papers, 1873 (49), p. 59.
[2] *Idem*, p. 51.

famous Constitution, had come into existence, and Governor Simpson had met the members thereof at Mankessim, in 1869, and there recognised the Fanti Confederation, the same being then designated the "Fanti Confederacy." Moreover, Her Majesty's Government had gone so far as to seek the assistance of the Confederacy in the matter of the ransom of certain Dutch naval officers captured by the Commendas; and King Ghartey, of Winnebah, then Prince Ghartey, as President of the Confederation, had joined in ratifying the treaty or convention entered into, by signing the same on behalf of the Confederation, Governor Simpson signing for Her Majesty's Government, and Governor Natglass signing for the Netherlands Government. Yet again, Governor Simpson had himself invited Prince Ghartey and Mr. George Blankson, the secretary of the Confederation, to Cape Coast, for the purpose of deliberating "as to the form best suited to the Confederation."

When, therefore, we come to examine the attitude of the local administration upon the presentation of the Constitution, it will be quite obvious that section 1 of Article 8 thereof could form no ground of objection.

SECOND OBJECT.—" To direct the labours of the Confederation towards the improvement of the country at large."

This section requires no comment.

THIRD OBJECT.—"To make good and substantial roads throughout all the interior districts included in the Confederation."

Article 26, which, really, should be construed with section 3 of Article 8, directs that the said roads should be made " fifteen feet broad, with good deep gutters on either side, and that the attention of the Confederation be first directed to the main road connecting Edgimacoe, Ayan, Ayanmain, and Mankessim, with the coast."

Fancy the Aborigines of the Gold Coast, thirty-two years ago, thinking of the necessity of good roads, fifteen feet wide, connecting the principal producing districts with the sea coast! But they were not suffered by the local Administration to try to open up their own country, and it so happens that it is only now that, under an energetic Administration, there is anything like a serious attempt to grapple with the question of good roads. Thus, waste, absolute waste, of golden opportunity is the record of a whole thirty-two years in the country's history. One is inclined, therefore, to agree with Mr. Salmon, speaking as a private British citizen, and not as the Administrator of the Gold Coast, that progress is not the keynote of the Crown Colony system.[1]

FOURTH OBJECT.—" To erect school-houses and establish schools for the education of all children within the Confederation, and to obtain the services of efficient schoolmasters."

[1] Crown Colonies of Great Britain, p. 90.

Articles 21 to 25 must be read with section 4 of Article 8, which directs the establishment of national schools in Brofoo country, Abrah, Ayan, Goomowah, Eckumfi, Edgimacoe, Denkira, and Assin; the attachment of normal schools to each national school for technical instruction in carpentry, masonry, agriculture, architecture, etc.; special provision for female education, and provision for meeting the expense of school building, and ensuring the attendance at school of all children between the ages of eight and fourteen.

What a far-reaching policy is foreshadowed in the "object" under discussion! Why, it meant the emergence of the country in two or three generations from a lower to a higher order of civilisation. It meant providing the country with that incalculable boon, good, intelligent mothers, to guide the growing minds of their offspring. It meant well laid out towns and sanitary arrangements, commensurate with an advanced stage of society. It meant lastly, and most important of all, the flooding of the country with contented men, each sitting under his own vine and fig-tree, close to Mother Earth, instead of a certain class of concessionmongers and breathless speculators on the Exchange. What a dream to be frustrated by stupid officialism and red tape!

Surely, whatever may be said against the Constitution now before us, it will be admitted by all fair-minded men that its policy was an enlightened one, and that it sought to do for the country what His Majesty's Government have not yet showed any visible signs of accomplishing.

Why, it looks like beginning afresh, does it not, for the Aborigines of the Gold Coast, thirty-two years after the Constitution, to inaugurate a scheme of national education, somewhat after the model foreshadowed in the said Constitution, which has received the hearty support of the present enlightened Administration? Yes, we have to weave it all over again, you see. What a waste of time, and the energy of a past generation!

FIFTH OBJECT.—"To promote agricultural and industrial pursuits, and to endeavour to introduce such new plants as may hereafter become sources of profitable commerce to the country."

It is conceivable that the Gold Coast might be a cotton-producing country to-day if the Confederation had been allowed to work out its constitution.

SIXTH OBJECT.—"To develop and facilitate the working of the mineral and other resources of the country."

The above are the modest objects of the Confederation. The remaining Articles, which the reader can examine for himself in the Appendix, deal mostly with the executive functions of the office-bearers of the Confederation. Throughout the Articles you trace in vain what could have been the cause of offence to the local Administration until you come to Article 44, where provision is made for the purpose of carrying on the administration of the Federal Government, to pass laws, etc., for the levying of such taxes as may be necessary. In other words, the question as to whether any native authority should be suffered to levy taxes in the country was the crux of the contention between the local Administration and the Confederators. Innocently asked the leaders of the movement, "How possibly are we to go to work at all without money?" They did not know then, as events proved subsequently, that, notwithstanding all protestations to the contrary, the intention of the British Government was not to allow the people self-government at all, but to govern the country as a Crown Colony. And, of course, the Constitution went diametrically against that policy.

Now, while Mr. Salmon disapproved of the movement *in toto*, and cast the leaders thereof into prison, it appears that his superior officers did not approve of his attitude towards the Confederators.

The Administrator-in-Chief of the West African Settlements, His Excellency J. Pope Hennessy, under date the 15th of March, 1872, wrote to the then Administrator of the Gold Coast thus:—

"No doubt you will observe that Mr. Salmon's proclamation disapproving, without any reservation, of the Confederacy, is in some passages at variance with the Secretary of State's instructions.

"Should you find on your arrival at Cape Coast that the Confederation is practically at an end, there will be no necessity for doing anything further in the matter. If, however, the agitation is still going on, it would be well to explain to any of the leaders of the movement that you may meet, that as long as they live under protection of Great Britain, the protecting Government should be consulted about any new institutions that may be proposed; but, at the same time, that Her Majesty's Government have no desire whatever to discourage any legitimate efforts of the Fantees to establish for themselves an improved form of government."[1]

The instructions were based upon the directions of the then Secretary of State for the Colonies, to wit, Lord Kimberley, expressed in these words, in a letter addressed to the Governor, Mr. Pope Hennessy, bearing date the 16th of June, 1872:

"Her Majesty's Government have no wish to discourage any legitimate efforts on the part of the Fantee kings and chiefs to establish for themselves an improved form of government which, indeed, it is much to be desired that they should succeed in doing; but it is necessary that all parties concerned should understand that as long as they live under the protection of Great Britain, the protecting Government must be consulted as to any new institutions which may be proposed."[2]

A feature of the official correspondence herein was an attempt on the part of the local Administration to throw suspicion on the leaders of the movement, and to treat them more as conspirators than as the natural representatives of the people.

[1] Parliamentary Papers, 1873 (49), p. 43.
[2] *Idem*, p. 14.

His Excellency Mr. Pope Hennessy had to examine matters for himself on the spot, and in his despatch to the Secretary of State he remarked, under date the 29th of October, 1872, as follows :—

"As far as I could observe, every educated native at Cape Coast sympathised with the Confederation. Mr. F. C. Grant, a native gentleman, who is certainly not the inferior of any European on the Gold Coast in character, ability, or mercantile position, is a strong supporter of the Confederation. If Mr. Ussher's judgment on their moral conduct and character were sound, it would be a painful commentary on the so-called Christianising and civilising effect of the Gold Coast Administration. But on the contrary, my inquiries on the spot, and an examination of the archives of the Local Government, convinced me that the educated natives have contrasted favourably as a body with the European residents. I was certainly impressed favourably by their tone and manner in their several interviews with me." [1]

There is a touch of humour in Mr. Hennessy's commentary on Mr. Ussher's censure upon Mr. Salmon, which reveals, in a striking manner, the want of consistency in official conduct which sometimes prevails in local Administrations.[2]

You see, Mr. Salmon had been acting as Administrator during Mr. Ussher's absence, and when the latter gentleman returned, he had, to a certain extent, followed the policy mapped out by his *locum tenens*; but when it subsequently transpired that the Colonial Secretary disapproved of the said policy,

[1] Parliamentary Papers, 1873 (49), p. 47.
[2] *Idem*, p. 47.

he then proceeded to find fault with the same in his report to Governor Pope Hennessy. Commenting upon the arrest of the leaders of the Confederators, Mr. Ussher says :—

"Here, however, Mr. Salmon committed errors, and grave ones. He caused the messengers of the Confederation (who should have been sacred) to be arrested, as well as others, on a charge of treason and conspiracy. The legality of this course was more than doubtful; it was imprudent, and calculated to give greater impetus to the movement. His further action in the matter of the search warrants was unjustifiable and irritating; the prosecution of Fynn took a political colouring and added fuel to the flame." [1]

Mr. Hennessy remarks with calm judicial impartiality upon this portion of Mr. Ussher's report thus :—

"As to Mr. Ussher's censure on Mr. Salmon, it is at variance with the opinions he had expressed before he knew my views on the subject, and it seems to be inconsistent with his own proclamation and circular." [2]

The reader gets here an inkling into how things work sometimes in the inner circle of officialism in the Crown Colony System. The man on the spot, as I have shown elsewhere, often has merely to feel his way in the dark, the chances being that he may be censured or applauded in so far as his line of conduct is successful or otherwise.

And herein lies the greatest danger of the Crown

---

[1] Parliamentary Papers, 1873 (49), p. 59.
[2] *Idem*, p. 47.

Colony System—this groping in the dark and seeking after effects inconsistent with political causes and facts in the past. For ourselves, we never blame a given official, or a given administration. How can we ? It is the system that is at fault—it is the system that must be righted. But how ? Simply by giving the merchants and the Aborigines of the Gold Coast a voice, an effective voice, in the administration of the Gold Coast and Ashanti.

Landmarks.

3. THE DEBATE ON THE SECOND READING OF THE LANDS BILL.

The "Lands Bill, 1897," was intituled "an Ordinance to regulate the administration of public land, and to define certain interests therein, and to constitute a Concessions Court."

The able speeches delivered by counsel[1] in the Legislative Council against the principle of the Bill amounted to a negation of the proposition that there were any public lands so-called on the Gold Coast, whose administration awaited governmental regulation. The point was emphasised, and that with great clearness, that every inch of soil in the country is owned by some person or other to whose stool it is attached. The authorities on the matter are simply overwhelming. Let me hasten to collect together a few of leading importance, among others, that were relied upon by learned counsel, for the benefit of posterity :—

HIS HONOUR MR. JUSTICE SMITH (acting Chief Justice) :

"*Land in the colony is distinguished under the following heads—stool land, private land, and family land. Under*

[1] Government Gazette, August 13th, 1897, pp. 296—312.

these designations, all the land in the colony, save what the Government have from time to time taken for public purposes, has, according to native law, an owner.

"Most carefully do the natives preserve and hand down all traditions connected with the ownership of such lands, and no matter how small may be the plot of land, they are always keen in preventing any encroachment on their rights in respect thereof."

The Hon. Bruce Hindle (Attorney-General, and afterwards Chief Justice of Sierra Leone):

"It is considered by the natives that all lands, whether reclaimed or not, are attached to the Stools of the different Kings and Chiefs, with the exception of the comparatively small portions attached in manner hereinafter mentioned. There is no land which is not or which has not been so attached. In the bush the boundaries are generally fixed by particular trees, by natural features, such as rivers or streams."

Major-General Sir Francis Scott (Inspector-General of the Gold Coast Constabulary):

"As a general rule among the real natives of the Gold Coast, the tenure of land is perpetual, whether cultivated or otherwise. All land on the Gold Coast is either the property of a (1) tribe, (2) country, (3) town, (4) company, (5) family, or (6) an individual."

W. H. Adams, B.A., Barrister-at-Law (District Commissioner):

"Every acre of land on the Gold Coast has an owner. There is no unoccupied land. Though no boundaries may be visible to the European, they are perfectly clear to the eyes of the various owners. It would seem as if in the remote past the whole land had been vested in the various Kings—each stool, with its boundaries, forming a commonwealth."

See Government Gazette Extraordinary, dated August 13, 1897, pages 298 and 299.

Other authorities are :—

THE HON. J. MENSAH SARBAH, Barrister-at-Law, (Member of the Legislative Council), in "Fanti Customary Laws," pages 55 and 56 :

"*The King, by the law of England, is the supreme lord of the whole soil. Whoever, therefore, holds lands must hold them mediately or immediately of him ; and while the subject enjoys the usufructuary possession, the absolute and ultimate dominion remains in the King (Co. Lit. 1 a).*

"*As far as the Gold Coast is concerned, this portion of the English law does not apply, for it is a group of territories under native rulers taken under British protection. It is British territory, but not so by conquest or cession ; as a matter of fact, the Colonial Office stated on the 11th day of March, 1887, as published in Parliamentary Blue Book of that year, that it is inaccurate to state that after the successful Ashanti expedition of 1874 the Protectorate was annexed by Great Britain and became a colony, inasmuch as the greater portion of the Gold Coast Colony still remains a Protectorate, the soil being in the hands of the natives, and under the jurisdiction of the native chiefs.*

"*According to native ideas, there is no land without owners. What is now a forest or unused land will, as years go on, come under cultivation by the subjects of the stool or members of the village community, or other members of the community.*"

His Excellency Sir William MacGregor, M.D., C.B., K.C.M.G. (Governor of Lagos) :

"*In dealing with the natives one must never touch their rights in lands, or compromise the authority of the chiefs. If one wished to stir up trouble in West Africa, all one would have to do would be to suggest that the land of the natives is about to be taken away from them. Unfortunately, their credulity in this respect is sometimes practised on.*"

I record the above pregnant paragraphs without comment.

LANDMARKS.

4. THE CONCESSIONS ORDINANCE.

From the foregoing authorities, and from the evidence discussed, equally emphatic in law as in fact, it was a foregone conclusion that the Colonial Office could not upon any show of reason declare the lands of the country public lands. *A fortiori*, there could be no governmental administration of the said lands. Accordingly, the mountain in labour produced but the " Concessions Ordinance " of 1900.

The " Concessions Ordinance " of 1900 is the best abused piece of legislation I have ever come across. Capitalists and speculators alike join forces in heaping invective upon it; and some have even gone so far as to charge those engaged in the arduous task of dispensing the law as it stands with obstruction.

The fact of the case is, that the average European knows nothing of the history of the law, and cannot comprehend its underlying principles. But that the facts are clear and just, and the principles in every way scientific, there can be no doubt. It is idle, therefore, to compare the mining laws of the Rand, or the land laws of Australia, with those of the Gold

Coast. The conditions are not the same, and, therefore, you cannot logically compare them. Gold, truly, there is in the country, and plenty of it. If you want to get it out, you must accommodate yourself to the situation, and go philosophically to work.

And, after all, it is not an impossible situation. To get a ninety-nine years' lease, with your measurements taken from a banket formation, is worth all the trouble to which you may be put. Let us consider the steps you have to take, and you will see that, after all, you have been making mountains of mole-hills.

Let us assume you have dependable agents in the country, who have made a proper selection of mining areas for you, and you have had the same carefully located, and favourably reported upon by a dependable mining expert, always remembering that there are experts *and* experts. You ought in that case, all things being equal, to be before the Concessions Court within four months from the time of obtaining execution of your leases. In taking leases, you will have taken the precaution to consult an experienced legal practitioner with a knowledge of the country, and taken care to obtain the sanction of the paramount King of the district. You may note that this is strictly and technically not always necessary; for there is a difference between a sub-chief having to report to his paramount King that he has leased his lands, tendering the latter a portion of the proceeds as a token of his allegiance to him, and the case where he must previously get the paramount King's consent to make the transaction valid. I have indicated elsewhere[1] the distinction between Ownership and Paramountcy in this connection. The fine legal distinction is gradually becoming accentuated, and soon the law upon the matter will be settled; but, as a working hypothesis, you may take it that, for the present, it will be safe to have had your leases confirmed by the paramount King.

Now you are before the Concessions Court. Pray remember that it is a division of the Supreme Court, and as regularly constituted as any division of the High Court of Justice in England. As such, the Court has rules and precedents to guide it. It does not go to work haphazardly. You must not expect, for example, that if in previous enquiries A. B. and C. have had to pay, as a fair rent for 1,000 fathoms square of leasehold premises, £200 a year, when you come before the Court, claiming property one half larger than the last, you will escape with the same rent. That will, of course, be absurd. Yet, I have heard sensible men grumble at their rents being raised in accordance with precedent.

Nor does it take long to get through a concession. I have known able counsel get through four unopposed concessions before lunch. But, remember, it is

[1] See pp. 44—62.

purely a matter of skill, gained by experience. It is perfectly possible for an inexperienced man to wreck the fortunes of a company before a morning sitting is over by ill-advised questioning of witnesses.

Assuming your concession has been carefully piloted through the Court, and you have a surveyor ready at once to take the Court's instructions, and the latter proceeds soon after to lay out the property, whose area is, say, 1,000 fathoms square, you ought, at the very outside, to get a certificate of validity well within six months from the time of the execution of your lease.

But what are the leading principles of the "Concessions Ordinance?" In order that we may understand one another clearly, please remember that I am not writing a treatise upon the land laws of the Gold Coast, or upon the "Concessions Ordinance." I am only taking a flying survey of the principal parts of the Ordinance, which, in my opinion, forms an important landmark in the history of the institutions of the country.

If you ask me, then, who may grant a concession in the country, I will beg of you to remember the following proposition: "All Natives, who are entitled by the Customary Law to rights in land, may make valid grants."

But who are "Natives"? To answer this with safety, you must go to Chief Justice Sir Brandford

Griffith's criticism of the definition of the term "native" upon the second reading of the Lands Bill.[1]

Chief Justice: "Your Excellency, 'native' in this definition does not include Mulattoes. I beg to point out that many Mulattoes have equal rights with the pure natives of this country, because they intermarry, and their children have rights through their mothers."

In this criticism you have the whole matter in a nutshell. Descent being traced through females by the Customary Law, where once a person can trace his or her line from a "pure native" *materfamilias*, he or she, no matter what his or her colour is, is a native, who may make grants in land in the country. In other words, that is to say, "Native" means all persons of African birth who can by the Customary Law make valid grants of land in the country.

What may be granted in a concession is "a right, interest, or property in or over land with respect to minerals, precious stones, timber, rubber or other products of the soil."[2]

Now, please remember that by a "concession" is not meant the piece of ground in which you have an interest: it means merely the paper writing by which you acquire such right.

[1] Government Gazette Extraordinary, August 13th, 1897, p. 313. Compare the case of *Hutton* v. *Kuta*: "Fanti Customary Laws," pp. 183 and 184.

[2] Concessions Ordinance, sect. 2.

The Ordinance would seem not to be very particular as to the form of the concession, for the interpretation clause says "any writing." Accordingly, it was argued by counsel in the Chidda Enquiry (the leading case in the Concessions Division, which I reported, and which is reproduced in this book by the kind courtesy of the editor of *West Africa* [1]) that it did not matter how informal a document was, so long as the intention of parties to grant and accept a leasehold tenure appeared clearly on the face of the paper writing, it would be a concession within the meaning of the Ordinance. The point was not covered by the judgment; but there is no doubt of an "option" agreement being a concession since the law expressly makes it such! [2]

However this may be, unless you are particularly desirous of having the point settled at your expense for the benefit of posterity, you would be well advised, in taking a concession, to have the same drawn by an experienced man, who would be sure to follow well-tested precedents.

The paper writing, whatever form it takes, must be signed by the "grantor or some person duly authorised by him." [3]

---

[1] See Appendix, pp. 289—310.
[2] Concession Ordinance, sect. 2.
[3] Concession Ordinance, sect. 11, sub-sect. 1.

Now, what amounts to signing under the Ordinance? If the grantor is an illiterate man, the ordinary mark in the shape of a St. Andrew's cross will do. The name of the grantor must be written by a person duly authorised thereunto in the presence of the grantor, who must touch the pen after his name has been written, whereupon the writer makes his mark. The writer then, usually, signs his name as a witness, and, as a guarantee of good faith, states his address and the date of the execution.

In case the grantor is unable to be present, what is to be done? He can in such a case be represented by some proper person, duly authorised by him. The Chief will, generally, when he cannot come to town for the execution of the deed, send his Linguist, or Cane-bearer, with some relative or other to represent him.

The next ground upon which your concession may be lost is whether or not the proper persons were parties to it. To find out who such proper persons are requires an accurate knowledge of native law. I have seen a good many concessions thrown out on this score. To state the law with any clearness would require a little book to itself. To avoid confusion of ideas, the concessionaire would do well, when the occasion arises, to consult an experienced native practitioner.

You must see, in the next place, of course, that every step taken by you in obtaining the concession is above board, if you will allow me to suggest such a thing. Respectable men have before now had doubts thrown upon their negotiations for leasehold properties. Whatever you do, never " jump " a property, whatever that means, for the chances are that you will break your neck in the attempt. Pray remember that in buying a concession, as in buying a flock of sheep, honesty is the best policy.

Your next difficulty will be to find out what is an " adequate valuable consideration." Here I can enlighten you a little. You know it is a general principle of the Common Law of England, as also of the Customary Law of the Gold Coast, that parties to a contract shall be free to settle *inter se* what is a fair consideration, its adequacy being " for the parties to consider at the time of making the agreement, not for the Courts when it is sought to be enforced."[1] So says the Customary Law. But the " Concessions Ordinance " says no : " There must be adequate valuable consideration, regard being had to the circumstances existing at the time of the concession." How is that ? you will ask. You will find the why and the wherefore in that valuable reply made to Mr. Grant in the memorable interview anent the " Lands Bill " at Downing Street, when

[1] *Per* Blackburn, J.: *Bolton* v. *Madden*, L. R. 9 Q. B. 55.

the Colonial Secretary solemnly impressed the fact that the Bill was an "entirely benevolent" one.[1]

You see, in the good old days, when far-seeing men were beginning to see, looming in the distance, the rich mineral possibilities of the country, it was nothing unusual for men having the fear of God in their hearts to give as consideration to a chief for a lease of a large tract of country a top hat. Now, as only one man could wear this head gear, usually the Chief, who kept it jealously to himself, sporting it on high days and holidays, the rest of the "tribe" went empty away. But the native law regards the "tribe"; and, so, a wise Government stepped in and said, Henceforth there shall be "adequate valuable consideration." Therefore, you and I need not chafe over the matter, or worry our heads over the law's inconsistencies.

You will, of course, having taken the land, pay the rents when due. Not to have done so before appearing in the Concessions Court would, probably, have the effect of throwing out your concession.

Then next the customary rights of the grantors to the use of the demised premises as to shifting cultivation, collection of firewood, etc., must have been duly protected in the concession.

Lastly, you will do well to bear in mind the fact that the Ordinance deals in "square miles" rather

[1] See p. 224.

than in "miles square," and if you would avoid shoals and quick-sands, it would be as well if you worked out the difference clearly in your own mind. I have seen deeds in which a good many intelligent men have not shown an appreciation of the difference here indicated.

The rest of the Ordinance deals with such matters as "duties on profits," and other revenue considerations, which are, of course, part of an "entirely benevolent" paternal scheme. The scheme may or may not be suggestive of the policy of killing the goose which lays the golden egg. But that is not my business: it may be yours, if you happen to be the goose in the parable.

Landmarks.

5. Native Jurisdiction.

The decision in *Oppon* v. *Ackinie* forms an important landmark in Native Institutions. The facts of the case may be briefly summarised here.[1]

Ackinie, King of Akumfie, in Fanti country, had brought before his Court one David Otchafoo, charged with receiving bribes, the complainant being one Ghartey. In accordance with custom, the accused had to find a surety to guarantee his meeting the award of the Court, and Oppon became the surety. The accused was mulcted in costs, and his surety called upon to pay. The surety refused, and the King promptly had him arrested. Oppon then sued the King in the District Commissioner's Court for damages, judgment going against the King, with costs. The King appealed from this judgment to the Divisional Court, which confirmed the judgment of the Court below. On the 24th of October, 1887, the decision of the Divisional Court came before the Full Court, consisting of their Honours Hector

---

[1] See pp. 273—281 for a full report of the case, reproduced from " Fanti Customary Laws " by the kind permission of the author.

Macleod, C.J., Smallman Smith, J., and Francis Smith, J., when the memorable decision was given affirming the judicial authority of the native Kings and Chiefs. It is a judgment which will repay careful perusal. It is remarkable for its breadth of view, its irresistible logic, and its freedom from outside influence.

One or two paragraphs from the judgment will show its scope. After discussing the bearing of *Quamin Fori's* case upon the case before the Court, the judgment proceeds :

"Without discussing whether a Governor has power to take away inherent jurisdiction, and without pretending to understand what the Full Court meant by the words ' unless those powers are taken away by the Governor,' we cannot help regarding the suggested line of criticism as unworthy of comment.

"Had it not been for the opinion of Bailey, C.J., we would have entertained no doubt upon the question which we have discussed. Now that we have considered it from every possible point of view, we are clear that the Supreme Court Ordinance, 1876, has in no way impaired the judicial powers of native kings and chiefs, and, so far as we know, it has not been suggested that any other Ordinance has taken them away."

Now, in the face of this important judgment of the Full Court, it becomes interesting to consider the effect of sect. 29 of Ordinance No. 5 of 1883, being the "Native Jurisdiction Ordinance." It is noteworthy that, whereas the Ordinance in question merely claims "to facilitate and regulate the exercise of certain powers and jurisdiction by native authorities," yet, in sect. 29, it reserves to the Governor in Council power to suspend or dismiss Chiefs. The very words of the section are:

"The Governor in Council may suspend for a stated time, or may dismiss, any chief who shall appear to him to have abused his power, or be unworthy or incapable of exercising the same justly, or for other sufficient reason, and thereupon such chief shall be disqualified to exercise any power or jurisdiction, unless and until he be expressly restored by the Governor in Council."

If sect. 29 means merely that the Governor in Council may suspend or dismiss a chief from exercising the power "facilitated and regulated" by the Ordinance, and that upon such suspension or dismissal he retains his "inherent jurisdiction," there is no ground for controversy. But if the words of the section, "shall be disqualified to exercise any power or jurisdiction," can by any possibility be construed to mean that upon the suspension or dismissal of the chief by the Governor in Council, he ceases, to all intents and purposes, to be a chief, incapable of discharging the functions of his stool, and practically destooled, then, indeed, there is grave cause for apprehension.

This matter is so vital to Native Institutions that I must ask the reader's indulgence to examine it fully. For, you see, once it is conceded that the

Legislature, under the guise of "facilitating and regulating" native jurisdiction—not conferring it, be it noted—may strike at the "inherent jurisdiction" of the native Chief, the whole fabric of native government falls to pieces.

The intelligent reader who has mastered the contents of the chapter on "*The Status of the Gold Coast*" will have no difficulty in seeing that, from the earliest times, the British Government have fully understood that the native Chief, in his own country and among his own people, has the undisputed right of exercising his functions administratively as well as judicially in accordance with the Customary Law.

But let us see how sect. 29, construed adversely, strikes at the root of this understanding. Let us say the King of Akumfie has been brought under the provisions of the Ordinance, and he has been provided with a pair of handcuffs as a symbol of authority under the Ordinance. Somehow the King comes under administrative displeasure, and he is adjudged to be unworthy of exercising his power, "or for other sufficient reason," he is dismissed by the Governor in Council, whereupon not merely does he cease to be a judicial officer of Akumfie *under the Ordinance*, but he ceases, to all intents and purposes, to be the King of Akumfie. The Administration directs a new man to be enstooled. The people kick, alleging that by the Customary Law they find no fault in the King. Direction becomes insistence. Through fear, the helpless people yield, and a new King is enstooled. *Important query:* Does the *de jure* King lose his "inherent jurisdiction," affirmed by the Full Court's decision of October 24th, 1887, and does the Government nominee succeed to any jurisdiction other than such as is embodied in the "Native Jurisdiction Ordinance"? For, mark you, the said Ordinance leaves untouched all other customary rights of the native Chief.

Surely, the people of the country have the right, in the election and destoolment of their Kings and Chiefs, to be governed by their own Customary Laws. So that, where the people see no infraction of the Customary Law thereto appertaining, it would be strange to say that a king ceases to be a king, if "for other sufficient reason" the Governor chooses to say he does not recognise him; and stranger still if the Government may obtrude upon an unwilling people its own nominee, and violate the sanctity of the kingly office.

If you construe the section favourably to the "inherent jurisdiction" of the native Kings and Chiefs, then, of course, you remove the necessity of urging upon the Legislature the importance of removing from the statute-book an ambiguity which is a danger and a snare to the "inherent jurisdiction" of the native Kings and Chiefs. For, as the law now stands, a native king or chief may unwarily bring himself under the Ordinance, only to find afterwards that his ancient freedom and "inherent jurisdiction" have been compromised.

CHAPTER VI.

THE CONFLICT OF SENTIMENTS.

"The object of our policy should be to encourage in the natives the exertion of those qualities which may render it possible for us more and more to transfer to them the administration of all the Governments."—*Parliamentary Committee*, 1865.

"If you will not allow a nation to govern itself through its best passions, you can only govern it yourself through its worst passions."—*Speaker*.

Of all the colonial possessions of the British Crown, the most disappointing have undoubtedly been the territories and protectorates in West Africa. Time out of mind great expectations have been formed of them, expeditions after expeditions have been undertaken, numerous wars have been fought, and all of them have been gloriously concluded, treaties have been made of the most satisfactory and binding character, the despatches of Governors have shown the most splendid results of an astute and far-seeing diplomacy, territories have been annexed and settlements founded, and large sums have been spent by the British Government in various ways; and in the latter half of the year 1885 the actual position, on the whole, looks wonderfully like what it was at any previous time during the last twenty or fifty years, or before. British administration in Western Africa has not been a success.

It must have been a failure; the elements necessary for the most temporary success have always been wanting. It is difficult at any time to rule a country against the wish of its inhabitants; but the West African system has been, as much as possible, to rule the country as if there were no inhabitants in it. They have been acknowledged to exist, it is true, in treaties, in wars, and in expeditions, and they must have been supposed to exist for taxing purposes; for few, if any, other reasons have been given for recent annexations except the necessities of the Custom-houses, or fear of other nations placing rival Custom-houses too near them.

* * * * * * *

If British dominion in Africa should ever be of any real good to the people, or of any lasting benefit to British commerce, it will only be by an entire reversal of the policy so long pursued. The various settlements should be looked upon only as stations or convenient outposts for opening up the interior portions of the vast continent to the advantages of commerce and industry, without which neither civilisation nor Christianity itself can make any headway in these lands. No attempt even should be made to govern the country anywhere except through the selected chiefs of the people, who are open to the best influences, and whom the people will implicitly obey. A noble career lies before any European people whose Executive adopts this simple method of dealing with a great and much-wronged race. British dominion in various forms has been established in portions of this Western Coast for two centuries and upwards, and there is more than enough experience to prove that white men can never inhabit it except in small numbers and at perpetual risk of life. In fact the country must be ruled and governed by a native element, and Great Britain can easily assist and guide it by laws and regulations—the fruit of ages of experience—engrafted on to and merged with such existing native systems and methods the people may desire to keep and to follow.— C. S. SALMON, *Ex-Administrator of the Gold Coast, in the " Crown Colonies of Great Britain,"* pp. 89—92.

CHAPTER VI.

THE CONFLICT OF SENTIMENTS.

It must strike the careful observer that the position of a man in the public service of the Gold Coast is often a difficult one. If such a man is honest and intelligent, he cannot fail soon to discover the peculiar conditions under which he is called upon to discharge his duties.

The first thing that will occur to him will be the dog-in-the-manger policy of the Administration, whose servant he is. He will find that, theoretically, the people are free, having their own laws and institutions. He will see that the Government, apparently, recognise this fact; but that in practice he, the public servant, is expected to interfere with the institutions of the people as far as he dares. Neither is he told to allow the natural development of the institutions of the people, nor is he directed, in so many words, to attempt to mould them. What he does to-day, which is considered wrong by his superiors, may be done to-morrow by another and applauded.

It is as if the Government were not sure of their own

position, if the truth may be spoken. They feel the force of the logic of facts against an aggressive policy, and they are content to feel their way gradually, until such time as such aggressive policy might boldly be asserted. Hence the difficulty in which a public servant finds himself. Being an honest man, if he were free to follow the dictates of his conscience, he would do so in the light of truth. Not being free, expediency must be his guide. He must bend or break.

And the climate and the conditions of life and the public service are largely responsible for this unsatisfactory state of things.

In the first place, entrance into the West African official life is not by competitive examination, as is the case in the Indian Civil Service. Patronage rules the day at Downing Street in official appointments to the West African Civil Service. You may be a very capable man; indeed, the best qualified by experience and natural ability for a particular appointment. But, unless you have influence with some one who has influence with the Colonial Office, you are sure to be left out in the cold. That being so, you naturally get a class of men who, as human nature goes, would be the most obedient, humble servants of the Colonial Office. That is clear.

Occasionally the service may, and does, show up a strong man, who stands up for truth, regardless of consequences; but such occasions are rare, and far between. You may sometimes observe the phenomenon of an independent man going to work on independent lines. But he does so only so long as his work has not attracted notice at head-quarters. It is sure to do so before long, and then he must either break or bend. The majority bend. The few—very few— to their eternal honour, elect to break. And why?

You see, when the average civil servant has successfully made his way to West Africa, it does not matter in what department, the present appointment is regarded by him as a stepping-stone to another in some better clime. It is not his fault. It is that of the climate. He cannot keep a family here, and so he takes the first opportunity of going away. To get away to a congenial clime with a promotion, or a C.M.G., is again a question of patronage. The Governor has the last say in the matter. Therefore, naturally, even strong men do bend in the end. It is only policy—a way, that is to say, to get on in life, no matter whether the better part of man approves or not.

If this is the case with the strong, what must it be with the weak members of the West African Civil Service? They are, of course, like chaff before the wind. Strangely enough, there are some Europeans who regard men of the other races as necessarily inferior to the European. Indeed, so weak-minded are they, that they cannot, even under circumstances where Nature proclaims the other man the master of the situation, divest themselves of the idea of superiority. On every possible occasion they try to inspire a sense of this so-called superiority over their coloured friends, the result being that they become the freest tools in the hands of the powers that be, in a policy which, in every way, conflicts with the written code of official sentiment.

Are the weak in their weakness a source of strength to the Government? Indeed not. It would be reversing the order of Nature, which makes for truth in every direction, were it so. Strange as it may seem, they serve Great Britain best who serve her in truth and godly fear. Men like Sir David Chalmers, Chief Justice Macleod, and others of like grit, who looked not to promotion or official applause in the manly discharge of their simple duty, are the ones who dig deep the foundations of British supremacy in West Africa. For, believe me, the Native of West Africa has profound respect for the qualities of justice and fair play. The careless observer may think that the fear of British guns and Maxims has hitherto kept the Gold Coast proper free from disturbances. A greater mistake could not be made. If you want to know what has hitherto been a tower of strength to the British Government on the Gold Coast, you will find it in the confidence which has been inspired in the native mind by the Judges of the

Supreme Court, who have been, taking them generally, men of singular uprightness, fairness and ability, independent of bureaucratic influence. But they have not worked alone. They have been supported by a strong and loyal Bar, a band of men in whom the clients have the most implicit confidence, and who generally succeed in throwing the oil of peace upon the troubled waters of popular passion and ferment. They help to make the administration of the country possible; "but the figure-heads generally receive all the praise, and the lawyers all the opprobrium."

You have only to suggest to a native chief, smarting under a sense of wrong, real or imaginary, that the Court will look into his case, and he will patiently bide his time for months till the whole matter has been thrashed out. If he is defeated, he will retire with good grace from the scene of conflict, and all because he has implicit confidence in both Bench and Bar. What honest man is there, I ask with all seriousness, who will dare to shake such confidence? It will be an evil day for the Gold Coast when the native client begins to lose confidence in either Bench or Bar. It will be but the beginning of the end, with chaos and black ruin attending it, of which, happily, I see no signs at present.

But to consider the bane of the conflict of sentiments in West African administration in another light, let me record the views of an experienced West African civil servant, an ex-Colonial Secretary and Administrator of the Gold Coast. He is none other than Mr. Charles Spencer Salmon, who writes in his able work, the "Crown Colonies of Great Britain," thus:

"British intervention in Western Africa should be an unmixed benefit to the people, and of immense value to British commerce; *but in order to accomplish any good the presence of the people must be acknowledged, and their co-operation enlisted in the work.* It is possible that the various settlements within the strict limits of their legal boundaries may have been managed, on the whole, as well as circumstances admitted, from the usual point of view of Crown Colonies; but British power and political influence have never been confined to these limits in Western Africa, nor have they ever pretended to be so. When a long line of coast has been declared British territory by the usual methods employed on such occasions, and Custom-houses and revenue officials hold sway over it, *all native rule is destroyed for a considerable distance inland.* Now it so happens that in such cases a reign of murder, plunder, and general disorganisation ensues in these hapless lands, and no one is held responsible. *The British Administration adheres to its strict limits, or to its supposed limits, under shelter of its forts and fleets, and takes no heed of its solvent influence over native rule, which falls to pieces by mere proximity.* It is curious to note how little heed is taken of the rights and claims of other and contiguous people by local administrations; and it is not too much to say that almost all wars, disputes, heart-burnings and troubles on the coast adjacent to the British settlements are entirely and solely due to this selfish and unpardonable oversight and deliberate injustice."[1]

[1] Pp. 90 and 91.

I am responsible for the italics, but the sentiments expressed in the above weighty words are wholly those of ex-Administrator Mr. Charles Spencer Salmon. He does not beat about the bush. The meaning will be clear to all. From the list of Governors supplied in Anaman's "Gold Coast Guide" for 1892, it does not appear that this independent-minded public servant retired from the Gold Coast Civil Service with a K.C.M.G., or even a C.M.G. But that is neither here nor there.

There is only one point in the above abstract calling for observation, and that is where Mr. Salmon says: "But British power and political influence have never been confined to these limits in Western Africa, nor have they ever pretended to be so." It is just possible that there has never been any doubt in the mind of the British Government what the final aim is in dealing with the native tribes; but it is altogether another question whether or no the British Government have not "pretended" to the protected tribes that they have no intention of interfering in any way with their institutions, which, according to Mr. Salmon, "fall to pieces by mere proximity" to the "solvent influence" of British administration.

A typical instance of official disclaimer we find in Mr. Chamberlain's reply to the "Lands Bill" Deputation at Downing Street on the 5th of August, 1898.

Mr. Chamberlain said :

" Now, Mr. Grant, I should like the chiefs to know what the object of the Government at any rate has been in proposing any legislation. The main object, almost the sole object, is to protect the chiefs against the action of speculators, who in many cases get hold of the land for insufficient consideration, and without regard to the various interests in the land. For instance, a chief sells his land for a perfectly insufficient consideration ; the interests of the tribe are not considered at all in that case, and the Government desires that the interests of the whole population—the whole of the tribe as well as of the chief and of the Government—should be taken into account ; that a speculator from this country should not be able, trading upon the weakness of a chief, to get his land for a mere nothing and to oust from it those to whom really it in right belongs. So far, therefore, the object is one entirely benevolent to the chiefs and their people, and I hope that there will be no difficulty whatever in coming to an agreement as to the method by which this object shall be secured."

The "Concessions Ordinance" has since been passed, and the Supreme Court is busily engaged casting the underlying principles thereof into imperishable moulds in the way of decided cases.

But it is interesting to notice the way the " solvent influence " of the local Administration is operating, or likely to operate, upon the revenues derived by the Chiefs under the very provisions of this " entirely benevolent" enactment. Section 23 of the Concessions Ordinance (1900) as amended stands thus :

"Any rent or other periodical sum payable under any certified concession to any native shall be paid in the prescribed manner by the holder of such concession to the treasurer and by the treasurer to such native, and such payment to the treasurer shall be complete discharge to the person making the same. Any such rent or periodical sum not paid within the prescribed time may be sued for by the person entitled to receive the same. In any such suit a certificate signed by the treasurer as to the amount due and as to the non-payment of any amount due shall be admitted without proof and shall be *primâ facie* evidence as to the amount due and as to such non-payment. Any money recovered or paid in any such suit shall be paid into Court and any receipt by the plaintiff shall not discharge the defendant. The Court after refunding the plaintiff any costs he may have been allowed shall order the residue to be paid to the treasurer."

Pray, mark the last two sentences of section 23. Why, in the name of all that is "entirely benevolent," should not the native landlord under the Ordinance, having recovered judgment for rents due to him, be able to give a good discharge for the same? Why should he be made use of merely to pluck the chestnuts out of the fire for the Colonial Treasurer? The truth is, the whole thing looks like the introduction of the thin end of the wedge. How far it may go it is difficult to divine.

Even now it is making steady progress. Mark the following winding up of a letter to the Gold Coast Aborigines' Rights Protection Society, dated 18th January, 1902, by the Colonial Secretary of the Gold Coast:

"His Excellency considers that if the Aborigines' Rights Protection Society could impress on chiefs that more profitable

G.C

ways of spending their money would be by the establishment of schools, the promotion of agriculture, and the proper maintenance of their roads and bridges, they would be doing good work for the colony and obviate the necessity for Government action."

Sound advice, surely, this, if only you could calm the fears of the people. You see, it might come to this in plain English. The Government Treasurer in an "entirely benevolent" way acts as treasurer for the Chiefs of the country. The Treasurer alone can give valid discharges for all revenue coming to the Chiefs. The Government in an "entirely benevolent" way take "Government action," deciding that in future the Chiefs shall maintain the roads and bridges of the country, and, being trustees for the Chiefs whose duty as wards is to obey, they perforce will obey, and obey they must. It is simple enough. It becomes simpler still when once you emphasise the suggestion, in a plausible way, that the Government have the right to depose any recalcitrant Chief. It is but a specimen of the "solvent influence" of British administration over native rights. Unhappy Gold Coast, unless thy sons are true to thee, the days of thy freedom are numbered!

Really, it is time all sentiment were done away with in such a practical matter as the moulding of a people's destiny. It would be better for all concerned to call a spade a spade, instead of this nauseous play with fine words. But whether you openly go to work in breaking down native Authority, or you prefer to arrive at the same result by a back door, mark this, that it is but an attempt to fight against Nature, which has decreed that the Gold Coast and Ashanti shall be only successfully administered, fairly and righteously, through the sons of the soil.

CHAPTER VII.

IMPERIAL GOLD COAST AND ASHANTI.

When politicians propose measures, the reasons they publicly give for them are those only which are intended to meet apprehended opposition; the objects really aimed at are often carefully hidden; but there is no doubt it is intended that Mauritius should enter the path of self-government. . . . The new Constitution granted to the Mauritians is, however, evidently inadequate, the bureaucratic Administration having complete and practical control in all matters—the very thing not wanted. What the people in the Crown Colonies really want is to be governed as little as possible by outsiders, to be able to live on their own land without being too much worried and meddled with by regulations and laws, to impose their own taxes, to have good cheap food, and above all, to enjoy their earnings themselves.—C. S. SALMON, *Ex-Administrator of the Gold Coast in the Crown Colonies of Great Britain*, p. 82.

Those who knew him best during his life and those who have most carefully studied the voluminous records of that life, one and all honestly declare themselves unable to detect any flaws in a most beautiful, most noble nature. He never could see that what was wrong for an individual to do was right for a nation or a Government.—SIR GEORGE ARTHUR on "The Personality of Sir Bartle Frere" (*Public Opinion*, October 10th, 1902).

The truth which needs recognition is that, while in Christian countries the value of a private conscience is recognised as an essential to individual honour, no high standard of public conscience has ever yet been set up.—*The Christian Commonwealth*, April 2, 1903.

CHAPTER VII.

IMPERIAL GOLD COAST AND ASHANTI.

BUILDING THE EMPIRE.

1.

WERE there such a thing as Political Ethics, or a pretence or semblance thereof among Christian nations, as there is a semblance of some sort of Christianity in so-called Christian countries, it might be permissible to enquire how far the conduct of Christian nations in relation to aboriginal races, sometimes charitably called subject races, conformed to the Christian standard of morality.

That different principles prevail in the life of nations is evident from the trend of modern history. Men ask, with apparent seriousness, "Who is my neighbour?" and when they receive the answer in the words of the Gospel, they immediately retort, "Am I my brother's keeper?"

But since, in the nature of things, there should be, if there is not, such a thing as Political Ethics, let me examine some of the fundamental ideas in this connection as they appear to an aboriginal mind in the first instance.

Let me premise that almost the first element which confronts the aboriginal mind, as it emerges from its primitive conceptions of things, and stands face to face with the forces of European civilisation, is the Christian propaganda. It is a favourite practice with European nations to precede the Flag with the Gospel of Jesus Christ. The missionary points to the present influence of the Christ life in moulding the life and character of the individual. He points to the cardinal lessons of truth, love, and brotherhood as proclaimed by that Gospel, which accord with the higher impulses of the Native, and command his ready respect and obedience. Moreover, the missionary hopes to prepare the way for civic life by specifically teaching the doctrines of the Ten Commandments. He particularly lays stress on the sixth, "Thou shalt not steal," which, in his view, becomes the groundwork of after respect for property rights on the part of the Native. What a deal of trouble, he fancies, the Flag would have afterwards, if this particular doctrine was not well rubbed in!

And so, in course of time, the Flag makes its appearance, and with it boldly the merchant and the tradesman, who before were merely sneaking round the corner.

Presently, the standard of truth held up to the

aboriginal mind receives a rude shock. The methods of the merchant and the tradesman are not always above board; and when the Native begins to adulterate his oil in retaliation for adulterated spirits, the Flag promptly legislates against the Native's dishonesty, which thing is not fair. Cunning for cunning, dishonesty for dishonesty—surely that is fair play. But it sounds like striking below the belt, where I may endure my neighbour's dishonesty, but he not mine, which thing is not an allegory.

The early stage of the acquaintanceship between the Flag and the Aborigines is in the nature of what is euphemistically called a protectorate. Now, the term "protectorate" connotes the dependence of a weaker upon a stronger. And as the Gospel of Jesus Christ, which, we shall say, in the first instance, was in good faith taught the Aborigines, insists upon the full brotherhood of the human race—and the Native, you must grant, whether you like it or not, is a member of that race—a protectorate, surely, must mean the dependence of a weaker upon a stronger brother. But here, again, facts falsify first impressions. The very missionary who preaches the gospel of universal brotherhood seems to scout the idea of the black man, cultured or uncultured, being on the same plane of life as himself. He beholds the Aborigines afar off, and believes in the Native being kept in his place. He merely intends to raise him a wee bit higher in order that he may be useful to his white brother by more intelligently hewing his wood and drawing his water, which the latter is too good to do for himself. This is the black man's burden. In all honesty, let the reader ask himself the plain question, When, in history, has the Caucasian approached the Negro, or the Mongolian—the black, the yellow, or the brown man—in the spirit of full brotherhood, in the spirit in which the Gospel of Jesus Christ teaches us one race should approach another—not because of its markets and rich natural products, but simply to raise up the race to the measure of true manhood and true freedom enjoyed by the Caucasian?

Talking of markets and rich natural products, there is hardly a European Power which will not fight its way to the possession of spheres of influence which are reputed rich in gold and diamonds, particularly if the country belongs to an aboriginal race that cannot work the maxim or the Long Tom. The cry of gold calls up the spirit of strife. The love of gold dissipates the love of man; for is not the love of gold the root of all evil? Ah! if it were not for the something which the Aborigines have which the white man wants, but cannot get otherwise than, if need be, by breaking the sixth and eighth Commandments at one spell, how dearly would the white man love his brethren the Aborigines of the waste places of the earth? Such surely is a wrong feeling! But Jesus Christ sought to change all that, and you say you are His followers, you Christian nations of the earth.

Really, it is about time in the earth's history that the swords were beaten into ploughshares. But, if strife there must be, then we beg of you, the mighty ones of the earth, to turn your armaments upon yourselves. Pray, give us peace; save us from internal dissensions and turmoil; grant that we may live under our own vine and fig trees in the portion of the earth where Providence has placed us.

2.

Surely, we can look to England for a certain amount of fair play. The history of your relations with weaker races is not altogether such as to fill us with despair, or to make us think that you will go the way of all flesh. We believe and hope that when the crooked has been made straight to your moral line of vision, you will stand corrected. We see and appreciate the huge efforts that you are making to reconcile the forces which make for national gain, as against the forces that make for the pure advancement and progress of the Aborigines; but we do not fail to notice at the same time your shortcomings so far. We notice, with aching hearts, for example, that, in your haste to fill the colonial exchequer, little regard is paid to what will work for the material advancement of the Aborigines, whose mites help mostly to fill those coffers, forgetful that the greatest good of the greatest number is the keynote of a healthy administration.

Again, we see what efforts you are making in constituting the country into districts, and consolidating your authority and rule; but we also see that you must fail in the end; for you have gone the wrong way to work. We see, for instance, that in Ashanti and elsewhere you are building upon the sand and not upon the rock, and presently the rains will descend and sweep the entire structure away. It is bound to come, if I am right in thinking that the destinies of nations are regulated with mathematical exactitude by a Power unseen.

If you earnestly sought the material advancement of the people, you would remove obstacles from their line of progress. What part have they in the government of their own country? To whom do the big appointments and the big salaries go? To their white brethren, of course. Why? Because they are competent, and the Natives are not? Time and again the Native does the hard work, and the European draws the hard cash. When the European does the work, it happens sometimes that he gains experience from the Native. He comes to know the work after a bit, and then there comes the rub. Of course, down goes the ladder by which he had climbed. This is brotherly love with a vengeance! We know we have only to point out these things and England will remedy them.

Again, take the labour question. It is dear to the heart of the European. Herein he shows his love for his black brother beyond all question. The black man fully understands that he has been expressly created by kind Providence to provide labour in the black man's country for the European. And do it he must. There are no two ways about it. If he does not obey the instincts of nature, he will be driven, if needs be, into labour compounds, and made to work, as the Israelites of old were made to work for their masters. He understands this so thoroughly, and it does not matter to the task-master if, in the process, he, the Native, loses all touch with the former habits of his ancestors, which made them contented men and women, when they stuck to the soil and caressingly coaxed from it what Mother Earth gave up liberally in response. It does not matter if, in the process, he exchanges all the finer manly qualities, which agriculture fosters, for the common-place dram-drinking,—the cursing and the devilment of the mining camp. It does not matter to some that the best manhood of the country is being drained for this sort of work, while the ancient farms lie neglected and unattended to, and food gets scarce, and yet more scarce, in some districts. Gold! gold! gold! that is what the white man wants; and gold he must have at any price.

Then there are some charitable people who suggest that if you cannot get the black man to work, and if you may not drive him into labour compounds, you must import the Chinaman. John Chinaman is John Bull's last hope. But have you never heard of the late Governor Maxwell's Chinaman, who declared that the Gold Coast was neither "fit" for a white man, nor a black man, nor a Chinaman, nor yet for a dog? He was a bit wrong though. The Gold Coast is, and will always be, "fit" for the Gold Coast man. So has God ordained it. Long after the members of your mining companies, with their huge speculations on the Stock Exchange, will have ceased to speculate in things temporal, and the cedar and the *odum*, the cotton and the *duben* trees will have reared their majestic heights to heaven where now stands the noisy mining camp, the Gold Coast Native will still be quietly toiling in the yam and corn-fields of his ancestors, grateful at last to have the opportunity of working out his own salvation. It may be that your very Government may grow sick and weary of bearing the white man's burden, when a just Providence indicates what that burden really means, and may give up the business in disgust.

History may here, indeed, repeat itself.. Have you not heard of Roman Catholic monasteries, with beautiful frescoes and paintings, crumbling to dust in the heart of Africa? Go along the coast, from Assinee to the Volta River, and mark how many are the castles and fortresses, emblems of European greed, that are now the habitations of owls and bats, as a native wit once put it. Instead of castles to-day, you build bungalows, those structures which take a few weeks to put up, and which, again, you can pull down, take, and carry away at will. Yes, we know fully well, our good Friends and Protectors, that if, on the morrow, you found the game was not worth the candle, you would close up 'business altogether, no matter what became of the black man or the black man's country. To you it may be a light thing. To us it will be incalculable loss—loss in the sense that we shall have to begin it all over again with, or without, your distorted version of the Gospel of love, truth, and universal brotherhood.

3.

Therefore, we say to you, we have a right to be heard in this matter, and we beg of you calmly to hear us. We ask you to apply a little common sense and practical statesmanship to the situation. Take the case of your own national evolution. It is a matter of history that, at the beginning of the

Christian era, you were worse off than we are to-day; greater darkness brooded over your intellectual horizon. By the absorption of Grecian and Roman culture and the science of Eastern worlds, you gradually emerged from darkness into light, and were able to develop what was natural and innate in you, and to, in time, contribute your quota to the world's work. In a word, given the conditions of development, you developed on your own lines, until you became the great nation you are to-day.

Surely, then, the first condition of the proper development of the peoples of the Gold Coast and Ashanti is the possession of knowledge in its fullest sense, that educational element which will draw out all the best qualities innate in the Gold Coast and Ashanti Native, preparing and making him ready to contribute to life's work. Remember, after all, that the Aborigines of the Gold Coast and of Ashanti, as Tennyson has it, are "the heirs of all the ages"; and who knows but that there may be higher things destined for their achievement than you can conceive of? But the responsibility rests primarily with you, and if you do not discharge it, Providence will raise others up to do the work. Assuming, then, that you have stretched out your hands in true brotherly fashion to the Native of the Gold Coast and Ashanti, not over a palm-oil cask, or a piece of elephant's tusk, but over the heart of Jesus Christ, thrilling your very being with true brotherly love and sympathy, and filled the land with schools and colleges, seminaries and seats of learning and culture, what is your next duty in the building up of the Empire?

It is plain and simple; but before grappling with it, you will take care that the spirit of pettiness does not creep in. You are now going to allow the free development of Native Institutions in a healthy atmosphere. You have before you the task of building up Imperial Gold Coast and Ashanti, as a basis for Imperial West Africa.

Your first stumbling-block will be the treatment of Ashanti. Shall the Ashantis be treated as a conquered people, or as friends and allies? This will be the question of questions, the test of true statesmanship. To answer this question, you must find out what you want to do. Now, you aim at nothing less than the fusion of the Fantis and the Ashantis into one people. Remember that by language, traditions, customs, and laws, they are practically one people. Remember that they are cousins, and that in remote times they lived together in brotherly unity and concord at Takiman, until one day they quarrelled and split. Remember, too, that the present difference in the characters of the two peoples, really one, is due to your own unwholesome influence over the Fantis. Therefore, it is the most natural suggestion that the two peoples should be merged into one; and it will be easier for you to entertain this suggestion, when you consider that the chastisement of Ashanti was really due to a mistake.

Surely, this is a sound proposition. You will find it so if you turn to history. For a century and a quarter, at the least, Nature has been preparing the way for this very consummation. The Fantis having settled on the littoral and established trade relations with the Europeans, the Ashantis did not see why they should be precluded from participating in the gains. Gradually the Ashantis worked their way to the coast, and diplomatic quarrels ensued, with the result that the King of Ashanti was, in the end, able to claim a right to the "notes" for rents in respect of some of the forts on the coast, thus establishing direct trade relations with Europe. That was his only ambition, his only sin. Said he in substance: "Elmina is my factory; I acquired it by force of arms, and established trade relations with the Dutch. Now, the Dutch are going to give up my factory to the English, and my people must henceforth deal through Fanti middlemen, which thing must not be." Hence the Calcalli war of 1873 and 1874, and the sequence of events culminating in the ruining of Ashanti trade with the Gold Coast. Soon after the war, the Ashantis began to trade directly with Assinee; and it is a question of time whether the English, or the French and German, will ultimately capture the hinterland trade.

The obtuseness in certain respects of the British Administration, since Governor Maclean's death, has been something amazing. That far-seeing man saw through it all, and framed his policy accordingly. He understood that the business of the Administration was not that of unduly interfering with the internal affairs of the protected people, and, therefore, sought to consolidate and strengthen Native Authority. What is more, he perceived that England's true interest in the Gold Coast was to make it an open market through which the trade of the hinterland might pass freely. Therefore, without overestimating his authority or his strength, by conciliation and moral persuasion he encouraged the Ashantis to come down freely to the open market of the Gold Coast, guaranteeing them safety by prevailing on the Fantis to be on their good behaviour.

In his mental vista, he beheld a prosperous Gold Coast, with Ashanti, as a great emporium of trade, interchanging with and pouring into the lap of the Gold Coast the rich resources and products of that now blasted land. He encouraged and was instrumental in the training in England of the Princes Quantamissa and Osoo Ansah to be the medium of intelligent influence in the hinterland; and who, having the slightest acquaintance with Gold Coast history, can say that the late Prince Osoo Ansah did not do his best to bring about a permanent friendly understanding, in his day, between Ashanti and the Gold Coast? It was a policy full of common sense and practical statesmanship. It was the work of the Colonial Office, in recent years, to have struck at Governor Maclean's work, root and branch, by attempting to discredit, but without success, the sons of the late Prince Ansah in the eyes of their countrymen and the British public.

A different policy was that of Sir Charles Macarthy, another British Governor, who flourished, as far as the Gold Coast is concerned, in the first quarter of the nineteenth century. He also saw in the distance, but saw differently. He was deeply conscious of the power of England—a power which, he considered, no subject race could withstand; and he was impatient of what seemed an impediment in the way of England's aggrandisement in these parts. If he could only pierce into the interior, what untold treasures would not be open to England to gather in? In this spirit, he, the faithful servant of the Crown, went forth with the drawn sword breaking down the power of the Chiefs, and subduing all before it. Impatient of obstacles, he was also impatient of counsel as to the best way to overcome such obstacles. Accordingly, he went forth in the faith and in the strength of the conqueror, seeking new territories which should own allegiance to Great Britain through his prowess. He considered the kingdom of Ashanti a barrier to British commerce and enterprise piercing the interior, and he fondly wished to see that barrier down. He tried to break through, and died in the attempt. To-day, a first-rate Colonial Minister, persistently pursuing that policy, has brought down that barrier, only to behold beyond, if the truth may be told, a land of dreams and disappointments.

4.

It is about time to pause and think. And the thinking must be done by the British nation. The matter must be reasoned out calmly and deliberately; and if there be fifty men in Israel who have the interest of the Aborigines at heart, the right course will certainly be taken, and the right thing done. Which is it to be? Will the British nation sanction a policy which will tend more and more to alienate the Ashantis, and drive them into the bosom of the French or German, or will it pursue a conciliatory policy? Will the nation consent to the utter destruction of all national spirit from the life of the Ashantis, or will it foster the spirit of self-respect and national development on natural lines? Will

Great Britain forget that Ashanti is a conquered country, and will the conqueror be benevolent and reckon the Ashantis, as their cousins the Fantis are reckoned, as the friends and allies of His Majesty King Edward VII. ?

Will the nation quietly look on while an agrarian grievance is engendered in the breast of the Ashantis, or will the lands be restored to their legitimate owners, gradually assimilating the land laws of the Gold Coast and of Ashanti? Please note that you are deciding the fate of a nation, a people with grit and backbone, of men and women richly endowed by nature with intellects and instincts which make for organised government of a high order. You are deciding also, let me entreat you to remember, the fate of Imperial West Africa. Yes, Imperial West Africa that shall be. Nature has decreed that it shall be, but not in your way—not with the sword, or the Maxim, or by coercion in any shape or form. The thing will be done with the free will and consent of all the peoples of West Africa upon native lines; and in all this the Gold Coast and Ashanti will lead the way, because their sons are richly endowed by Nature with the qualities for leadership and guidance.

If you believe me that the Gold Coast and Ashanti will lead the way in what will prove the grandest conception of the twentieth century — grandest because Ethiopia will have at length raised up her hand unto God,—allow me to indicate what sort of an empire this shall be, and on what lines it shall work. You will allow, as a working hypothesis, that all the other races of mankind have had their day, and that the black man is about to have his day. The common Father of the human race is bringing it about that the white man shall warmly shake the hand of his fellow black man in true brotherly grip. There will be fraternity without hypocrisy, intercourse without compunction, and the question of colour will be a trifle, because there will be equality of intellect and oneness in aim and purpose.

The black man, you know, has had no chance in America. How could he? The environment has been dead against him, and, though emancipated, he remains in many respects a bondman. The American white would like to get rid of the American black, but he cannot. It is the law of compensation. It is like the law-breaker trying to shake off from his memory the image of his victim, and the circumstances attending his wrong act. How can he? No more can white America. This is Nemesis indeed—the sins of the fathers upon the third and fourth generation. Nor is it much different in the case of Hayti, or Liberia, or even Sierra Leone. The nightmare lingers, only in a different form.

But out here, in the primeval forests of the Gold Coast and of Ashanti, with a simple faith in God, the

Aborigines may be trusted to work out for themselves a civilisation whose fruits shall abide and influence sister communities, because they will be the fruits of peace and good-will among men.

How do I know that? I know this, that out here we shall not have the cry of the working-man for the comforts of life which his next-door neighbour enjoys. We shall have no question of the housing of the poor, or an eight hours a day labour trouble. Whoever heard on the Gold Coast or in Ashanti of a native who had no home, or not enough to eat, or more work to do than was physically good for him? Why, such cannot happen in the nature of things out there. The founders of the African State System were men of wisdom and forethought. They cut the Gordian knot of social unrest in the distant future at a stroke. They ordained that the interests of the members of a family should be identical. They evenly balanced the interests of the peoples of a given community, so that, when swords should have been beaten into plough-shares in the new civilisation, there would be truly peace and good-will among men.

Therefore do I hold that, while the social systems of the old civilisation will be torn asunder by communism and socialism, the new civilisation will enjoy rest and quietness, for the foundations of society are here based upon a rock, and that rock is the native law of Inheritance. We have no poor laws out here. Every man or woman you meet claims connection with some family or other. And the members of a family share the fortunes or misfortunes of each other. Hence it is that we have no excessively rich men or the excessively poor. Talk of the dead upheaval of the lower classes! Here all members of a family are equal, and yet there is one above all, namely, the head of the family. To him the members of the family pay patriarchal honours. While there prevails this equality, there is yet scope for individual effort, success, and distinction. We have, in the family system of the Fantis and Ashantis, the panacea for all the ills of the socialism of the present day.

5.

To return to the argument: when you have two peoples so nearly related as to be, in fact, one people, welded together by a common language, by common customs, common laws, common aims, hopes, and aspirations, it is madness to try and keep them separate. It is like trying to keep away the sun from kissing the sea on an African summer day. The only question is, who will work this fusion and bring about this long-wished-for union? It is obvious that the foreign intermeddler is an utterly hopeless individual for this task. He has neither the requisite knowledge, nor the patience and coolness necessary for the great consummation. It must be the work of the educated Native, if the British Government will trust him to do it. On what lines will he proceed? He will take the Native State System as he finds it, and develop and improve it on aboriginal lines, and on scientific principles.

Let me indicate how harmoniously this System works, how free from internal strifes and heart-burnings. We have seen, in the earlier chapters of this book, that every individual of a given community is, by distinct stages in the working of the body politic, connected with the central State, and, in a measure, shares in the government thereof. To accentuate the proposition, let me summarise here briefly how the System works.

Every Native of the Gold Coast or Ashanti is a member of a family. He sinks or swims by the fortunes of the family. There is a community of interest among the members of such family, who, as a rule, trace their ancestry from a common *mater-familias*. The male members of such family regard the children of their sisters with peculiar feelings of kinship. In former times, in a case of pecuniary difficulties, the nephew or niece would willingly go into servitude to relieve the uncle, who invariably redeemed his kith and kin at the first opportunity.

The relationship existing between an uncle and a nephew or a niece is tersely expressed by the phrase, *na dzi yinaä*, meaning, "he is his all in all." You have here the bed rock basis of the Native State System. Let us proceed a step higher in the order of development.

Now, a given community, it may be a village community or a township, consists of individual families, whose heads represent such individual families in the Village or Town Council. So that you have here an elective system which is at once natural, and commands the confidence of the electors. In large townships you will have the different wards (being, for convenience sake, the different sections into which the community is divided), consisting of a given number of families, such wards having the right to elect their most intelligent and influential members into the Town Council. The heads of the families are known as *Panins*, or Elders, and the head of the ward is the Head *Panin*, or Chief Elder. To him all the members of the ward pay the greatest homage and respect.

But how came families to be congregated together thus into wards, or into given sections, of the township? If you examine the matter carefully, you will find that the original members of the ward are members of the same tribe; for it is a thing practised to this day that when a stranger enters a village or a township, and desires to become a member of the community, he finds out where the members of his tribe live, and would invariably live among them, rather than dwell with a different tribe.

Now, since a man belongs to his father's Company, and his father generally lives with the members of his family, it does, indeed, happen that the sons of the male members of a given ward join themselves to such ward. We have thus the beginnings of the *Arsafu*, or Company System, the word *Arsafu* being a corruption of *Insefu*, meaning friends, and by extension friends in arms. A son, in early life, lives with his father, and, naturally, the friends of his youth would be the youth of his father's ward, and he would, therefore, as he grew to manhood, associate himself in arms with the friends of his father's ward, who together would form an *Arsafu*, or Company. The principal *Panins* of the ward and the principal Captains of the *Arsafu* would be entitled to represent the ward at the Council meetings of the township.

We come next to the Civil Chiefs who form part of the Town Council. These generally represent the aristocracy of the township, in most cases their ancestors having first settled in the country with the ancestor of the King or Head-Chief. Then comes the Linguist, who, as I have shown in an earlier chapter, is the Spokesman of the King.

We have thus in the Council of an aboriginal township, analytically, first the King, then the *Tufuhin*, then the Civil Chiefs in their order of importance, then the Captains according to their rank, then the Linguists, then the *Panins* of the several wards.

We have seen that a Village Council is only a miniature Town Council. Even so is the Town Council but a miniature District Council, the latter being but a miniature of a Provincial Council, which again is a miniature of a State Council, the great Parliament of the people.

Now, to elucidate the foregoing, take for example the township of Agambra, whose stool is under that of the district of Princes, whose stool is under that of the province of Axim, whose stool is under that of the State of Ahanta. Imagine for a moment, then, that there is a big political issue affecting the whole State of Ahanta to be discussed. Notice by gong-gong would be given in every village community and township throughout the entire State. The *Panins* and Captains of the wards of a township, who would be joined by the *Panins* of the village communities, would discuss the matter and arrive at a conclusion among themselves. They would next appoint the most intelligent of their number with a Linguist to represent them at the Council of the district, where also the matter would be discussed a second time, and a decision come to. Next, each district would send its representatives with the Head Linguists to the Provincial Council. Lastly, the several Head-Chiefs of the provinces would attend the State Council in great state, with their several principal Councillors and Linguists, where the King paramount would sit in solemn conclave with his vassals, and finally dispose of the matter, such *plebiscite*, of course, binding the entire State. It is a beautiful system, this wheel within wheel, which brings satisfaction to the minds of the adult members of the entire State, when any matter affecting their vital interests happens to be under discussion. When you add to this the further consideration of the almost communistic method of holding property, you have a perfect system, which, properly developed and worked, would usher in a new civilisation, the like of which the world has probably never seen.

Now imagine, if you can, the Gold Coast and Ashanti flooded with knowledge and culture of the best order, and the several States of the two countries federated together in one Union—with the same laws, the same customs, the same hopes, and the same aspirations; working under conditions and amid environments peculiar to themselves as unto a peculiar people. Imagine, if you can, all flying the Union Jack, not by coercion in any shape or form, but by free choice, as becomes a free people. Think of them developing the natural resources of the land—a rich legacy bequeathed unto them by kind Providence—and pouring into the lap of Britannia gold, myrrh, and frankincense, the swords for ever beaten into plough-shares as far as the Gold Coast and Ashanti are concerned. Imagine what all this would mean! You may call it a picture of Utopia. I call it a picture of the new civilisation that is to be, when a portion of down-trodden Ethiopia will have at length raised up her hand unto God.

It is bound to come. The world is moving fast, and the Gold Coast and Ashanti with it. Will British capital, energy, and intelligence do it, or will the millionaire from the other side of the Atlantic, in these days of combines, come along and sweep the stakes? In any event, the country must move with the times, and we do not intend to stand still.

CHAPTER VIII.

WRECKING THE EMPIRE.

. . . In one breath Europe declares that African customs, all based on the assumption of slavery, are so wicked as to justify all wars of aggression upon the natives. In another, Europe declares that the African cannot be left free. . . . It is hard to resist the conclusion that in Sierra Leone, in Ashanti, and now in Hausaland, war has been brought on by pursuing a highhanded policy of very doubtful justice, and the result of these wars is not merely to confiscate the independence of a people, but to abolish the institutions, the customs, the laws and the rights which the people has created for itself. What is common to our notions and to theirs, the principle that a bargain must be adhered to, that a friend should not hurt a friend, we disregard. What we do not understand in their rules of life we abolish, and we lay upon them rules of life that they do not understand.—STEPHEN GWYNN, *Fortnightly Review*, March, 1903, p. 457.

CHAPTER VIII.

WRECKING THE EMPIRE.

1.

We have seen the true way in which it is suggested Imperial West Africa, with federal Fanti and Ashanti as a basis, may be solidly built up. Let us now see how the powers that be set to work steadily to make this ideal impossible of realisation.

We have seen also that at the Head of the Native State stands prominently the King, who represents to his people what a civilised monarch does to his subjects. His person is sacred to them, and so is his stool. Any affront to the majesty of the King is an affront to the sovereignty of the people. Any attempt to break up the kingly office and the traditions surrounding it, is an attempt to destroy the nationality of the people. Any restraint upon the liberty of the King is a restraint, for the time being, upon the freedom of the nation. The King means this and much more to the State System of Fanti and Ashanti. Moreover, every successful attempt on the part of the Authorities, in ignorance possibly, to set a minor chief against the authority of his paramount King, or, again, to partition a native state, is a deadly blow struck at the very root of the fundamental idea of the Native State System.

But our rulers do not appear to trouble much, if at all, to study Native Institutions; and so we find that in the year 1896 Cudjoe Imbrah, King of Cape Coast, was actually put in prison, his hair clipped, and made to don prison clothes, in connection with the "Compulsory Labour Ordinance, 1895." This imprisonment and the gross indignity consequent thereupon were preliminary to his paying a fine of one hundred pounds. I appeared subsequently for the King in the Appeal Court, and succeeded in getting the conviction quashed and the fine remitted.[1] But what of the indignity? I am not aware that Her Majesty's Government even offered the King an apology upon the reversal of the judgment of the Court below.

Now, who is Cudjoe Imbrah, and what sort of a community is that of Cape Coast? By common consent, Cape Coast is the leading town of the Gold Coast. It contains within its walls the best intelligence of the country. It is the political centre of all the interior provinces. Thither the native Kings are wont to send their big Linguists on important occasions to consult with their intelligent "sons" and

---

[1] Regina on the prosecution of *D. A. Donovan* v. *Cudjoe Imbrah*, on appeal. *Coram* Redwar, J. 17th Feb., 1897. See pp. 281 288.

chosen representatives, to wit, the members of the Gold Coast Aborigines' Rights Protection Society. It is, moreover, a commercial centre of no mean order. Before the Ashanti trade was practically ruined by unnecessary expeditions, Cape Coast was the great port for all the interior trade. Here stands Gothic House, as representing the glory of private mercantile enterprise, and here stands Cape Coast Castle, the harbour of the foreign kidnapper in pre-abolition days. As such, the King of Cape Coast must be a comparatively important person.

See, for a moment, how Cudjoe Imbrah was chosen King of Cape Coast. At the time I was editing the *Gold Coast Echo*, and I remember the facts so clearly. Kweku Atta, the immediate predecessor of Cudjoe Imbrah, had died, and for some time there had been no King of Cape Coast. When a Deputation of the representatives of the Companies and the community generally, including the educated people, waited upon the future King, he said: "I am not anxious to be your King. I am satisfied with my present position of a 'gold taker.' Leave me alone in peace." But the Deputation insisted upon his accepting the office. They said, "We must have a King, and you being the rightful heir, you cannot well refuse." They pressed him and gave him no rest until he consented to be their King. The Administration of the late Governor Griffith attempted to interfere in his election, but the people simply ignored Governmental interference, and Cudjoe Imbrah was put upon the stool of his ancestors, to reign King of Cape Coast.

It may seem to you, decent civilised reader, that this was a retrograde step. You may even have on your lips the enquiry: " Can the leopard change its spots?" Here was a set of educated Natives clamouring with their illiterate brethren for an illiterate King, when they had the good White Queen for their Queen, and the good Governor as her representative! Can anything be done with such a people? No, I grant you nothing can be done with these people, unless and until you condescend to study Nature. The people yearned for a King as an orphan child yearns for a lost parent. It was the sentiment of nationality which prevailed. They are a people yet. They could breathe freely when once they had Cudjoe Imbrah upon his ancestral stool.

But the wreckers of empire come along, and this self-same Cudjoe Imbrah, over whose enstoolment sensible men had shown such enthusiasm and such national spirit, and they coolly clap him in gaol. Nay, worse, the King is treated as a common felon! Heavens! What was there to have prevented the people rising up as one man to avenge the insult to a crowned head? But this—that wise counsel prevailed, the same wise counsel which is steadily carving the happy destiny of the Fanti as the predominant partner in the coming Imperial West Africa.

But what had Cudjoe Imbrah to do with the "Compulsory Labour Ordinance"? Nothing at all, if you please. The Government having objected to his enstoolment, and having done all they could to place obstacles in the way, and to weaken his influence, suddenly woke up to the fact, after his enstoolment, that there was a King in Cape Coast, who could find labour for the Government, while the Government could not find labour for themselves. And, so, they approached him. Said he, in substance, "By your own act, I have not that control over my people now that my ancestors had; give me time, and I will try and find you the labourers that you want." But, no, the Authorities must have the men on a certain day, and by a certain hour. He fails; a writ issues; he is tried, convicted, and imprisoned. Worse still, he suffers ignominy unparalleled in the history of the country, and he is saved from a heavy pecuniary loss by technical points raised by his counsel. Such is British statesmanship. Such is British commonsense. This is the way Great Britain wrecks the chances of Imperialism in West Africa.

2.

Or, again, take the case of King Prempeh of Ashanti, now pining away his days in exile. I will take the *Times* for my guidance as to what policy should have guided Downing Street in the matter of war with Ashanti. It is true that policy is some thirty-nine years old. But still it was the policy of the *Times* all the same, and the *Times* is a very great authority as you know. I will indulge in a quotation. Mr. Fox Bourne, of the Aborigines' Protection Society, has made the matter easy by placing that policy on record on page 22 of his pamphlet, *Blacks and Whites in West Africa*. Referring to Governor Pine's threatened war with Ashanti in 1864, which did not come off, the *Times* asked, "What good can come out of that? If we capture Kumasi, a couple of English regiments will be needed to hold it. If we destroy it, we destroy at once the commercial value of Cape Coast. It would likewise be the grossest political blunder to undermine the power and authority of the King of Ashanti. . . . Instead of harbouring culprits against his Crown, instead of disregarding the treaties between himself and us, instead of trying to sap the foundations of his throne, we should strive to cultivate acquaintance with him by the tranquil arts of peace." Wiser words were never penned. I wonder if the Editor of the *Times* ever looks up his back files? Perhaps he does. But I am not sure whether there was the same statesmanlike appeal to British common-sense in subsequent mischievous expeditions as was the case in 1864.

Now, I have pointed out before that the war of 1873—1874 was mainly due to the transfer of Elmina by the Dutch to the English, and the latter failing to treat with respect and consideration the claims of the King of Ashanti to suzerainty. In the result, Lord Wolseley succeeded in capturing Kumasi, whereupon the Authorities promptly inflicted an indemnity of 50,000 ounces of gold upon the Ashantis. Then Mensa succeeded to the stool; and when he was followed by Prempeh, the Authorities stoutly maintained that he was only King of Kumasi, and not of *all* Ashanti. That was true only in so far as there were at the time internal disturbances in the kingdom. But mark official perversity. In the expedition of Major-General Scott, the non-payment of the war indemnity was made a cause of Prempeh's degradation and transportation. The Authorities, that is to say, saddled the sins of omission of *all* Ashanti upon Prempeh, whose claim to the sovereignty of *all* Ashanti they had previously denied. It may be British justice; but it certainly does not appeal to the sense of justice of the untutored Ashanti now roaming in the wilds of the back country, an outcast from his former home. This is, again, another way in which is wrecked the hope of empire in West Africa.

Let us take up another theme altogether. Now it is not a matter of policy, but the way in which is carried on the business of government. You know when Governor Hodgson was unfortunately locked up with Lady Hodgson in Kumasi fort, and popular imagination was active in that, if the good lady came out, the Governor never would alive, both civilians and officials were loud in their condemnation of the good Governor. He was freely charged with folly, and a member of Council eased his conscience by the simple remark: "You know he never asked any of us if it was safe to go." The circumstance revealed in the clearest light how very badly the Gold Coast is governed.

We have seen how beautifully arranged is the system of aboriginal representative government, which practically gives the franchise to every adult member of the community in the National Assembly, presided over by the paramount King. When the Native recalls to mind his own System, the way he is at present governed, and the suggestion on the part of the British Government that they are training him up for self-government, he knows that such a suggestion is not sincere, and that his national spirit and independence are being dwarfed the whole time, which, surely, is another way of wrecking the empire.

But the Native is sure of his destiny, and, therefore, calls loudly for reform. He did so in 1898 in the humble petition of the Kings and Chiefs of the Western Province of the Gold Coast Protectorate to Her Most Gracious Majesty the Queen in Council, and will do so again and again, until his prayer is heard. Thus ran the prayer :

"Your petitioners respectfully suggest as a first step that the Letters Patent whereby the Executive and Legislative Council was created should be altered so as to enable the Kings and Chiefs of the colony and the protectorate to elect to the Legislative Council eight additional members, of whom three shall also be members of the Executive Council.

"Your petitioners respectfully suggest that for the purpose of the election of such members of the Legislative and Executive Councils, the Gold Coast Colony and Protectorate be divided into four provinces, viz. :—

"*A*. From the River Volta to the River Sccum.
"*B*. From the Secum to the Sweet River.
"*C*. From the Sweet River to Dixcove.
"*D*. From Dixcove to Half Assinee.

"And that each province have the right of electing two members of the Legislative Council, the members thus elected themselves electing from amongst themselves the three members of the Executive Council.

"Your petitioners, therefore, humbly pray your Majesty to grant an amendment of the existing Letters Patent for the Gold Coast Colony and the Protectorate whereby the present system of government and protection may be altered so as to provide that the natives of the colony and the protectorate may elect members to the Legislative Council and Executive Council and thus take part in the work of legislation for their native land.

"And your petitioners will ever pray." [1]

This was a modest prayer. Why it was not granted one is at a loss to know. The petition was in 1898. The ill-advised hunt for the golden stool by Governor Hodgson was in 1900. A member of Council then said the Legislative Council had not been consulted. See what a waste of money and blood would have been saved if this simple prayer had been granted. Had the representatives of the people from the Volta to the Assinee River been sitting at Victoriaburg, with eight votes in the Legislative Council and a controlling voice in the Executive Council of three votes, the greatest blunder of the last decade in Gold Coast and Ashanti affairs could never have been committed. For every Native knows, as a fundamental principle, that to ask for a king's stool is to ask for the surrender of the national integrity, which is the one thing, as an abstract idea, that a native will keep hold on to after he has lost all.

Moreover, an honourable member could have urged that the policy of the Gold Coast Government should be the gradual healing up of the wounds so grievously inflicted upon the sense of

[1] "The Report of the Proceedings of the Deputation from the Kings and Chiefs of the Western Provinces of the Gold Coast (1898)," page 2.

justice and fair-play of the people of Ashanti, rather than to keep them open. For, mark you, the talk about human sacrifices and barbarous customs and slave-raiding is all cant. What lies behind it all is the desire for the good things of Ashanti that would come into the pockets of the British capitalist. How many thousands are mowed down by the Maxim in a single expedition? And in times of peace are not "rebel chiefs" freely hanged? The Ashanti loathes the hangman's noose, but gladly lays his neck upon the execution block. The latter he accounts honourable death, if death he has deserved; the former he regards as a disgraceful exit which his soul abhors. I do not personally approve of executions and slave-raiding, or of slavery in any shape or form. But what calls for loud protest is, that these should be made a cloak for cant—an apology for the use of the Maxim gun—when all the time all the world knows that you are simply taking part in the scramble for the black man's country. It is unpalatable, I know; but it is true all the same.

I dearly love this ideal of Imperial West Africa, and I sincerely desire that the golden hope may not be wrecked. The country is flooded even now with intelligence. With hardly sixty years' educational advantages, we have a remarkable band of able men in all walks of life, a sign of the coming greatness of the people in the new century and in the new civilisation. We only ask for opportunity, that opportunity being fundamentally the prayer that the Aborigines may now be allowed to take part in the work of legislation for their native land.

Will Great Britain do her duty to the Gold Coast and to Ashanti, or will she turn away from the prayer in scorn?

APPENDICES.

APPENDIX A.

DECIDED CASES.

Oppon *v.* Ackinie.

October 24th, 1887.

"Before Hector Macleod, C.J., Smalman Smith, J., Francis Smith, J.

This is an appeal against a judgment of the Divisional Court of Cape Coast, dated February 14th, 1887, confirming a judgment of the District Commissioner, Saltpond, ordering defendant Ackinie to pay damages to Oppon in the amount of £5, with 11*s.* costs.

Mr. Eminsang, Mr. Williams, and Mr. Renner for appellant (Ackinie).

Oppon in person.

Judgment, October 24th, 1887 :—

This is an appeal by the defendant Ackinie against a judgment of the Divisional Court of the Western Province, dated February 14th, 1887, affirming a judgment of the District Commissioner of Saltpond, dated February 25th, 1886, by which the defendant was ordered to pay to the plaintiff the sum of £5 as damages, with 11s. costs.

The facts of the case are practically not in dispute. A person named Ghartey (formerly one of the defendants in this action) charged another person, named David Otchafoo, before the defendant Ackinie, who is the King of Aikunfie, with receiving bribes. According to the custom in such matters a surety had to be found, and the plaintiff Oppon, one of Ackinie's own subjects, became surety for the payment of any costs to be found due by Otchafoo, in the matter of that complaint. Otchafoo was found liable to costs.

If Oppon was dissatisfied with the decision, his remedy, according to one of the witnesses called on February 14th last, was to pay the costs and cause an appeal to be brought to the British Courts; but Oppon refused to pay the costs, alleging that he was not satisfied with the decision of King Ackinie. Thereupon Ackinie caused Oppon to be arrested and imprisoned in respect of the refusal to pay the costs.

The power of arrest and imprisonment under such circumstances has been exercised by the defendant and his predecessors as far back as the memory of living witnesses can carry us, as one of the royal prerogatives.

Upon these facts there arises a short but very

important point in law—important, because it affects the whole judicial powers of kings and chiefs throughout the Protected Territories. Short, because it is all summed up in this question: 'Has the Supreme Court Ordinance, 1876, swept away the previously existing judicial powers of native kings and chiefs?'

Before we proceed to discuss this question, we desire to make one preliminary observation, and it is so important that we shall direct it to be recorded in red ink.

We are not here engaged in any inquiry as to the extent of Her Majesty's power and jurisdiction in and over the Protected Territories. We are only inquiring whether, through the medium of the Colonial Legislature, she has, in virtue of the power and jurisdiction vested in her, yet chosen to say that the judicial powers of native kings and chiefs shall no longer exist.

King Ackinie has, in the course of this case, had the benefit of nearly all the local legal talent. Oppon has had no such aid. Nevertheless, had Bailey, C.J., still been alive, he would doubtless have given judgment in Oppon's favour. That is evident, from several cases decided by him in the Divisional Court of the Central Province. In none of these cases did the learned Chief Justice enter into any discussion upon the point, which one must suppose appeared to him so clear as to require no consideration.

We know, however, the reasons upon which he founded his judgments, and we think it only right that we should state them. He founded his opinion upon sects. 11 and 12 of the Supreme Court Ordinance, 1876. Regarding sect. 11, he would in substance say, if he were here to-day, 'The Supreme Court Ordinance, sect. 11, vests all the jurisdiction of the High Court of Justice in England (Admiralty excepted) in the Supreme Court of the colony. That being so, whatever jurisdiction the native chiefs formerly possessed was from the date of the passing of that Ordinance extinguished.'

Regarding sect. 12 he would doubtless say, 'What jurisdiction, civil or criminal, was, or is not, exercisable by Her Majesty in these territories? Absolutely none. All, then, is vested in the Supreme Court, and, according to the concluding words of the section, shall be exercised under and according to the provisions of the Ordinance and not otherwise.' If Oppon had all the legal talent in the world to plead for him, we do not see how his case could be more powerfully stated.

But we think Bailey, C.J., failed to apprehend the object and scope of this Ordinance. First, however, let us consider sects. 11 and 12 by themselves. While these sections contain words affirmative of the

Supreme Court, we find in them no negative words, no words of conclusion, nothing to indicate that jurisdiction, other than Her Majesty's, is to cease. We see no words that lead us to think it would be inconsistent with the object of the Legislature that Her Majesty's jurisdiction and the jurisdiction of the kings and chiefs should be co-existent. The civil and criminal jurisdiction of Her Majesty exercisable in the Protected Territories at the commencement of the Ordinance was one, to a great extent, occurrent [concurrent?] with the jurisdiction exercisable by the native kings and chiefs; and that is, to our minds, a conclusive answer to the arguments which we have put into the mouth of Bailey, C.J.

But we must not confine our attention to sects. 11 and 12 of this Ordinance. It is not by any means the only Ordinance that created a Supreme Court of the Gold Coast, and regulated its procedure. Various such Ordinances were passed from 1853 downwards, and we think we are right when we say that not one of such previous Ordinances referred to the Local Native Courts, yet these Native Courts exercised jurisdiction side by side with the Supreme Court so created.

The key to the successful interpretation of sects. 11 and 12 already mentioned is, we think, to be found in sect. 20 of the same Ordinance; from which it appears that, prior to this Ordinance of

1876, Her Majesty had been exercising her jurisdiction by the help of a very confusing arrangement of Courts and magistrates. All these were to cease, and the one Supreme Court, whose powers and jurisdiction are described in sects. 11 and 12, took their place.

Two years later the Colonial Legislature passed an Ordinance (No. 8 of 1878) ' to facilitate and regulate the exercise, in the protected territories, of certain powers and jurisdiction by native authorities.' Can anyone read that Ordinance, and particularly sects. 3, 4, 10, and 30 thereof, without coming to the conclusion that the jurisdiction of the kings and chiefs is there treated as existing, but requiring regulation? That Ordinance was confirmed by Her Majesty, though it was not thought expedient to proclaim any head chief's division under it.

In 1888 it was repealed, not because it did not speak the truth, but that an Ordinance more in harmony with the views of the Legislature for the time being might take its place; and that successor is No. 5 of 1883. It also treats native tribunals as existing, but requiring regulation.

It might be observed of these two native jurisdiction Ordinances that, by mere recital, they could not restore what was taken away by the Supreme Court Ordinance of 1876. Perfectly true; but, when considering whether the Supreme Court Ordinance of

1876 did or did not take away jurisdiction from native tribunals, do not these native jurisdiction Ordinances give us considerable light?

Again, the point seems covered by authority. In the end of 1880, or beginning of 1881, the Divisional Court of the Central Province ordered Quamin Fori, King of Aquapim, to pay damages to one Bruce, as compensation for illegal arrest.

Bruce was charged with violating a girl in the bush, and Quamin Fori ordered his arrest. The Divisional Court was of opinion that Quamin Fori had used such violence in having Bruce brought before him that he must pay £30 damages and costs.

Upon the 1st of April, 1881, this judgment was reversed by the Full Court (Marshall, C.J., and J. W. Smith, Ag. Judge), whose judgment says: 'We are of opinion that the king, in all that was done, acted within the powers which have always been recognised and allowed to the Native Courts unless those powers are taken away by the Governor; and that if he was in fault, it was in not proceeding further with the case, and inquiring more fully into the charge against Bruce.'

As a criticism upon that judgment, it might be observed that it only recognised powers in kings and chiefs which can be taken away by the Governor; and that, as the Governor has no power to take away inherent jurisdiction from a king, that cannot have been the jurisdiction recognised in Quamin Fori's case, and therefore his case cannot apply to the present one.

Without discussing whether a Governor has power to take away inherent jurisdiction, and without pretending to understand what the Full Court meant by the words 'unless those powers are taken away by the Governor,' we cannot help regarding the suggested line of criticism as unworthy of comment.

Had it not been for the opinion of Bailey, C.J., we would have entertained no doubt upon the question which we have discussed. Now that we have considered it from every possible point of view, we are clear that the Supreme Court Ordinance, 1876, has in no way impaired the judicial powers of native kings and chiefs, and, so far as we know, it has not been suggested that any other Ordinance has taken them away.

The defendant (appellant) in the present case has exercised a very ordinary judicial power, and therefore we think the judgment of the Court below ought to be reversed and judgment entered for the defendant Ackinie.

We are not inclined to give him costs, for the impression made upon our minds is that he has brought this action upon himself. It must be distinctly understood that there is to be no imprisonment without an adequate and regular supply of food, means of washing daily, and ample opportunities for obeying the calls of nature, being given to every prisoner."

IN THE SUPREME COURT OF THE GOLD COAST COLONY, WESTERN PROVINCE.

17th February, 1897.

Before HIS HONOUR HAYES REDWAR, Puisne Judge.

REGINA, ON THE PROSECUTION OF D. A. DONOVAN *v.* KUDJOE IMBRA.

Case stated by the District Commissioner of Cape Coast, Mr. J. A. McCarthy, under sect. 157 of the Criminal Procedure Ordinance, 1876, upon a conviction by the District Commissioner of Cape Coast, Dr. D. K. McDowell, under the Compulsory Labour Ordinance, 1895, on the 30th November, 1896.

The case, dated 11th February, 1897, upon an application made on the date of the conviction by defendant's counsel to the District Commissioner, who heard and determined the charge, was laid before the Court by the Registrar, as also the notes of evidence taken before the District Commissioner and accompanying the case.

Hayford, for appellant, states that he is holding Mill's brief in this case, and is instructed to press on this appeal.

The officer on whose prosecution the conviction was made (sub-Assistant Commissioner D. A. Donovan, of the police) does not appear, but the Registrar reports that in the absence of Mr. Donovan notice had been served on the present Senior Officer of Police at Cape Coast. Superintendent Penny now appears and states that he has been served with notice to attend on the argument upon this case, but has received no instructions in the matter from Mr. Donovan, who is absent at Accra; he further states that in the absence of Mr. Donovan, the District Commissioner, Cape Coast, is the officer in command of the police in the district.

The Court refers to the Police Ordinance, 1894, and discovers that by sect. 6 the Superintendent is in command of the police in any district where there is no police officer of higher grade. The Court then directs the argument to proceed.

Mr. Penny states that he has not been instructed and has no argument to offer.

Hayford, for appellant, is heard against the conviction. He refers to the Ordinance under which this conviction was made and to the evidence upon which it was founded.

He contends.

*   *   *   *

By the Court :—

It is to be regretted that no steps have been taken to ensure the prosecution being represented on this appeal. There can, however, be no difficulty in dealing with it, as the facts of the case are as simple as the law governing them, and argument is scarcely necessary upon so obviously simple a matter, and, indeed, in the view which I have taken of the law, the case is not arguable, as it depends upon the meaning to be placed upon a clearly expressed enactment of the Legislature of a penal character, which must, of course, be construed strictly, according to the established principle of interpreting Statutes which operate in restriction of common right and the liberty of the subject.

The case shortly stated is this : the charge in the summons stated verbatim is, "Being a head chief, neglecting to call out carriers for public purpose, when ordered to do so by District Commissioner, Cape Coast, on the 19th November, 1896, contrary to sects. 2 and 4 of Ordinance No. 9 of 1895."

In the first place it is necessary to consider the question whether a District Commissioner other than the District Commissioner who made the conviction has power to state a case of this kind under sect. 157 of the Criminal Procedure Ordinance, 1876. As to this I hold that the Court referred to in that section must for necessary reasons of convenience in a colony so subject to changes of officials as this be extended so as to include a District Commissioner other than the one convicting, if application be made for a case within the four days limited in the section.

I am of opinion that the word "Court" wherever it appears in the Criminal Procedure Ordinance must, unless the context contains something repugnant to the definition, be deemed to be the "Court" as defined in the Interpretation clause (sect. 2) of the Supreme Court Ordinance, 1876, and must therefore include a "District Commissioner" engaged in any judicial act or proceeding. There being nothing repugnant to this definition in the context, I hold that the District Commissioner according to sect. 157 of the Criminal Procedure Ordinance, even although not the District Commissioner convicting the defendant, may state a case, especially when, as here, application was made on the day of the conviction to the District Commissioner who heard and determined the charge. The present District Commissioner of Cape Coast has, therefore, acted correctly in stating this case.

It is matter for surprise, however, that the District Commissioner convicting this defendant did not adopt the course indicated by sect. 159 of the Criminal Procedure Ordinance, 1876, and respite execution of the judgment, when application was made to him for stay of execution pending this appeal according to the notes of the case taken by himself.

Evidence was given for the prosecution, and upon this evidence the District Commissioner convicted the defendant, and the two questions for this Court to decide are :—

First, whether the conviction was or was not wrong on the ground of misreception of evidence.

Secondly, whether the facts proved did or did not warrant a conviction.

First. As regards the question whether the conviction was or was not wrong on the ground of misreception of evidence, I am of opinion that if it were deemed necessary to give in evidence the document referred to in the proceedings as a " notice to supply carriers," the original should have been produced, or upon proof of service of notice to produce it on defendant, then, and then only, should a copy have been received in evidence.

The document was not a step to initiate proceedings, like a summons, and should have been proved as all documents are proved before reception in evidence. If, however, the original notice had been produced, it would not have been evidence of such an order or requisition for carriers as the Ordinance requires. As regards the telegram referred to in the proceedings, it is extremely doubtful from the District Commissioner's notes of evidence whether it was ever formally put in, nor does it appear that sufficient foundation was laid for its admission in evidence. There is only one " exhibit " accompanying the notes, and that is the copy of the " notice to supply carriers," and this exhibit bears no distinguishing letter or serial number indicating that it is one of a series of exhibits.

Second. As regards the question whether the facts proved did or did not warrant a conviction, I am of opinion that no satisfactory evidence was given of the *status* of the defendant, whether as head chief, or inferior chief, Mr. Donovan's evidence amounting in reality to a mere expression of his opinion on this point. Sect. 2 of the Compulsory Labour Ordinance, 1895, provides (in its latter portion, upon which these proceedings must be founded) that " it shall be lawful for any head chief, captain, or headman to order any inferior chief, officer, captain, or headman, subject to his authority, to co-operate in calling out the labourers of his towns or villages for service as carriers for any public purpose, and such inferior chief, officer, captain, or headman shall be legally bound to comply with such order." Now, the only punishment in connection with chiefs under this Ordinance is provided for by sect. 4, which says that " whoever being legally bound under sect. 2 to comply with any order refuses or neglects to comply therewith, shall be liable on conviction to fine or imprisonment." It is to be observed that this punishment can only be inflicted on an inferior chief ordered to co-operate with a superior chief, and refusing or neglecting to comply with such order. What evidence is there that defendant was ever ordered by a superior chief to co-operate with him in calling out carriers? There is absolutely no such evidence on the Commissioner's "Notes." Assuming the most in favour of the District Commissioner's "Notice," he is not a head chief within the meaning of this Ordinance, and only refusal or neglect to comply with a head chief's order by an inferior chief is made an offence under sects. 2 and 4 of the Ordinance, the sections under which this summons is expressed on its face to have been issued. Nor is there on the record the evidence required by sect. 9, viz., a certificate under the hand of the Colonial Secretary that any head chief, chief, headman, or captain has been required by the Government to call out carriers for service under the Ordinance. Neither was any evidence given for a general or special order being issued under sect. 7, nor that defendant or anybody else had prior to the passing of the Ordinance been required by the Governor to furnish carriers, so as to bring the case within the provisions of sect. 8.

Under these circumstances I am of opinion that the facts proved did not warrant a conviction. The conviction must therefore be set aside, and I order that an entry be made in the minutes of the Court below that, in the judgment of this Court, the defendant in this case ought not to have been convicted, and that the fine be repaid to the defendant.

Hayford asked for the costs of the appeal, and urged that, as the proceedings against defendant had been most negligently conducted, and he had been put to much inconvenience and expense, he was entitled to costs as a sort of compensation for the inconvenience and expense entailed upon him by this prosecution.

The Court refused to allow costs on the ground that most probably the police officer who conducted the prosecution deemed it to be his duty to take the proceedings, although he had acted erroneously.

(Signed) HAYES REDWAR, J.

Certified true copy.
(Signed) P. W. BERNASKO, *Registrar*,
Cape Coast,
20 . 2 . 97.

The Chidda Concession.[1]

Enquiry No. 5 (Cape Coast), March 1st, 1901.

Before His Honour Mr. Justice Nicoll.

The claimants were the Gold Coast Amalgamated Mines, Limited. The opposers were—(1) Chiefs Cudjoe Buaful, guardian to the King Quamina Enimil, Cudjoe Enimil Koomah II., Quasie Ankuma, Cudjoe Ammoo, and Quamina Innuama; (2) the Sekondi and Tarkwa Company, Limited. The grounds of opposition for the first opposers were —(1) fraud, (2) misrepresentation; for second opposers—(1) deceit, (2) fraud, (3) misrepresentation, (4) prior lease. This was the first enquiry under the Concessions Ordinance, 1900. In the course of the enquiry so many important points as to the construction and the working of the substantive law and the rules thereunder were raised and discussed, as to make this enquiry the leading case of the Concessions Division of the Supreme Court. The enquiry had been transferred from the Concessions Division, Cape Coast, to the Concessions Division, Axim, on February 11th, 1901; and the latter Division had fixed it for hearing on March 1st. On that day there appeared for the claimants Mr. J. Mensah Sarbah, barrister-at-law, leading counsel,

[1] Reproduced from *West Africa* of May 25, 1901, pp. 665—667.
G.C.

supported by Mr. Casely Hayford, barrister-at-law, and Mr. A. W. Osborne, solicitor, Mr. P. A. Renner, barrister-at-law, who was leading for the claimants when the enquiry was first called at Cape Coast, subsequently joining the counsel for the claimants. The counsel for the opposers were Mr. J. Renner Maxwell, barrister-at-law, leader; with him Mr. G. H. Savage, barrister-at-law, Mr. Charles J. Bannerman, barrister-at-law, and Mr. R. Alade, barrister-at-law. The actual hearing of the enquiry up to the date of judgment occupied twenty-two days.

The Case for the First Opposers.

The first opposers, in their statement of particulars of grounds of opposition, filed on March 2nd, alleged, *inter alia*:—

1. That on August 28th, 1896, an indenture of lease had been executed by Enimil Koomah II. and Quasie Ankuma, chiefs of Busumchie Abosso, granting to William Edward Sam, acting for Messrs. F. and A. Swanzy, of No. 147, Cannon Street, London, the concession of all that piece or parcel of land known as Cinnamon Bippo Range, bounded on the north by the village of Chidda, on the south by the northern boundary of Swanzy Estate and Gold Mining Company's Cinnamon Bippo Concession, and extending half a mile beyond the western bank of Huni River, as it runs on the east by a line one

mile from the centre line of the range, and running parallel with the said range, on the west by a line half a mile distant from the western bank of the Huni River.

2. That upon the said concession of August 28th, 1896, being repudiated by Chief Cudjoe Buaful, guardian to the King Quamina Enimil, on the ground that he had not been made a party thereto, it was agreed in or about the month of September, 1896, between Sam, Buaful, and the Chiefs of Busumchie that a new concession of the same land should be granted to Sam for his principals, which should include Buaful's name for the King as one of the grantors.

3. That upon April 24th, 1897, Sam invited Buaful and the Chiefs of Busumchie to Tarkwa, to execute the new lease before mentioned.

4. That when the chiefs were assembled at Sam's house at Tarkwa, the interpreter, Aggrey, Sam's clerk, interpreted to them that the land leased extended from the end of Cinnamon Bippo Concession of Swanzy's Concession to the Chidda Creek; whereas, in truth and in fact, the lease, then executed, granted that piece or parcel of land in the district of Busumchie Abosso, and situate on the range of hills commencing from the village of Chidda to the village of Busumchie, known as Busumchie Cinnamon Bippo Range, divided into six concessions of 1,000 fathoms square.

5. That, relying upon the truthfulness of the said interpretation, they had executed the lease of April 24th, 1896 (thereby hanging the allegations of fraud and misrepresentation).

6. That upon discovering the fraud, they had repudiated the said lease.

Answers by the Claimants.

The reply of the claimants was substantially this:—

1. Denial that the lease of April 24th, 1897, was a substitution for that of August 28th, 1896, or that it was in any way connected with or had reference to the six Chidda concessions, the subject-matter of the present enquiry.

2. That before the execution of the lease of April 24th, 1897, samples had been sent for by Buaful and Enimil Koomah II., the Chief of Busumchie, for Sam from the land in dispute; and, upon notice by Sam, Buaful, and other grantors of the lease of April 24th, 1897, had come to Tarkwa and executed the same after it had been correctly interpreted to them by Villars, the King's Secretary, in the presence of Lemaire, the clerk of the Chief of Busumchie, and others.

3. That after such correct interpretation, and with full knowledge that the concession referred to the land mentioned by Sam in his letter of April

16th, 1897, which was acknowledged on April 19th, the chiefs executed the lease of April 24th, 1897.

4. That in August, 1897, after the grant of the concession under enquiry, Sam, with Gowans, a mining engineer, had surveyed and measured the land granted by the concession, and that the work and movements of Sam and Gowans were not unknown to the chiefs.

5. That previously to the execution of the lease in dispute, the Chiefs had received in advance the sum of £250 towards rents.

6. That the Chiefs had received rents under the said concession, and that, as recently as February 15th last, Quasie Ankuma, the present Busumchie Chief, had applied to Sam for his share of the rents.

The concession under enquiry had been duly registered under Ordinance No. 1 of 1895.

Upon application by counsel, the names of Cudjoe Enimil Koomah II., and Cudjoe Ammoo were struck out from the names of the opposing chiefs.

The Court upon hearing counsel for the claimants and the opposers respectively, ruled that the *onus* was with the claimants.

Correspondence with the Chiefs.

Mr. Sarbah opened for the claimants, accentuating the allegation that the concession of August 28th, 1896, related to land to the south-west of

Chidda village, whereas the concession under enquiry related to land to the north-east of Chidda.

For the claimants Sam affirmed that Villars read and interpreted the lease to the chiefs, and that he did so correctly, specifying the land given by the concession, namely, from Chidda village to Busumchie village. Before the execution of the deed in question, he had, on December 16th, 1896, paid to the chiefs the sum of £250 for six concessions on the Cinnamon Bippo Range, and produced correspondence relating to the transaction. In a letter dated March 25th, 1897, he wrote to Buaful, *inter alia*, the following :—

"I beg also to inform you that, if you do not come and give me the six concessions or mines, for which you have received £250 on account, within one week from now, I shall call upon you to return the money, with interest agreed upon."

Buaful and Enimil Koomah having ordered samples for him (Sam) from the land in dispute, Buaful wrote to him (Sam) on the 13th of April, 1897, thus :—

"Please kindly let me know, per the return of this bearer, if Chief Enimil Koomah has presented to you the samples of quartz as we arranged, and, if so, are they good or what? You will inform me if the documents have arrived from Cape Coast.

"I am always ready to go over when you send for me.

"I am, dearly yours,
"KING KWAMINA ENIMIL,
"Writer, his
"JACOB PA VILLARS, "Per Kudjoe × Buaful.
"Bensu." mark.

On April 16th, 1897, he (Sam) wrote to Buaful:—

"Being very busy yesterday, and your messenger, like a madman, hurrying me on to send him away, I forgot to reply to your other letter of the 13th, asking if the samples from the new property (concession) have been sent to me, and if so, they are good.

"In reply, I beg to inform you that conglomerate samples have been sent to me from a range of hills between Chidda and Busumchie. I have made a deed to take the whole of the six concessions on this range—that is, if we get more than six concessions I will pay extra retaining fee for the odd piece. If, on the other hand, I find less than the six concessions you offered to me on the aforesaid range, I can take the balance anywhere you and your chiefs may direct me, provided always that I have the option of selecting what land within your district.

"I shall go to Tarkwa on Monday next to sign the deed, and I ask you particularly to be present in order that you may make your mark with your chiefs, and at the same time to settle other matters. I send this letter by special messenger, and expect to meet you in Tarkwa on the day above mentioned.

"Trusting you are well, and with kind regards,
"Yours faithfully,
"W. E. SAM,
"Manager."

On April 19th Buaful replied to him as follows:—

"Your favour of the 16th instant received. I am going to Amantsin to leave the King there and come over to Tarkwa. I have been ill these few days, and as you want me I shall go to Tarkwa as requested. With due regards—Villars joins,
"I am, your,
"KING KWAMINA ENIMIL,
his
"Per Kudjoe × Buaful.
mark.

"Writer,
"JACOB PA VILLARS,
"Bensu."

After this correspondence the chiefs met him at Tarkwa, and executed the lease of April 24th, 1897. Surveys were subsequently made of the land in dispute, and the chiefs, or some of them, knew of same.

Aggrey corroborated Sam as to what transpired upon the execution of the lease of April 24th, 1897, and witnesses were called who supported the fact of samples having been sent for by the chiefs for Sam from the land in dispute, and as to the survey of the land.

The Custom of Giving Earnest Money.

At the close of the claimants' case, Mr. Savage, for the opposers, submitted that there was no case to answer, having regard to sect. 11 of the Ordinance. His grounds were :—

1. That the receipts of claimants for rents had not been put in evidence.

2. Sam did not give chiefs copy of lease until February 1st, 1900.

3. That there was no consideration for the lease in dispute, consideration being synonymous with earnest money.

By the Court: Do you argue that the consideration under sect. 11 must be earnest money?

Mr. Savage: The consideration must be earnest money, plus rent.

By the Court: Is the native practice of giving earnest money binding where the bargain is between a European and a native?

(Refers counsel to sect. 19 of Ordinance No. 4 of 1876.)

Mr. Savage, proceeding, urged:

4. That the rents had not been paid.

The Court pointed out that there was oral evidence that the rents had partly been paid.

Mr. Savage opened the case for the opposers, dwelling upon the main issues raised by the pleadings.

For the opposers Buaful flatly denied the correct interpretation of the lease in dispute, and stated that the interpretation by Aggrey as to the land granted did not correspond with the land covered by the lease in dispute. He denied that he had ever sent for samples for Sam, or that he had ever caused the letter of April 13th to Sam to be written. He affirmed that Sam had steadily avoided supplying him with a copy of the lease in dispute, and that, upon the same being supplied, he at once repudiated the lease. Previously to the execution of the lease in dispute there had been a meeting with Sam relative to the lease agreed to be substituted for that of August 28th, 1896.

Villars generally supported the evidence of Buaful. He admitted, in cross-examination by Mr. Hayford, that all letters written for Buaful by him were first read over to him before he touched the pen, his mark thereto made, and forwarded; and that letters read to the chief were correctly read by him to the chief, and his instructions taken before replying thereto. In answer to the Court, after being severely pressed, he said he remembered the correspondence above quoted. He affirmed that Sam knew before the 24th day of April, 1897, that the land in dispute had previously been given to Bridges.

The other chiefs and some of their headmen also supported Buaful generally in his evidence.

The Case for the Second Opposers.

The particulars of the grounds of opposition of the second opposers were as follows:—

1. That on January 7th, 1897, Cudjoe Buaful, for and on behalf of Quamina Enimil, King of Tarkwa and Lower Wassaw, granted to George John Bridges an option to select and acquire twenty gold concessions of not less than 1,000 fathoms square each, five of which said concessions were to be situated on the north of the village of Chidda, in consideration of the advance of a loan of £2,000 by the said George John Bridges to the said Quamina Enimil.

2. Renewal of the said option, firstly on March 31st, 1898, secondly on November 29th, 1898.

3. Fraud and misrepresentation in connection with lease of April 24th, 1897.

It may be noted that the option agreement had not been registered under Ordinance No. 1 of 1895.

The Claimants' Reply.

The claimants replied :—

1. That they had no notice of the said option of Bridges until Bridges entered upon the land in dispute in June, 1900, whereupon an action of ejectment had been brought against the second opposers.

2. Denial of allegation of fraud and misrepresentation.

Upon Mr. Savage opening on above allegation—

The Court to Counsel: Assuming the chief had given the lease to Sam, can Bridges' option stand ?

The Court said this question went to the root of the matter, and suggested Counsel considering it.

On resumption, the Court, addressing Counsel, said: Supposing Bridges filed his option and the Amalgamated Mines filed their lease subsequently, do you contend that the option will stand in the face of the lease, or will Bridges merely have a right to an action for damages ? A. sells to B. and gets purchase-money, but does not get title-deeds executed and delivered. Meanwhile, A. sells to C., who pays purchase-money, and gets title-deeds executed and delivered; will C. or B.'s title stand ?

Counsel replied that his strongest point was the definition of a concession—sect. 2 of No. 14, of 1900.

The Court: What would be the position if a certificate of validity were granted for an option, and a lease subsequently granted for the same premises? (The Court drew attention to sect. 21 of the Ordinance.)

Counsel: The Ordinance overrides the common-law principles herein, and a certificate of validity by sect. 21 will be good against all adversaries.

Bridges gave evidence in support of the option as to execution and the agreements renewing them.

Counsel informed the Court that there had been an assignment of the option to the Sekondi and Tarkwa Company, Limited.

The witness stated the deed was in his despatch-box in his house, but it was not subsequently produced.

Villars supported the evidence of Bridges.

Mr. Bridges, on application of Counsel, was made a party to the suit.

Priority Claimed for the Option.

Mr. Bannerman, in closing for second opposers, submitted :—

1. That the option of January 7th, 1897, took priority over the lease of April 24th, 1897. He

discussed sect. 2 of the Ordinance to show that an option was of equal degree with a lease.

2. That registration did not give priority in this case, sects. 19 and 20 of No. 1 of 1895 not affecting agreements.

3. That Sam had notice of Bridges' option. He quoted the case of *Le Neve* v. *Le Neve*, White & Tudor's Leading Cases; *Punchard* v. *Tomkins*, 31 Weekly Reports, 286; *Yates Brothers and Shattuck* v. *Garshong*, Gold Coast Appeal Cases.

The Court: Section 11, sub-sect. 1, of the Concessions Ordinance merely says, before a concession can be entertained there must at least be a writing, but it does not say one kind of writing or instrument shall be necessarily as good as another; that is a matter of general law.

Mr. Sarbah, in reply, submitted:—

1. That the so-called option of Bridges was not really an option. Before the payment of the £2,000 mentioned therein as consideration for the option Bridges could not go upon the land. He had no choice of exercising option at all until he had paid the £2,000 within twelve months.

2. That the area of the lands comprised in the option was not defined.

3. Non-registration of the option.

4. That a lease is of a higher nature than an option.

5. The lease made during subsistence of option comes into operation upon the expiration of the option, but it is not void during subsistence of option.

6. Application of Registration Ordinance to Options. Assuming there was notice to Sam, what effect would it have upon the claimants? None, there being no evidence of fraud on their part. A *bonâ fide* purchaser for value is not affected by the fraud of his assignor.

The Court: Does sub-sect. 3 of sect. 11 not apply to third parties claiming under fraudulent leases? It goes to the root of the whole Ordinance.

Counsel, resuming, urged :—

7. Laches on the part of the chiefs.

8. Knowledge of second opposers as to possession of Sam.

The Judgment.

The Court reviewed in the clearest manner the voluminous evidence adduced for and against the case for the claimants. Referring to the incident of sending for the samples, the Court pointed out that Sam's evidence therein was corroborated by several witnesses. Buaful denied the incident absolutely. But letter of April 13th showed that Buaful knew of the sample being given to Sam, and Sam's reply thereto, dated April 16th, 1897, was of the greatest importance. His Honour, continuing, said: "The letter clearly brings home to Buaful's mind that Sam had made a paper to take six concessions from Chidda to Busumchie, and that he and his chiefs were to go to Tarkwa to execute the same. Buaful replied on April 19th. Buaful's evidence respecting the letters of April 13th, 16th, and 19th is most unsatisfactory. He admits getting letter of April 16th, but did not go to Tarkwa for a year after." The Court, having considered the whole evidence *re* the execution of the concession under inquiry and the subsequent conduct of the parties, had no hesitation in coming to the following conclusions :—

1. That the evidence of the first opposers was untrustworthy.

2. That the grantors of the concession knew they had been summoned to execute a document *re* land from Chidda to Busumchie.

3. That they went there to execute such a document.

4. That the interpreter accurately interpreted to them the contents of the lease.

5. That the chief signed the lease, knowing they were giving land from Chidda to Busumchie.

6. That they knew the terms of the lease before signing it, and that they were not induced by fraud.

The Court, therefore, declared the first opposition bad.

The Court next dealt with the case for the second opposers, observing that Bridges, on or about September 28th, 1897, had not deposited the £2,000 under the option agreement, and that it was clearly of opinion that Bridges had no right to Sam's concession by the agreement of January 7th, 1897. That the concession of April 24th, 1897, having been registered, and the option of January 7th not having been registered, even though Bridges had the right under his option, Sam's lease would have priority. His Honour continued: "It has been argued for second opposers that the Registration Ordinance does not apply to the Concessions Ordinance. I am not aware of any grounds for such an argument. The Registration Ordinance should be looked upon as having special reference to concessions. It has great bearing on the Concessions Ordinance." Referring to the question of notice to Sam of Bridges' option, the Court said it did not believe the evidence of Villars, and observed that whether an option of a concession took precedence of a lease subsequently granted did not arise for discussion in the present case.

The Court declared the second opposition also to have failed, and found as follows:—

That the claimants were entitled to the benefit of

the concession of April 24th, 1897, and that the conditions laid down in section 11 of the Ordinance had been fulfilled. That—

1. Concession was in writing, duly signed by grantors.

2. Proper persons, parties to it, who understood the nature and terms thereof.

3. Concessions not obtained by fraudulent or other improper means.

4. Adequate valuable consideration paid therefor.

5. All the terms and conditions thereof reasonably and satisfactorily performed.

6. Customary rights of natives reasonably protected.

Declared, however:—

(*a*) That so much of the concession as exceeds five square miles was invalid.

(*b*) Limit of concession ninety-nine years.

Mr. Sam having delayed in giving the chiefs copy of the concession under enquiry, which circumstance probably led to the opposition, the Court ordered the several parties to pay their own costs.

COLONIAL SECRETARY'S OFFICE,
ACCRA,
16*th November*, 1901.

The following Certificate of Validity issued at Axim by His Honour Mr. Justice William Nicoll

for No. 5 (Cape Coast) Chidda Concession, is published for general information.
By His Excellency's Command,
C. H. HUNTER,
Acting Colonial Secretary.

Wednesday the 16th October, 1901.

Before HIS HONOUR WILLIAM NICOLL, JUDGE.

Certificate of Validity.

In the Supreme Court of the Gold Coast Colony, Western Province. (Concessions Division.)

No. 5 (Cape Coast). Chidda.

Subject as below the Concession of Chief Cudjoe Buaful, guardian to the King Quamina Enimil, Chief Cudjoe Enimil Koomah II., Quasie Ankuma, Cudjoe Ammoo and Quamina Innuama, Chiefs of Busumchie Abosso, Wassaw, to William Edward Sam of Adja Bippo, acting for Messrs. F. & A. Swanzy of 147, Cannon Street, London, dated the 24th day of April, 1897, registered at Cape Coast Registry Office to which this Certificate is attached, is hereby declared to be valid.

APPENDIX A.

Boundaries, Extent, and Situation of Land in respect of which this Certificate is given.

The lands are situate between the village of Chidda and the village of Busumchie. The boundaries thereof are shown on the plan attached hereto and signed as relative hereto. The said lands measure two thousand seven hundred and eighteen (2,718) fathoms in length, extending from the village of Chidda to the village of Busumchie, and one thousand (1,000) fathoms in breath, and the extent or area of these said lands is 3·5098140 square miles.

Nature of Concession.

Mining with timber rights.

Limitations imposed by the Court.

1. The Concession shall not be construed so as to deprive any native of his customary rights as to shifting cultivation, the collection of firewood, and hunting and snaring game on the land.

2. The Concession shall be construed to include only such timber as is necessary in connection with mining operations.

3. The Concession shall extend for a period of ninety-nine years only from the 24th day of April, 1897, and no longer.

4. The Concession shall not be construed to confer any right to have it renewed.

5. The Concession shall be read and construed as if the following clause were omitted from the Concession : " It is mutually agreed and understood between the lessors and the lessees, their heirs, successors, executors, administrators, and assigns that in the event of cessation of crushing operations through want of funds or other lawful causes, the yearly rent of two hundred pounds for that particular mine shall be reduced to one hundred pounds per annum during such cessation provided it does not exceed three years from the date of such cessation."

6. The Concession shall be read and construed as if the word " three " in the clause " This lease may be determined at any time by the lessees, their heirs, executors, administrators, and assigns on their giving three months' notice in writing to the lessors, their heirs, successors, and assigns " were deleted therefrom, and the word " twelve " inserted in lieu thereof.

7. The Concession shall be read and construed as if the following clause were inserted therein : " Provided always that if the lessees or their successors in title shall make default in payment of any rent reserved under the Concession for three calendar months after the same shall become due, it shall be lawful for the lessors, their successors, or assigns by writing under their hand to give three months' notice

to the lessees or their successors in title of their intention to determine the Concession, and in the event of the rent in arrears at the time of giving such notice not being paid before expiration of three months, the rights, privileges, and powers granted by the Concession shall cease and be at an end, and the lessors, their successors, and assigns, shall be at liberty to re-enter upon the said lands and take possession of the same.

8. Notice of intention to terminate the Concession shall be given on a rent day only.

Rent.

(i.) The retaining rent payable in respect of the Concession shall be sixty pounds *per annum*, and shall continue to be payable until the working rent, as hereinafter mentioned, becomes payable.

(ii.) The working rent shall be seven hundred pounds *per annum*.

(iii.) The working rent of seven hundred pounds per annum shall be payable as from the 15th day of October, 1904, whether mining operations have then been commenced or not. In the event of mining operations being commenced before the aforesaid date, the said rent of seven hundred pounds per annum shall be payable as from the date of the commencement of such mining operations.

(iv.) The rents under the Concession shall be

paid quarterly—on first January, first April, first July, and first October in each year.

Maintenance of Boundaries.

The holders of the Concession having undertaken :—

(*a*) To keep the boundary road clean ;

(*b*) To keep the pillars marking the boundaries in good condition and repair ;

(*c*) To keep the name of the Concession (Chidda) legible on each pillar ;

(*d*) To lay down the said lands with reference to the Government *Datum point* when such Government *Datum point* has been fixed in the district of Tarkwa ;

The Concession shall be read and construed as if the lessees had bound themselves accordingly.

Date of Final Order for issue of Certificate of Validity.

15th October, 1901.

Given under my hand and the seal of the Court at Axim this 16th day of October, 1901.

(L.S.)   W. Nicoll, *Judge.*

APPENDIX B.

The following extract appeared in an article in the *Gold Coast Methodist Times* of April 30th, 1897, the contributor being the Rev. Attoh Ahuma, who was then editing that paper:—

THOUGHTS ON THE PRESENT DISCONTENT.

Addressed to the Gold Coast Aborigines' Rights Protection Society, Cape Coast Castle.

* * * * *

Colony or Protectorate?

Colony or Protectorate—which? Some one may say this is a purely technical point, and that it is solely for purposes of convenience that the Gold Coast is called a colony at all. But it must never be forgotten that technical points have before to-day been the means of saving many a wretch from the hangman's noose, and technical points have consigned an innocent victim to perdition. We cannot, in these circumstances, afford to minimise the importance and effect of such points. If by doing away with them, once and for all, there is shown a possibility of ensuring the safety, honour, and welfare of the body politic, we shall have accomplished more than enough. The comparative study of Her Majesty's foreign possessions accentuates the fact that our country holds a unique position upon the world-wide map of the British Empire. We know of no other place similarly situated. We labour in vain to find one spot where the people possess in their own right such a rich and unhampered legacy of liberty, freedom, and enfranchisement as we should enjoy on the Gold Coast. If the sovereignty of the people is entitled to recognition and respect, we, also, have undisputed claim to such political distinction. This undeniable status is not unknown at the Colonial Office, Downing Street, London; and, therefore, from facts which are happily historic, he wins golden opinions whoever manfully strives to bring the country in line with others; and it is just here that, as a society, we must, at all costs, maintain our individuality, come what may.

There is nothing new under the sun; but the old, old story must be rehearsed.

From Stormouth's English Dictionary—a book that has found its way to the Gold Coast through the Government—we learn that a " colony means a body of persons sent out from their native country to a distant district or a new country, in order to settle and cultivate it; the country thus settled or planted."

From Webster's International Dictionary we read:—

"*Colony:* (1) A company of people transplanted from their Mother-Country to a remote province or country, and remaining subject to the jurisdiction of the parent State, as the British *Colonies* in America.

(2) "The district or colony colonised; a settlement.

(3) "A company of persons from the same country sojourning in a foreign city or land; as the American *Colony* in Paris.

(4) "(Natural history) a number of animals or plants living or growing together beyond their usual range."

Settlement: "The act of peopling or state of being peopled; act of planting as a colony; colonization; occupation by settlers, as the settlement of a new country."

Settler: (1) "One who settles, becomes fixed, established; (2) especially, one who establishes himself in a new region or a colony."

Our contention is this: If, as Aboriginals of the country, we have allowed and still do allow ourselves to be described as a colony, without transplantation or emigration, we should not resent, we cannot legitimately and reasonably resent, when we are called settlers, and the only rights sought to be conceded to us—settlers' rights!

But a colony, as you are aware, is not only so called by transplantation from the Mother-Country or by emigration alone; it is often so by treaty cession, or conquest, or transfer, or by annexation. In the archives of the Government we are supposed to be a colony by treaty cession. But there are treaty cessions *and* treaty cessions. Gibraltar, for example, was acquired by treaty cession in 1713; but the student of English history knows this much, that that rocky promontory was captured by the combined forces of England and Holland during the war of the Spanish Succession in 1704, under Sir George Rooke, and that it was after that insanguinary war that Gibraltar was ceded by the Treaty of Utrecht in 1713. It cannot, therefore, be urged that we should be treated in every respect as all countries obtained by the British Government by treaty cession. It is the incumbent duty of the members of the "Gold Coast Aborigines' Rights Protection Society" to inwardly digest the precise terms of the treaty by which the Gold Coast became part and parcel of the British Empire.

These necessary informations are set forth in the plainest possible language, as shall be seen in the Bond of Fantee Chiefs, dated March 6th, 1844;

Lord Stanley's letter to Governor Hill (November 22nd, 1844); draft of an order of the Queen in Council determining the mode of exercising her acquired power and jurisdiction within the Gold Coast Colony (Osborne House, 6th day of August, 1874); the Earl of Carnarvon's letter to Governor Strahan (August 20th, 1874); "the proclamation defining the nature and extent of the Queen's jurisdiction on the Gold Coast;" British Letters Patent constituting the office of Governor and Commander-in-Chief of the Gold Coast Colony, and providing for the government thereof (January 13th, 1886)—a welcome collection of which Mr. Mensah Sarbah, Barrister-at-law, has most timeously embodied in his invaluable work "Fanti Customary Laws." A careful, diligent, and intelligent perusal of these highly important documents, which form the exclusive bases of whatever powers, authority, and jurisdiction Her Majesty exercises in the Gold Coast, will not only disclose the extent and limit of such powers, authority, and jurisdiction, but will likewise incidentally bring to the light of day in how many instances the local Government have, from time to time, infringed the law, and trespassed upon our sacred rights and privileges, thereby breaking with impunity the contract or bond betwixt us, made and provided before our alliance with the Queen, and to which Her Most Gracious Majesty most solemnly plighted her troth.

The very names or titles of King [1] Tackie of Accra, King Ghartey IV. of Winnebah, King Amonoo IV. of Anamabu, and King Dawuna of Christiansborg are proofs, positive, irrefragable and final, if proofs were needed, that the Gold Coast could not be thought or spoken of in the same sense as Australia, the Straits Settlements, Jamaica, or, to come nearer home, Sierra Leone. The natural concession of kingship to us while Her Majesty remains the Queen of England and the Colonies is in itself significant of much. Mention anywhere else but in West Africa where kings reign concurrently with Victoria Alexandrina; and the logical inference is that Her Majesty's Government simply exists "*by usage, and by the sufferance and tacit assent*" of the natives of the soil.

Our rulers are our friends and nothing more—valuable acquisitions, friends in need and in deed, true friends, good friends—to use Governor Griffith's time-honoured formula, but still friends; and being friends, and nothing but friends, to seek insidiously to enslave us, to brand us with the hall-mark of conquered subjects, is to outrage good faith and commit a breach of confidence. But Punic faith is impossible to the genius of the British Constitution, and our budding ideas of British jurisprudence are fraught with peace,

[1] There has been of late years a curious tendency of describing our provincial or district Kings as *Chiefs* or *Recognised Chiefs*. This is very much to be regretted. The erroneous appellation is obviously a disturbing element in the native economy of concentric government.

fair play, and justice—especially justice. From sources of information available, we learn that Elmina is the only place that may be rightly called a settlement or colony, having been founded by the Portuguese in 1481,[1] under the auspices of King John II. We can have no objection to this statement so far as *Elmina* is concerned. The Portuguese may have founded *St. George della Mina*, but certainly not *Dina*, so that even this point can only be conceded with a very large grain of salt.

How then did we come into contact with Her Majesty's Government?

Three hundred and sixty-one years ago, in the reign of Edward IV., certain English adventurers made their first appearance on the coast in competition with the Portuguese traders already in possession. It was not until eighty-eight years after, however, when James I. was King of England, that the successors of those English enterprising merchants obtained a firm footing in the country. They found their way to Grand Cormantine, where in course of time they established friendly relations with the people and built a fort, in 1624. Not being molested by the natives, they extended their borders. In process of time Europe scrambled for places on the coast where she might be permitted to trade,

---

[1] Some writers make out that Elmina was founded by a French Company of Dieppe and Rouen, who built the first Gold Coast fort in 1383.

and so it came to pass that not only Portuguese and English, but Dutch, Danish, Swedish, French, and German merchants arrived in our midst and established forts and factories. But they proved to be treacherous specimens of European civilisation. These colonists, or settlers, who will ever merit the severest censure and the utmost reprobation, repaid the kindness and hospitality of our ancestors by making human traffic a most lucrative industry, and by deporting thousands of the people as slaves for their cotton-fields in the West Indies and America. In 1662 a charter was granted to an English company for the purpose of trading with the Gold Coast. Ten years subsequently the Royal African Company appeared on the scene, and after making some extensions and improvements on the Castle at Cape Coast Castle, proceeded to build other fortifications, such as Fort James (Accra, 1662), Commenda (1681), Sekundi (1685), Dixcove (1691), Winnebah (1694), and Anamabu (1753). Seventy-eight years afterwards "the African Company of Merchants" was constituted by Act of Parliament, "with liberty to trade and form establishments on the West Coast of Africa, between 20 degrees N. and 20 degrees S. Lat."

These places, known as settlements from the point of view of the natives, by reason of the Europeans who had settled in the country, were transferred seventy-one years afterwards, rightly or wrongly, to the Crown and placed under the Government of Sierra Leone, from which they were finally separated in 1874 under the ill-starred title of the Gold Coast Colony.

In 1872 the Dutch Government exchanged their forts (fifteen in number), *and only their forts*, with Great Britain (which had prior to that taken over by purchase all the Danish forts), an action the clumsiness of which brought about the Ashanti War of 1873—74.

So, then, history establishes the fact that the term Gold Coast Colony, or Settlement, has no reference to us whatsoever as natives of the soil, but is exclusively applicable to those European merchants and followers who came to settle in the country for the purposes of trade, in years gone by. British possessions on the Gold Coast, therefore, are the actual forts dotted here and there on the littoral, *many of which are to-day inhabited by colonies or settlements of bats and moles*. We somehow, either through lack of intelligent appreciation of the fact, or through the peculiar conditions of scattered interests in political matters in the country, acquiesced in a sense to be called a colony, where we should have made a firm stand against the applicability of the misnomer; and thereby hangs our tale of woe. But if not a colony or settlement as natives, what then is our relationship to the British Empire ? How should we be designated ? There is happily another word with which we are all familiar, and which accurately explains on the face of it the position of affairs, and that is the term "protectorate." Up to the time of His Excellency Sir William Brandford Griffith, K.C.M.G., and until quite recently, the country was officially known as the "Gold Coast Colony and Protectorate," to distinguish, let us suppose, the people inhabiting the littoral and those in the far interior. And what is a Protectorate? We refer to Webster's International Dictionary again: "The authority assumed by a superior power over an inferior or a dependent one, whereby the former *protects* the latter from invasion and *shares* in the management of its affairs."

The description portrayed in this definition suits the country and its inhabitants most admirably, and the Government should, therefore, be known as the Gold Coast Protectorate and not a colonial Government pure and simple. If we had insisted on this ancient but correct title, such anomalous Ordinances as the Native Jurisdiction Bill, the Land Bill, 1897, the Compulsory Labour Ordinance, and others after their kind, could never have had in this country a local habitation and a name.

Hitherto our successive Governors have been leading us on a down-grade tendency in respect of our inalienable aboriginal rights; it was left, however, for the present Administration to give the stroke of policy, hence the vigorous attack of the Legislative Council to make null and void the immemorial titles of the natives to the land of their ancestors. Yet in our heart of hearts we cannot in strict justice or in reason blame our present Governor.

Sir William Maxwell hails from the Straits Settlements, or Colony—for the terms are interchangeable—on the West Coast of the Malay Peninsula to the Gold Coast Settlements, or Colony, on the West Coast of Africa. He arrives with preconceived notions and ideas. He comes fully *au courant* of those elements that constitute a colony. If he leaves one colony to administer the affairs of another colony under the same authority and power, he cannot be held as having committed an unpardonable offence if he proceeds to carry out conscientiously and faithfully the *régime* that obtains in the colony from whence he comes. He shows himself more consistent than most of his predecessors, and for taking such a bold attitude he should be worthy of our admiration and respect; for until he learns more of the peculiar history of the Gold Coast, until he is forced to admit that there must have been a reason, an irrefutable reason, why those he succeeds could not promulgate such a law as the Land Bill without detriment to the ethical code of civilised Governments, we should be charitable enough to put the very best possible construction upon all

G.C.

measures he may innocently introduce against our interests.

Just a word or two touching the *locus standi* of the Straits Settlements from a political standpoint. We have all the more reason to do this since His Excellency the Governor appears to be fond of making, in season and out of season, invidious comparisons between West Africans and Asiatics without any appreciable regard being paid to the number of years the formative and civilised influences that raise up one nation above another had been in active operation in the Orient before the tide broke its maiden spray over this part of the world. Our usual catalogue of sins of omission as they appear to Europeans with centuries of schooling, discipline, and advantages of time behind them might indeed be tolerable if due consideration were given to such indispensable factors as time and tide. But enough of this, and perhaps more than enough. The Straits Settlements are—

(1) Singapore—first occupied in 1819, and finally ceded to the British Government by the Sultan of Jahore in 1824.

(2) Penang—ceded to H.M. Government of India in 1786 by the Rajah of Kedah.

(3) The Province of Wellesley—also ceded by the Rajah of Kedah, in 1800.

(4) The Dindings—included in the Settlements for administrative purposes under a Resident Councillor.

(5) Malacca—captured by the English in 1795 and retained until 1818, when it was given back to the Dutch; but in pursuance of the treaty in Holland in 1824, it became a British possession, the place having been exchanged for British settlements in Sumatra. We need hardly point out that there are other States, such as Perak, Selangor, Nigri Semblia, and Pahang, which by reason of the fact that they have never been conquered or ceded, are called the Protected Malay States, administered under the advice of the British Resident-General, and subject to the paramount authority of the Governor of the Straits Colony; and we take leave to submit that the case of the Gold Coast is analogous to that of the Protected Malay States, governed by native rulers as chiefs under British control.

The Legislative Court, therefore, fails to understand the pertinence of our claims to respect, and the reasons which compel a hostile attitude against any drastic Bill wherein the liberty, property, and other rights of the subject are seriously threatened.

We urge then that the Gold Coast Aborigines' Rights Protection Society, with or without the co-operation of other organisations for the protection of aboriginal races in the British Empire, must begin by claiming the rightful name of "Protectorate" for this country, and all other things will follow in time as a matter of course. *Sublata causa, tollitur effectus*—" Remove the cause and the effect is destroyed."

Such a change of front might at once secure authority for our kings and chiefs, and all coercive measures be done away with for ever. Once get England to acknowledge and baptise the colony with the old name, and their sense of the moral fitness of things would naturally induce Englishmen to afford us such protection as is consistent with our dignity and place in the Empire.

If the society omits to regard and labour this initial step, and we still continue to vegetate under the blighting name of Colony or Settlement, we may clamour, clamouring never so loudly, but nothing good will come out of the effort; the society will be, in that case, but another mountain in labour, and then this splendid organisation, which we feel sure is divinely inspired, will only exist to make confusion worse confounded; but the consummation devoutly to be wished will still elude our grasp when so near to it.

We implore the society first and foremost to clear the ground by casting away the rock of offence to which we allude, lest, with mighty protestations in other directions and a loud fanfare of trumpets, the Gold Coast Aborigines' Rights Protection Society parades a great name and pretensions which, on being subjected to the test of exact logical deductions, may be found wanting; lest its precious promises of something exceedingly great may be inevitably accompanied by a performance ridiculously disproportionate.

One word of assurance. The patriotic members of the society have no need to furnish or secure arguments in justification of their name and title. We are the lineal descendants of the Aborigines of the land known as the Gold Coast. We scorn to descend into puerilities in refutation of those ill-advised deliverances which regard the natives of this country as foreigners because forsooth our forbears were immigrants from Timbuctoo or Takieman, through Mohammedan aggressions and consequent expatriation. First principles should teach us all that the Garden of Eden is the only battle-ground for rival claimants to acres of land in their absolute right. Such are the consolations of the exhaustive process on the last analysis. As human beings we are not sufficiently developed to create by successive *fiats* islands and capes, mountains and plains, &c. But the English law provides sufficient *data* in support of those who by long possession lay claim to any portion or portions of our planet as their very own. We do not base our indefeasible rights on the fact that as natives we originally sprang from the soil like the products of the teeth of the dragon Cadmus slew in Bœotia. We do maintain with the emphasis of simplicity that we are *ab origines*, and that, therefore, every inch of ground is ours and ours irrevocably, to have and to hold and to administer, and all because our ancestors were the first and earliest inhabitants of the protectorate, thousands of years ago, even before the traditional voyage of Hanno the Carthaginian to the Gold Coast. The Latins, first settling in the Apennines and afterwards in the Lower Tiber, have always been acknowledged in the history of pre-Roman Italy as *Aborigines*, and we might go on *ad infinitum* and show in what respects England, France, Germany, and other European countries could be said to be the *bonâ fide* possessions of the English, the French, the Germans, &c. But to what end? We are the undisputed masters of the soil, and that should suffice. Stand then, my countrymen, shoulder to shoulder. Let unity of thought and unanimity of purpose prevail, and your love for the Motherland, its institutions and traditions, be without dissimulation. Above all, strain every nerve to remain loyal to the Queen, our Protector. Quit you like men, standing square to the great work before you, and with a pull, a long pull, and a pull altogether, depend upon it there is nothing that will ever be impossible to our beloved country, the Gold Coast Protectorate.

APPENDIX C.

1.

CONSTITUTION OF THE NEW FANTEE CONFEDERACY.

To all whom it may concern.

Whereas we, the undersigned kings and chiefs of Fanti, have taken into consideration the deplorable state of our peoples and subjects in the interior of the Gold Coast, and whereas we are of opinion that unity and concord among ourselves would conduce to our mutual well-being, and promote and advance the social and political condition of our peoples and subjects, who are in a state of degradation, without the means of education and of carrying on proper industry, we, the said kings and chiefs, after having duly discussed and considered the subject at meetings held at Mankessim on the 16th day of October last and following days, have unanimously resolved and agreed upon the articles hereinafter named.

ARTICLE 1.—That we, the kings and chiefs of Fanti here present, form ourselves into a committee with the view of effecting unity of purpose and of action between the kings and chiefs of the Fanti territory.

ARTICLE 2.—That we, the kings and chiefs here assembled, now form ourselves into a compact body for the purpose of more effectually bringing about certain improvements (hereafter to be considered) in the country.

ARTICLE 3.—That this compact body shall be recognised under the title and designation of the " Fanti Confederation."

ARTICLE 4.—That there shall be elected a president, vice-president, secretary, under-secretary, treasurer, and assistant treasurer.

ARTICLE 5.—That the president be elected from the body of kings, and be proclaimed king-president of the Fanti Confederation.

ARTICLE 6.—That the vice-president, secretary and under-secretary, treasurer, and assistant treasurer, who shall constitute the ministry, be men of education and position.

ARTICLE 7.—That it be competent to the Fanti Confederation thus constituted to receive into its body politic any other king or kings, chief or chiefs, who may not now be present.

ARTICLE 8.—That it be the object of the Confederation—

Section 1. To promote friendly intercourse between

all the kings and chiefs of Fanti, and to unite them for offensive and defensive purposes against their common enemy.

Section 2. To direct the labours of the Confederation towards the improvement of the country at large.

Section 3. To make good and substantial roads throughout all the interior districts included in the Confederation.

Section 4. To erect school-houses and establish schools for the education of all children within the Confederation, and to obtain the service of efficient schoolmasters.

Section 5. To promote agricultural and industrial pursuits, and to endeavour to introduce such new plants as may hereafter become sources of profitable commerce to the country.

Section 6. To develop and facilitate the working of the mineral and other resources of the country.

ARTICLE 9.—That an executive council be formed, composed of the vice-president, secretary, undersecretary, treasurer, and assistant treasurer, who shall be *ex-officio* members thereof, together with such others as may be hereafter from time to time appointed.

ARTICLE 10.—That in order that the business of the Confederation be properly carried on during the course of the year, each king and principal chief shall appoint two representatives, one educated, the other a chief or headman of the district of such king and principal chief, who shall attend the meetings which the secretary may deem necessary to convene for the deliberation of State matters.

ARTICLE 11.—That the representatives of the kings and chiefs assembled in council shall be known under the designation of the "Representative Assembly of the Fanti Confederation," and that this assembly be called together by the secretary as State exigency may require.

ARTICLE 12.—That this representative assembly shall have the power of preparing laws, ordinances, bills, &c., of using proper means for effectually carrying out the resolutions, &c., of the Government, of examining any questions laid before it by the ministry and by any of the kings and chiefs, and, in fact, of exercising all the functions of a legislative body.

ARTICLE 13.—That the representative of each king and chief be responsible to the nation for the effectual carrying out of the bills, resolutions, &c., passed at such meetings, and approved of by the king-president.

ARTICLE 14.—That the appointment of the representatives nominated by the kings and principal chiefs be notified to the secretary, who shall make it known to all the members of the national Government.

Article 15.—That the National Assembly shall appoint an educated man to represent the king-president, and act as vice-president of the Confederation; and that the vice-president shall preside over all meetings convened by the secretary.

Article 16.—That there shall be in the month of October of each year a gathering of the kings, principal chiefs, and others within the Confederation, when a recapitulation of the business done by the Representative Assembly shall be read, and the programme of the ensuing year discussed.

Article 17.—That at such meetings the king-president shall preside, and that it be the duty of the king-president to sanction all laws, ordinances, &c., passed by the Representative Assembly, so far as they are compatible with the interests of the country.

Article 18.—That the king-president shall not have the power to pass any, or originate any, laws, resolutions, ordinances, bills, &c., nor create any office or appointment, excepting by, and under the advice of, the ministry.

Article 19.—That the representatives of the kings and principal chiefs hold office as members of the Representative Assembly for three years, at the expiration of which it shall be competent for the kings and chiefs to re-elect the same or appoint other representatives.

ARTICLE 20.—That the members of the ministry and Executive Council hold office for three years, and that it is competent to the National Assembly to re-elect all or any of them and appoint others.

ARTICLE 21.—That national schools be established at as early a period as possible in the following districts: Braffoo Country, Abrah, Ayan, Gomowah, Eckunifi, Edgimacoe, Denhia and Assin.

ARTICLE 22.—That normal schools be attached to each national school for the express purpose of educating and instructing the scholars as carpenters, masons, sawyers, joiners, agriculturists, smiths, architects, builders, &c.

ARTICLE 23.—That schools be also established, and schoolmistresses procured to train and teach the female sex, and to instruct them in the necessary requisites.

ARTICLE 24.—That the expense of erecting each school be defrayed from the national purse, but that each king and chief be requested to render all possible aid to facilitate the movement by supplying men and materials.

ARTICLE 25.—That in districts where there are Wesleyan Schools at present established the kings and chiefs be requested to insist on the daily attendance of all children between the ages of eight and fourteen.

Article 26.—That main roads be made, connecting various provinces or districts with one another, and with the sea coast; that the roads be made after the following standard, viz., fifteen feet broad, with good deep gutters on either side, and that the attention of the Confederation be first directed to the main road connecting Edgimacoe, Ayan, Ayanmain, and Mankessim, with the sea coast.

Article 27.—That the kings and principal chiefs be allowed a stipulated sum for the express purpose of maintaining the roads in proper order.

Article 28.—That a site or town, unanimously agreed upon, be chosen as the nominal capital of the Confederation, where the principal business of the State should be conducted.

Article 29. — That provincial assessors be appointed in each province or district, who shall perform certain judicial functions, and attend to the internal management thereof.

Article 30.—That it shall be the duty of the secretary of the Confederation—

Section 1. To convene meetings of the Representative Assembly, for the purpose of considering State matters, as may appear to the ministry necessary.

Section 2. To forward the decision of the Executive Council to the representatives of the various provinces or districts, with instructions thereon.

Section 3. To be the medium through which all important State matters be conducted.

Section 4. To inform the king-president of the decision of the Representative Assembly on any resolutions, &c., and to explain to him the nature of whatever resolutions, &c., are passed, as well as to carry to the Representative Assembly his sanction thereof.

Section 5. To promulgate in each province, either through the provincial representatives or otherwise, whatever resolutions, laws, &c., have been passed and have received the sanction of the king-president.

Section 6. To appoint, under the advice of the Executive Council, subject to the sanction of the king-president, but countersigned by the vice-president, all subordinate officers in the provinces.

Section 7. To receive the revenue of the country, keeping a strict account thereof, and to transmit monthly to the treasurer all moneys in his possession, stating the sums obtained from the different sources of revenue.

Section 8. To sign all vouchers for the treasurer's guidance in the payment of moneys.

ARTICLE 31.—That it be the duty of the treasurer—

Section 1. To receive monthly from the secretary all moneys in his possession, keeping accounts thereof and giving him a receipt for the same.

Section 2. To make no disbursements excepting under instructions, accompanied with approved vouchers from the secretary authorising the payments.

Section 3. To furnish quarterly to the secretary, for the information of the Representative Assembly, an account showing the receipts during the quarter and the disbursements.

ARTICLE 32.—That at the end of each quarter a board of officers, consisting of the vice-president, secretary, treasurer, and one of the kings, to be held for the purpose of verifying the cash in hand.

ARTICLE 33.—That in case the cash in hand in the possession of the treasurer should exceed a sum hereafter to be considered, the surplus should be placed in a depôt chest, furnished with three keys, one of which shall be in the possession of the vice-president, another in that of the treasurer, and the third shall be retained by one of the kings.

ARTICLE 34.—That it be the duty of the under-secretary—

Section 1. To aid the secretary generally.

Section 2. To hear and determine, with an assistant appointed by the secretary, cases which may be brought from the provincial courts.

Section 3. To arrange important appeal cases for the hearing of the Executive Council, which shall constitute the final court of appeal of the Confederation.

Section 4. To draw up a report from accounts received from the provinces of the state of the roads, schools, &c., for the guidance of the Executive Council.

ARTICLE 35.—That it be the duty of the assistant treasurer—

Section 1. To receive all moneys from the provincial courts, receipt the vouchers thereof, and hand same to the secretary.

Section 2. To keep an account of the various sources of revenue, and to receive the moneys accruing therefrom, and pay the same over to the secretary every fortnight.

ARTICLE 36.—That it be the duty of the provincial assessors—

Section 1. To hold courts in the districts to which they are appointed, with the assistance of the king or principal chief.

Section 2. To transmit to the secretary a statement of all cases tried during each month, showing the decisions arrived at thereon according to a form hereafter to be prescribed by the Executive Council.

Section 3. To keep an account of the summonses, writs, &c., issued during the month, showing the costs and fees thereon, as well as all fines imposed by them.

Section 4. To transmit weekly to the assistant treasurer all moneys received by them as court fees or fines, with an accompanying voucher.

Section 5. To see that the roads are made according to the approved standard, and that they are kept in proper condition.

Section 6. To see that the national schools are attended by all children between the ages of eight and fourteen, and report thereon to the secretary.

Section 7. To see that summonses, writs, &c., issuing from the British courts on the sea coast to any of the provincial towns are carried into effect with as little delay as possible, and to aid in the apprehension of criminals.

ARTICLE 37.—That in each province or district provincial courts be established, to be presided over by the provincial assessors.

ARTICLE 38.—That it be the duty of the Ministry and Executive Council—

Section 1. To advise the king-president in all State matters.

Section 2. To see that all laws, bills, ordinances, resolutions, &c., passed by the Representative Assembly, after receiving the sanction of the king-president, are carried into effect with as little delay as possible.

Section 3. To examine carefully the financial condition of the Confederation.

Section 4. To hear, try, and determine all important appeal cases brought before it by the under-secretary, option being allowed any party or parties dissatisfied with the decision thereof to appeal to the British Courts, on application from which the minutes of the proceedings therewith will be forwarded.

Section 5. To hear, presided over by the king-president, and assisted by any king or chief whom it may deem necessary to summon for that purpose, all disputes between any of the kings and chiefs or their peoples.

Section 6. To determine, according to the majority of votes of the people, the succession to the stool of any king or chief.

Section 7. To prepare laws, bills, ordinances, &c., for the consideration of the representative body.

Section 8. To issue notices to the kings and chiefs appointing time for their annual meeting, and frame out the programme of such meeting.

Section 9. To consider all applications of alliances from surrounding tribes, to present them for the consideration of the Representative Assembly, and to frame a reply thereto.

ARTICLE 39.—That three of the *ex officio* members of the Executive Council, or two *ex officio* and two non-official members, shall form a quorum of said council, and be competent to deliberate on all matters laid before it for the consideration by the secretary or under-secretary, or any other member thereof.

ARTICLE 40.—That one-third of the members composing the Representative Assembly shall form a quorum to discuss and deliberate on all questions brought before said Assembly.

ARTICLE 41.—That all laws, bills, regulations, ordinances, &c., be carried by the majority of votes in the Representative Assembly or Executive Council, in the latter the vice-president possessing a casting vote.

ARTICLE 42.—That it be the duty of the National Assembly, held in October of each year—

Section 1. To elect from the body of kings the president for the ensuing year, and to re-elect, as often as may appear to it fit and proper, the outgoing president.

Section 2. To consider all programmes laid before it by the executive council.

Section 3. To place on the stool, in cases of disputed succession thereto, the person elected by the executive council, with the concurrence of the principal inhabitants of the town, croom, or district.

ARTICLE 43.—That the officers of the Confederation shall render assistance as directed by the executive in carrying out the wishes of the British Government.

ARTICLE 44.—That it be competent to the

Representative Assembly, for the purpose of carrying on the administration of the Government, to pass laws, &c., for the levying of such taxes as it may seem necessary.

ARTICLE 45.—That all the articles herein above passed be designated "The Constitution of the Fanti Confederation."

ARTICLE 46.—That oaths of allegiance to the Fanti Confederation be taken by the kings and principal chiefs, which shall be held binding on their subjects and peoples, as well as by the principal officers of the Confederation and others joining it.

ARTICLE 47.—That the following oaths, in conjunction with that peculiar to each province, be administered as soon as the "Constitution" becomes law, to all the kings and chiefs present, to their captains and headmen, to the educated persons who express a wish to join the Confederation, and to all the office-bearers.[1]

2.

THE FANTI NATIONAL EDUCATION SCHEME.

To all to whom these presents shall come Kobena Entiree, Chief of Bamianko, and the undersigned headmen, elders and councillors, hereinafter called the grantors, we send greeting.

[1] Parliamentary Papers, 1873 (49), p. 3—7.

Whereas we desire to provide for the proper education and technical training of the people still under our stool, and to aid and promote sound learning and religious education in the Gold Coast by raising a fund hereinafter to be called Mfantsi National Education Fund, and to appoint trustees to administer such fund. Now these presents witness :—

1. That the said grantors do hereby of our own free will authorise and fully empower the treasurer of the Gold Coast Colony, or other officer or person empowered by the Concessions Ordinance, 1900, to receive the rents due to us or any of us for any concessions granted by ourselves individually or collectively or our predecessors in title, to deduct 10 per cent. out of and from all rents and monies so received from time to time, which shall be a first charge on such rents, and the same to set aside and pay into the Bank of British West Africa, Limited, at Cape Coast Castle, or some other bank, to the credit of the trustees of the said Mfantsi National Education Fund; and we declare that the receipt of the said sum by the Bank of British West Africa, Limited, or any person duly authorised by the said trustees to receive the same, shall discharge the said treasurer or other officer or person from seeing to the application thereof.

2. We do hereby appoint His Excellency the Governor of the Gold Coast Colony, the senior

native unofficial member of the Legislative Council of the Gold Coast, the President of the Gold Coast Aborigines' Rights Protection Society, the Rev. Andrew William Parker, of Cape Coast Castle (Wesleyan Minister), William Edward Sam, of Adja Bippo in Tarkwa, and Joseph Ephraim Casely Hayford, of Axim, barrister-at-law, to be the trustees of this fund.

3. The said trustees shall have full power to nominate and add to their number not more than four persons, and on any of them ceasing to be a trustee the remaining trustees shall by vote fill up such vacancy.

4. The said trustees shall stand possessed of and interested in the said money hereinbefore charged and made payable upon trust—

(i.) To establish and maintain a school or schools in the district of   or other parts of the Gold Coast, in which children shall receive religious training, and be taught—

(*a*) To read and write the Fanti language;

(*b*) The history and geography of the Gold Coast, having special reference to the local institutions, customs, and usages;

(*c*) Industrial and technical training;

(*d*) English education.

(ii.) To establish secondary or higher-grade schools.

(iii.) To found scholarships, to be called Queen Victoria scholarships, in aid of a liberal and professional education, and to encourage local literature.

5. In the event of other chiefs, headmen, and persons in like manner contributing or providing to the aforesaid objects, power is given to the said trustees to add the monies hereby granted, and the same to administer together.

6. Power is given to the said trustees and their successors to make such rules and regulations and to apply to the legislature of the Gold Coast Colony for such further powers and authorities as they may consider fit and proper for more perfectly and completely carrying out the objects of these presents, and it is hereby declared that in every case of difference the decision of the majority shall prevail, subject to any rules and regulations then in force.

7. And each and every one of us for himself and his successors in title, doth and do hereby covenant with each of the said trustees and their respective successors, that the aforesaid authority to deduct, set aside and pay the said ten per cent. shall not at any time hereafter be cancelled or recalled, and it is hereby declared to be irrevocable, and that each and all of us will from time to time and at any time hereinafter at the request of any of the trustees or their successors, do, execute and perform or cause to be done, executed and performed all things that may

be requisite and necessary for fully and effectually vesting the said money in the said trustees and their successors, so as to secure and promote among the aboriginal inhabitants of the Gold Coast from henceforth for all future generations, sound learning and religious education.

As witness our hands, marks and seals, this day of

The contents of this document were fully explained and interpreted to the said grantors in their own language, and it was executed after each of them had stated he perfectly understood the same, in the presence of

APPENDIX D.

OFFICIAL CORRESPONDENCE AND OTHER INFORMATION.

1.

DRAFT of an order of the Queen in Council for determining the mode of exercising the power and jurisdiction acquired by Her Majesty within divers countries on the West Coast of Africa, near or adjacent to Her Majesty's Gold Coast Colony.

At the Court at Osborne House, Isle of Wight, the 6th day of August, 1874.

Present: The Queen's Most Excellent Majesty, Lord President, Mr. Secretary Cross, Mr. Disraeli.

Whereas, by an Act made and passed in the session of Parliament, holden in the sixth and seventh years of Her Majesty's reign, intituled "An Act to remove doubts as to the exercise of power and jurisdiction by Her Majesty within divers countries and places out of Her Majesty's dominions, and to render the same more effectual," it was, amongst other things, enacted that it should be lawful for Her Majesty to hold, exercise, and enjoy any power or jurisdiction which Her Majesty then had, or might at any time thereafter have, within any country or place out of Her Majesty's dominions in the same and as ample a manner as if Her Majesty had acquired such power or jurisdiction by the cession or conquest of territory. And whereas by certain letters patent, under the great seal of the United Kingdom of Great Britain and Ireland, bearing date at Westminster the 24th day of July, 1874, in the thirty-eighth year of Her Majesty's reign, Her Majesty's settlements on the Gold Coast and of Lagos were constituted and erected into one colony, under the title of the Gold Coast Colony, and a Legislative Council was appointed for the same colony, with certain powers and authority to legislate for the said colony, as by the said Letters Patent, reference being had thereto will more fully appear. And whereas Her Majesty hath acquired power and jurisdiction within divers countries on the West Coast of Africa, near or adjacent to Her Majesty's said Gold Coast Colony, and it is expedient to determine the mode of exercising such power and jurisdiction. Now, therefore, it is hereby ordered, with the advice and consent of her Privy Council, as follows :—

1. It shall be lawful for the Legislative Council for the time being of the said Gold Coast Colony,

by ordinance or ordinances, to exercise and provide for giving effect to all such powers and jurisdiction as Her Majesty may at any time, before or after the passing of this order in council, have acquired in the said territories adjacent to the Gold Coast Colony.

2. The Governor for the time being of the said colony has a negative voice in the passing of all such ordinances as aforesaid. And the right is hereby reserved to Her Majesty, her heirs and successors, to disallow any such ordinances as aforesaid, in whole or in part, such disallowance being signified to the Governor through one of Her Majesty's principal Secretaries of State, and also to make and establish from time to time, with the advice and consent of Parliament, or with the advice of her or their Privy Council, all such laws or ordinances as may to her or them appear necessary for the exercise of such powers and jurisdiction as aforesaid, as fully as if this order in council had not been made.

3. In the making and establishing all such ordinances, the said Legislative Council shall conform to and observe all such rules and regulations as may from time to time be appointed by any instruction or instructions issued by Her Majesty with the advice of her Privy Council, and, until further directed, the instructions in force for the time

being as to ordinances passed by the said Legislative Council for the peace, order, and good government of the said Gold Coast Colony shall, so far as they may be applicable, be taken and deemed to be in force in respect of ordinances passed by the said council by virtue of this order in council.

4. In the construction of this order in council, the term "Governor" shall include the officer for the time being administering the Government of the Gold Coast Colony.

And the Right Honourable the Earl of Carnarvon, one of Her Majesty's principal Secretaries of State, is to give the necessary directions herein accordingly.

(*Signed*) ARTHUR HELPS.

2.

LORD STANLEY TO LIEUTENANT-GOVERNOR HILL.

Assessors' Jurisdiction.

DOWNING STREET,
November 22nd, 1844.

SIR,—I have had under my consideration the correspondence noted in the accompanying schedule and of which papers and copies are herewith enclosed, and I have to acquaint you that upon the report of the law officers of the Crown, Her Majesty has been pleased to pass an order in council, herewith enclosed, under the Acts 6 & 7 Vict., cc. 13 and 94, appointing Her Majesty's settlement of Cape Coast Castle as a place to which persons coming within the operation of the last mentioned of those Acts may be sent for trial or punishment.

The order, you will perceive, provides for two distinct classes of cases. The one, that of persons whom it may be deemed expedient to send from the neighbouring countries to be tried within Her Majesty's settlement; the other, that of persons who may have been tried in the neighbouring countries, but whom it is considered advisable to send into Her Majesty's settlement for the purpose of undergoing their sentences.

As regards the first class of cases, you will of course bear in mind that in any trial which takes place the provisions of the 6 & 7 Vict., c. 94 applicable to that event must be strictly observed; and also, that as the jurisdiction for the trial of offenders sent under the provisions of the Act is given to the Supreme Court of the Colony only to which they are sent, that in the present state of the judicial institutions on the Gold Coast, such offenders would require to be forwarded thence to Sierra Leone for trial.

For practical purposes, therefore, as yet at all events, his power is not likely to be of any general utility. The powers, however, given under the second head will, I apprehend, greatly facilitate the working of the system which has grown up in our relations with the tribes surrounding the forts under your government.

It being necessary to provide for the appointment of persons to be specially empowered to exercise the powers conferred by the different sections of the 6 & 7 Vict., c. 94, I send you additional instructions, under the sign manual, giving you the requisite authority, both to act yourself and to nominate others for the same purpose; and I have, as you will perceive, taken the opportunity of providing for Mr. Maclean's absence or inability to discharge the duties of assessor to the sovereigns and chiefs of the neighbouring tribes by making a fresh appointment to the office, including yourself and others with him, as such assessors having power to act either jointly or severally.

Should Mr. Cloustun, the gentleman whom you have appointed as reported in your despatch, No. 27 of June 16th last, to officiate for Mr. Maclean, not be already in the commission of the peace, or his name not stand first or second upon it, it will of course be necessary that a new commission should be issued.

I presume that the magistrates and gaoler at the gaol at Cape Coast Castle are already the persons to whom it appertains to carry into effect there any sentences which may have been passed by the Supreme Court at Sierra Leone.

Should that, however, be not the case, appointments to that effect ought forthwith to be made, and I have instructed the Governor of Sierra Leone accordingly, it being necessary, under the 5th section of the 6 & 7 Vict., c. 94, that the persons to give effect within any colony to sentences passed out of it should be " magistrates, gaolers, or other officers to whom it may appertain to give effect to any sentence passed by the Supreme Court exercising criminal jurisdiction within such colony."

The royal instructions, you will perceive, also provide for the appointment of persons having the authority to exercise the powers given by the 6th section of the 6 & 7 Vict., c. 94, relative to the transportation of convicts; but you will clearly understand that, although it has been considered expedient to provide by the instrument the machinery necessary for bringing into operation all the powers conferred by the Act, yet that you are not to consider yourself at liberty, in any case, to exercise or permit the exercise of that relative to transportation without special instructions from the Secretary of State.

Although likewise the instructions, as before observed, provide for the exercise of the office of assessor by several persons jointly, as well as by one person, you will not on that account make any alteration in the practice which has hitherto prevailed of leaving the duties to be executed by one person.

You will bear in mind that the power of the assessor, in his judicial capacity, is not derived from either the Acts of Parliament above referred to, or from the order in council; and further, that it cannot be exercised by him as such within Her Majesty's dominions. It must be founded on the assent and concurrence of the sovereign power of the State within which it is exercised, either express, as in the case of the treaty transmitted by you in your private and confidential despatch of the 6th of March last, or implied from long usage, as in the case of the long and general acquiescence, which can be shown in many districts, in the authority hitherto exercised by Mr. Maclean.

You will understand that the system upon which Mr. Maclean has proceeded, in the exercise of judicial powers over the natives, is to be taken as the guide for the exercise of the powers of assessor for the future.

It consists, in fact, in combining with an impartial investigation of the cases brought before him, a mitigation of the severity of the sentences which in such cases would be awarded by native judges in the event of conviction. I need not therefore instruct you to caution the assessor of the necessity for a lenient exercise of the discretion entrusted to him ; but in the event of his deeming capital punishment in any case inevitable, you will instruct him that the execution must be carried into effect by the native authorities, and take place in the country in which the offender is tried.

Having thus, as far as possible, brought the very peculiar case of the jurisdiction exercised among the tribes in the neighbourhood of the forts on the Gold Coast within the operation of the Acts of Parliament referred to in the commencement of this despatch, it only remains for me further to observe that I am not to be understood as affirming that the exercise of that jurisdiction is not capable of being justified and maintained independently of any such express sanction of the Legislature.

It is a jurisdiction which had its origin in a desire to mitigate, by the influence of Christianity and civilisation, the effect of cruel and barbarous customs; it has been brought into operation upon a state of society, and under relation to savage tribes, necessitating a neglect of all technical rules and observances. In its effects, it has undeniably been the means of insuring justice, preventing cruelty, and promoting civilisation; and I must guard myself against being supposed, because I endeavour to give it the aid of the forms I have averted to, to assume that the general principles of the law of England are not comprehensive enough to allow for the necessities which such a state of circumstances as exist on the Gold Coast unavoidably creates, and to justify those measures by which such necessities, when created, can alone be adequately provided for.

I have, &c.,

(*Signed*) STANLEY.

Lieut.-Governor Hill, &c.

3.

THE EARL OF CARNARVON TO GOVERNOR STRAHAN.

DOWNING STREET,
August 20*th*, 1874.

SIR,—In my despatch of the 20th instant, I had the honour to forward to you an order made by Her Majesty in Council, which delegates to the Legislature of the Gold Coast the exercise by ordinance or ordinances of such power and jurisdiction as Her Majesty has or may at any time have acquired in the territories adjacent to the Gold Coast Colony.

2. The Legislature of the Gold Coast settlements has from time to time enacted ordinances which were intended to take effect beyond the local limits

APPENDIX D. 355

of the British settlements of the Gold Coast. Doubts, however, have been entertained as to the validity and force of such legislation, and in 1855 the law officers reported that such assumption of authority was not justified.

3. Her Majesty's Government having decided to establish a new colony and legislative council for the settlements of the Gold Coast and Lagos, vesting in that council the power to legislate for the protected territories on the Gold Coast, the law officers were requested to report upon the subject; and in accordance with their opinion, of which I annex a copy for your private information, the order in council already transmitted to you was passed. By this order the local Legislature is (subject to the conditions and reservations therein specified) clothed with whatever legislative authority Her Majesty has or may hereafter claim to exercise on the Gold Coast.

4. This having been done, it becomes advisable to define as clearly as may be the extent of Her Majesty's power and jurisdiction, so as to prevent misunderstandings in future, and to enable the colonial Legislature to know on what subjects it may properly legislate.

5. I need not here examine in detail the origin and history of the peculiar jurisdiction exercised by this country in the protected territories of the

Gold Coast. Carried to its highest development under Governor Maclean, its existence is first authoritatively recorded and recognised in the report of the House of Commons committee of 1842, which, in recommending the continuance of the system, suggested that it should be made the subject of distinct agreement with the native chiefs. That recommendation resulted in the negotiation with the native chiefs of the document called the "Bond" of the 6th of March, 1844, which is the only document purporting to define the extent of the Queen's jurisdiction on the Gold Coast in other than strictly political matters. But that definition, either from being an inadequate representation of the facts as they then existed, or from change of circumstances, no longer truly expresses what Her Majesty's Government believe to be the extent and scope of Her Majesty's power.

6. The Bond grants to Her Majesty's officers the right to try and punish crimes and offences and to repress human sacrifices, panyarring, and other unlawful acts and barbarous customs. It is silent as to the Queen's right by her officers and delegates, to collect customs, to administer civil justice, to legislate for the public health, or erect municipalities, to provide for education, to construct roads and regulate the industrial and social economy of the protectorate. On all these matters the Legislature

or Government of the settlement has, with or without the co-operation of the native rulers, exercised authority to an extent which, strictly speaking, could only be justified on the assumption (the justice of which I am satisfied is not open to question) that these matters have by usage and by the sufferance and tacit assent of the natives fallen within the province of the Queen's authority.

7. The necessity of some more adequate definition of the Queen's authority than the obsolete Bond of 1844 being thus apparent, it remains to be considered whether that definition should take the form of a bond to be negotiated with the chiefs, as in 1844, or a proclamation emanating from the sole authority of the Queen.

8. In 1844 the method of proceeding by negotiation was recommended by obvious considerations of prudence. But in the thirty years which have since elapsed the power and resources of the British Government have been gradually increasing, until, by the recent victories of the British forces, they have been so strengthened and consolidated as to render an act of sovereign power, such as a proclamation of the Queen, the only appropriate mode of proceeding for the attainment of the desired object. It may be added that there are many objections of policy to proceeding by way of negotiation. It is not for Her Majesty to take as a grant

what is already claimed and held as a right; whilst, looking to the number of petty chiefs on the coast, and the obscurity in which their relations with one another are involved, there would be some danger of not inviting the concurrence of chiefs who might afterwards allege, and with a certain show of reason, that their consent was as requisite as that of others whose co-operation had been asked and given. Besides this, the Government would be placed in a position of much embarrassment if any considerable body of chiefs refused their consent in part or in whole to the proposed treaty.

9. On the other hand, I should be anxious to avoid the risk, if any, attendant upon this manner of proceeding of alienating the feelings of the natives; and I am fully alive to the importance of their willing co-operation in the work of promoting the civilisation and prosperity of the protectorate. The nature of the proposed terms are such as, if not fully and clearly explained, might excite the alarm and aversion of the less intelligent rulers, whilst a too hasty assumption of authority might create a feeling of discontent, and possibly lead them to seek alliances beyond the protectorate with tribes hostile to our power.

10. Before coming to any conclusion as to the best mode of procedure, I desire to know your opinion on a question which is, perhaps, as difficult

as any that you may be called on to deal with, and one that demands the exercise of the most delicate tact and judgment. I enclose a draft of a proclamation which I have caused to be prepared for consideration.

11. In defining the nature of the Queen's protectorate on the Gold Coast, it may be well also to define and limit the local extent of that protectorate.

12. What may be termed the natural boundaries of the protectorate to the north and east are to a great extent marked out by a course of the Prah and the Volta, and the lagoon dividing Quittah from the sea; but considerations connected with the protection of trade and the collection of revenue may compel your Government to plant establishments or exercise jurisdiction in parts of the Ahoonah country lying to the east of the Volta and behind the lagoon. The question of the northern limit of the protectorate towards the Croboe and Aquamoo country will also call for careful examination in connection with the request of the Aquamoo people to be included in the protectorate, recently reported by Dr. Gouldsbury; and it may be worthy of consideration whether some limitation should not be put on what are usually regarded as the boundaries of British jurisdiction in the little known regions of the north-west.

13. Up to this point I have confined my observations to the protectorate adjacent to the Gold

Coast settlement; but a further question of grave importance presses for consideration, with reference to the boundaries of British territory and the British protectorate at Lagos, for it will not have escaped your notice that the language of the order in council in effect delegates to the local Legislature Her Majesty's rights over the protectorates. As bearing upon this point, I may refer you to Lord Kimberley's despatch of April 5th, 1873, to Governor Keate.

14. You are well aware that the effect of including, under the same provisions and procedure, the area of country which has been called the Protectorate of Lagos, would have to be seriously considered as possibly involving us in difficulties with the neighbouring nations, which might prove deeply injurious to the prosperity of that settlement. The history of our relations with the protected territories of Lagos differs entirely from that of our relations with the protected territories on the Gold Coast. Her Majesty's Government have not assumed to so great an extent at Lagos as at the Gold Coast the direction of political and other affairs, and the Queen's forces have not at Lagos, as on the Gold Coast, been associated with the native powers in hostile alliances against a powerful common foe. For these reasons I am inclined to think that the Queen's authority as a protecting power need not, under present circumstances, be declared to extend to the Protectorate of

Lagos, as proposed to be defined in the draft proclamation ; although, of course, under our treaty engagements, we must continue to exercise a control over the affairs of that part of the coast, and in some sense to discharge the functions of a protecting power.

15. I have to request your opinion and criticisms, together with those of Mr. Chalmers, on the draft proclamation, as well as on the form it should assume, and the territories to which it should be declared to extend. I shall be glad to receive your answer as soon as you feel yourself able to come to a conclusion on the various questions contained in this despatch.

16. If, contrary to my expectations, it should seem desirable to proceed by treaty engagements with the native chiefs, the draft proclamation, with due alterations of phrase, will probably suffice as a draft of the bond which those chiefs would be required to sign. But I have to request that you will apply to me confidentially for further instructions before taking any open action in the matter.

17. I need hardly add that, in the meantime, it will not be desirable for the Legislative Council, unless some very special emergency should arise, to attempt to exercise the powers vested in them by the recent order in council.

18. There remains the question of the existence

of slavery within the range of the Queen's influence and authority. It is one surrounded by many and serious difficulties, but it is also one which affects, by its existence, not only the honour and traditional policy of this country, but the welfare and good government of the Gold Coast. It has ever since I received the seals of this office engaged my anxious attention; and though Her Majesty's Government could not consent to have the decision of it forced upon them and to be pledged to some precipitate and probably ill-considered course of action, they have at no time abandoned the hope and intention of extinguishing an evil which they have been compelled to tolerate, but in which they have never acquiesced. The time has now, in my opinion, arrived when at least the possibility of dealing with this important question may receive a careful and dispassionate consideration; and I propose to address you in another despatch on this subject.

      I have, etc.,

        (*Signed*) CARNARVON.

4.

DRAFT OF A PROCLAMATION DEFINING THE NATURE AND EXTENT OF THE QUEEN'S JURISDICTION ON THE GOLD COAST.

Victoria, by the Grace of God, of the United Kingdom of Great Britain and Ireland, Queen, Defender of the Faith, to all to whom these presents shall come, greeting :

Whereas, by an Act of Parliament made and passed in the session of Parliament holden in the sixth and seventh years of our reign, intituled, "An Act to remove Doubts as to the Exercise of Power and Jurisdiction by Her Majesty within divers Countries and Places out of Her Majesty's Dominions, and to render the same more effectual," it is, amongst other things, enacted that it is and shall be lawful for us to hold, exercise, and enjoy any power or jurisdiction which we now have, or may at any time hereafter have, within any country or place out of our dominions, in the same and as ample a manner as if we had acquired such power or jurisdiction by the cession or conquest of territory :

And whereas we have by grant, treaty, usage, sufferance, and other lawful means acquired, and do hold, exercise, and enjoy power and jurisdiction in divers countries on the West Coast of Africa, near or adjacent to our Gold Coast Colony :

And whereas by an Order made by us in Council, bearing date at Osborne House, on the 6th day of August, in the year of our Lord one thousand eight hundred and seventy-four, it was, amongst other things, ordered that it should be lawful for the Legislative Council of our said Gold Coast Colony for the time being, by ordinance or ordinances, to exercise and provide for giving effect to all such power and jurisdiction as we might at any time, either before or after the passing of the said Order in Council, have acquired in the said territories adjacent to the Gold Coast Colony :

And whereas the extent and nature of our power and jurisdiction, as now actually holden, exercised and employed by us in the said territories, have not been anywhere by us fully declared :

And whereas it is expedient, for the guidance and information, as well as of the Legislature of our said Gold Coast Colony as for that of the native chiefs and rulers living under our protection in the said territories, that the nature of our power and jurisdiction, as well as their local limits, be declared by us. Therefore we do declare as follows :—

Our power and jurisdiction which we have acquired as aforesaid extend, amongst other things, to—

I. The preservation of the public peace and the protection of individuals and property.

II. The administration of civil and criminal justice, including:—

(1) The constitution and regulation of a superior court of justice, such as that which has been hitherto known as the Judicial Assessor's Court, of district magistrates' courts, native courts, and such other courts as it may from time to time be deemed expedient to create.

(2) The enactment of laws relating to crimes, wrongs, personal rights, contracts, property rights, and fiduciary relations similar to those prevailing in our Gold Coast Colony, but framed with due regard to native law and customs where they are not repugnant to justice, equity, and good conscience.

(3) The determination of appeals from native tribunals to magistrates or to some superior Court.

(4) The apprehension and trial of criminals and offenders of all kinds in any part of the said territories.

(5) The supervision and regulation of native prisons.

III. The extinction of human sacrifices, panyarring, judicial torture, and other immoral, barbarous, and cruel customs.

IV. The abolition of slave trading.

V. Measures with regard to domestic slavery and pawning.

VI. The protection and encouragement of trade and traders, including the construction, maintenance, and improvement of roads, paths, bridges, harbour works, waterways, telegraphs, and other public works which benefit trade and promote civilisation.

VII. The maintenance of an armed police force for the preservation of internal order and the prevention of foreign aggression, and the organisation of the military forces of the native rulers in alliance with her Majesty.

VIII. The settling by the authority of the Governor of our Gold Coast Colony of disputes arising between different chiefs and rulers in the said territories.

IX. The promotion of the public health, including the imposition, with the assent of the native chiefs, of sanitary rates in towns and villages.

X. The establishment of municipalities.

XI. Public education, including industrial and religious training.

XII. The raising of a revenue by licences and customs, and by such direct imposts as the native chiefs and rulers, or a major part of them, may agree to.

And further, we declare that the undermentioned

territories are those within which at the present time we have power and jurisdiction as aforesaid.

(List of territories to be inserted by the local authorities in the first instance.)

5.

Fantee Chiefs.

(Bond, 6th March, 1844.)

1. Whereas power and jurisdiction have been exercised for and on behalf of Her Majesty the Queen of Great Britain and Ireland, within divers countries and places adjacent to Her Majesty's forts and settlements on the Gold Coast, we, chiefs of countries and places so referred to, adjacent to the said forts and settlements, do hereby acknowledge that power and jurisdiction, and declare that the first objects of law are the protection of individuals and of property.

2. Human sacrifices and other barbarous customs, such as panyarring, are abominations, and contrary to law.

3. Murders, robberies, and other crimes and offences, will be tried and inquired of before the Queen's judicial officers and the chiefs of the district, moulding the customs of the country to the general principles of British law.

Done at Cape Coast Castle, before His Excellency

the Lieutenant-Governor, on this 6th day of March, in the year of our Lord 1844.

Their
- × Cudjoe Chibboe, King of Denkera.
- × Quashie Ottoo, Chief of Abrah.
- × Chibboe Coomah, Chief of Assin.
- × Gebre, Second Chief of Assin.
- × Quashie Ankah, Chief of Donadie.
- × Awoossie, Chief of Dominassie.

(Signed) Quashie Ankah.
- × Amonoo, Chief of Annamaboe.
- × Joe Aggrey, Chief of Cape Coast.

Witness my seal on the 6th day of March, 1844, and the 7th year of Her Majesty's reign.

(Signed) H. W. Hill,
Lieutenant-Governor (L.S.)

Witnesses, and done in the presence of—

(Signed) George Maclean, J.P. and Assessor (s.).
F. Pogson, 1st W.I. Regiment (s.), Commanding H.M. Troops.
S. Bannerman, Adjutant of Militia and Police (s.).

Blue Book: "Africa, Western Coast," p. 419.

6.

BRITISH CHARTER, PROVIDING FOR THE GOVERNMENT OF HER MAJESTY'S SETTLEMENTS ON THE GOLD COAST AND OF LAGOS, AND CONSTITUTING THOSE SETTLEMENTS INTO A SEPARATE COLONY TO BE CALLED THE GOLD COAST COLONY, AND PROVIDING FOR THE GOVERNMENT THEREOF. *Westminster*, July 24th, 1874.

Victoria, by the Grace of God of the United Kingdom of Great Britain and Ireland, Queen, Defender of the Faith, to all to whom these presents shall come, greeting.

1. Whereas, by certain Letters Patent under the Great Seal of our United Kingdom of Great Britain and Ireland, bearing date at Westminster the 19th day of February, 1866, in the 29th year of our reign, provision was made for the government of our settlements on the West Coast of Africa, as therein is more particularly described;

And whereas, by a supplementary commission under the Great Seal aforesaid, and bearing date at Westminster the 8th day of November, 1872, in the 36th year of our reign, we did empower our Governor and Commander-in-Chief of our West Africa settlements to grant pardons to offenders in the manner and upon the terms therein mentioned;

And whereas, by our commission under the Great

Seal aforesaid, bearing date the 25th day of July, 1873, in the 37th year of our reign, we did constitute and appoint our trusty and well-beloved George Berkeley, Esquire (now Companion of our Most Distinguished Order of St. Michael and St. George), to be, during our will and pleasure, our Governor and Commander-in-Chief in and over our said West Africa settlements; and whereas it is expedient that provision should be made for the government of our settlements on the Gold Coast and of Lagos, apart and separate from the government of our other settlements in the West Coast of Africa;

And whereas, by an Act made and passed in the sixth year of our reign (cap. 13), intituled "An Act to enable Her Majesty to provide for the Government of her Settlements upon the Coast of Africa and in the Falkland Islands," it was enacted that it should be lawful for us, by any commission under the Great Seal of our United Kingdom, or by any instructions under our sign-manual and signet accompanying and referred to in any such commission to delegate to any three or more persons within any of the settlements aforesaid, either in whole or in part, and subject to all such conditions, provisions, and limitations, as might be prescribed by any such commission or instructions, the power and authority to make and establish all such laws, institutions, and ordinances, and to constitute such courts and officers, and to make such provisions and regulations for the proceedings in such courts, and for the administration of justice as might be necessary for the peace, order, and good government of our subjects and others within our then present or future settlements on the said coast—

Now know ye that we do by these our Letters Patent, under the Great Seal aforesaid, declare our pleasure to be that our said Letters Patent of the 19th day of February, 1866, our said supplementary commission of the 8th of November, 1872, and our said commission of the 25th day of July, 1873, shall be, and they are hereby revoked so far as regards our said settlements on the Gold Coast and of Lagos, or any part or parts thereof; and we do further declare our pleasure to be that those settlements shall constitute, and they are hereby erected into a separate colony under the title of the Gold Coast Colony.

2. And we do further declare our pleasure to be that our settlements on the Gold Coast shall, as heretofore, and until otherwise provided by us, comprise all places, settlements, and territories which may at any time belong to us in Western Africa, between the 5th degree of west longitude and the 2nd degree of east longitude. And our settlement of Lagos shall, as heretofore and until otherwise provided by us, comprise all places, settlements,

and territories, which may at any time belong to us in Western Africa between the 2nd and 5th degrees of east longitude.

3. And we do further declare and appoint that the government of the said colony shall be administered by a Governor duly commissioned by us on that behalf.

4. And we do further declare our pleasure to be that there shall be within our said colony a Legislative Council, which shall consist of our said Governor for the time being, and of such other persons or officers, not being less than two in number, from each of our said settlements, as shall be named or designated by or by virtue of any instruction or instructions or by any warrant or warrants to be by us for that purpose issued under our sign-manual and signet, and with the advice of our Privy Council, all of which persons or officers shall hold their places in the said council during our pleasure.

5. And we do further, by this our commission under the Great Seal of our United Kingdom aforesaid, delegate to the persons who within our said colony shall compose the Legislative Council thereof, full power and authority, subject always to such conditions, provisions, and limitations as may be presented by any commission or instructions, to establish such ordinances not being repugnant to the law of England, or to any order made or to be

APPENDIX D.

made by us with the advice of our Privy Council, and to establish such courts and officers, and to make such provisions and regulations for the proceedings in such courts, and for the administration of justice, as may be necessary for the peace, order, and good government of such colony.

6. And we do further declare our pleasure to be that our said Governor shall have a negative voice in the passing of all such ordinances aforesaid: and we do also hereby reserve to ourselves, our heirs and successors, our and their right and authority to disallow any such ordinances as aforesaid, in the whole or in part, such allowance being from time to time signified to him through one of our principal Secretaries of State, and also to make and establish from time to time, with the advice and consent of Parliament, or with the advice of our and their Privy Council, all such laws or ordinances as may to us or them appear necessary for the order, peace, and good government of our said colony as fully as if these presents had not been made.

And we do further declare our pleasure to be that in the making and establishing of all such ordinances, the said Legislative Council shall conform to and observe all such rules as may from time to time be directed or appointed by any instruction or instructions issued by us with the advice of our Privy Council.

7. And we do further declare and establish that the laws now in force in our said colony shall continue in force as long and as far only as they are not repugnant to or repealed by any ordinance passed by the Legislature of our said colony.

8. And we do further declare our pleasure to be that, for the purpose of advising our said Governor, there shall be for our said colony an Executive Council, which shall be composed of such persons and constituted in such manner as may be directed by any instructions which may from time to time be addressed to our said Governor by us under our sign-manual and signet, and all such persons shall hold their places in the said council at our pleasure.

9. And we do further authorise and empower our said Governor to keep and use the public seal of our said colony for sealing all things whatsoever that shall pass the said seal, and we do direct that until a public seal shall be provided for our said colony the public seal of our settlement on the Gold Coast shall be used as the public seal of our said colony for sealing all things whatsoever that shall pass the said seal.

10. And we do authorise and empower our said Governor to make and execute in our name and on our behalf, under the said public seal, grants and dispositions of any lands which may be lawfully granted or disposed of by us within our said colony

either in conformity with instructions under our sign-manual and signet, or in conformity with such regulations as are now in force, or may be made by him in that behalf, with the advice of our said Executive Council, and duly published in our said colony.

11. And we do further authorise and empower our said Governor to constitute and appoint all such Judges, Commissioners of Oyer and Terminer, Judges of the Peace, and other necessary officers and ministers as may lawfully be appointed by us, all of whom shall hold their offices during our pleasure.

12. And we do further authorise and empower our said Governor as he shall see occasion, in our name and on our behalf, when any crime has been committed within our said colony, or for which the offender may be tried therein, to grant a pardon to any accomplice, not being the actual perpetrator of such crime, who shall give such information and evidence as shall lead to the apprehension and conviction of the principal offender, and further to grant to any offender convicted of any crime in any court, or before any judge, justice, or magistrate within our said colony, a pardon either full or subject to lawful conditions or any respite of the execution of the sentence of any such offender, of such period as to him may seem fit, and to remit any fines,

penalties, or forfeitures which may become due and payable to us.

13. And we do further authorise and empower our said Governor, upon sufficient cause to him appearing, to suspend from the exercise of his office within our said colony any person exercising the same under or by virtue of any commission or warrant, granted or to be granted by us in our name or under our authority, which suspension shall continue and have effect only until our pleasure therein shall be known and signified to him. And we do hereby strictly require and enjoin him, in proceeding to any such suspension, to observe the directions in that behalf given to him by any instructions under our sign-manual and signet as may be hereafter addressed to our said Governor for the time being.

14. Our will and pleasure is, and we do hereby direct that, in the execution of this our commission, and in the exercise of the command hereby vested in our Governor for the time being, he be resident in our settlement on the Gold Coast, or at such place or places in the territories adjacent thereto as may from time to time be appointed for the residence of our said Governor, except when the interests of our service may render his presence desirable in our settlement of Lagos.

15. And whereas it is necessary that provision be made for the execution of this our commission in

the event of the death or incapacity of our said Governor, or of his removal from his command, or of his absence from the limits of his said government: Now, therefore, we do further declare our pleasure to be that, in any such event as aforesaid, all and every the powers and authorities hereby vested in him shall be, and the same are hereby vested in such person as may be appointed by us and our sign-manual and signet, to be our Lieutenant-Governor of our said colony, or if there be no such Lieutenant-Governor therein, such person or persons as may be appointed by us under our sign-manual and signet to administer the government of our said colony, and in case there shall be no such person or persons within our said colony so appointed by us, then is the person for the time being administering the government of our said settlement of Lagos, who shall for such time as he administers the government of our said colony, be called the administrator of the Gold Coast Colony. Provided always, and we do further declare our pleasure to be, that our Governor for the time being during the period of his passage by sea from either of the settlements aforesaid to the other of the said settlements, or while visiting or residing at any place in any of the territories adjacent thereto, shall not, for any of the purposes aforesaid, be considered as being absent from the limits of his said command.

16. And we do further declare and direct that, during his absence from our said settlement on the Gold Coast, but while he is within the limits of his said command as aforesaid, our Governor may, if he think fit, appoint some person to act as his deputy in administering the government of our said Gold Coast settlement, upon such terms and conditions, and for such time, as he may think desirable for the good government of our said settlement; and all or such of the powers and authorities aforesaid as our said Governor in his discretion shall from time to time think it necessary or expedient to assign to such deputy shall, as far as the same shall be exercisable within such settlement, be vested in such deputy.

17. And we do further declare that so long as our said Governor, or (as the case may be) Lieutenant-Governor, or administrator of the Gold Coast Colony, shall be absent from our settlement of Lagos, all and every the powers and authorities, except the powers of suspension and pardon, hereby vested in our said Governor, and so far as the same shall be exercisable within such settlement, shall be vested in such person within the same as may be appointed by us by warrant under our sign-manual and signet to administer the government thereof; and in case there shall not be within such settlement any such administrator, then we declare that the said powers and authorities shall, in our said settlement of

Lagos, be vested in such person, and upon such terms and conditions, and for such time, as our said Governor, Lieutenant-Governor, or administrator of our Gold Coast Colony, as the case may be, shall provisionally from time to time appoint, subject to our approval. And we do further declare and provide that the officer for the time being administering the government of our said settlement of Lagos shall, in the discharge of such his office, conform to and observe such instructions as shall, for that purpose, be addressed to him by our said Governor in the execution of this our commission; subject, nevertheless, to all such rules and regulations in that behalf as may from time to time be contained in any instructions under our sign-manual and signet, addressed to our Governor for the time being of our said Gold Coast Colony.

18. And we do further direct and enjoin that this our commission shall be read and proclaimed within our said respective settlements on the Gold Coast and of Lagos, and that a transcript thereof shall be deposited and duly recorded in our said settlements, this our original commission being preserved within our settlement on the Gold Coast.

19. And we do hereby require and command all officers, civil and military, and all others the inhabitants of our said colony, to be obedient, aiding and assisting unto our said Governor for the time

being, and to the officer appointed to administer the government of our settlement of Lagos, in the execution of this our commission, and of the powers and authorities herein contained.

20. And we do hereby reserve to ourselves, our heirs and successors, full power and authority from time to time to revoke, alter, or amend this our commission as to us or them shall seem meet.

In witness whereof we have caused these our letters to be made patent.

7.

AT A PALAVER HELD AT GOVERNMENT HOUSE, CAPE COAST, MAY 10th, 1865.[1]

Present:

His Excellency Wm. Hackett, Lieutenant-Governor; the Hon. M. R. Barry, Acting Chief Justice.

Chiefs of Cape Coast: J. R. Thompson, Isaac Robertson, Quamina Mayan, Quamina Acquah, Quacoe Gapee.

Quamina Acquah states, on behalf of himself and chiefs, that, with reference to the request of the Lieutenant-Governor that they should sign a paper ceding a portion of the town of Cape Coast to the

[1] Parliamentary Papers, 1867 (198), xlix. 45.

Government, after consultation they had arrived at the following decision, which they desired should be interpreted to His Excellency :—

That they, the chiefs and people, knew that the lands in Cape Coast belong to the Queen; that they themselves are under the Queen, and are protected by her; that wherever the Governor resides in Cape Coast they considered as the Castle. That, knowing these things, the people think it unnecessary for the Governor to make such a request, viz., that they should sign a document giving land to the Queen, when the Queen had for a series of years given and granted the said lands without any question on their part. The Governor having previously explained to them that he had discovered in the records of the Government that lands were granted by the Government during fifty years past, the chiefs replied that the signing of a paper is what is doubtful to them and people, but they wished to remain under the Queen, as they were under the late King, and that the signing of a paper had never been required by any of the Lieutenant-Governor's predecessors; that every one knew the land to be the Queen's, and that therefore they begged the Governor to let them remain in the same position.

(*Signed*) W. THOMPSON,
Interpreter.

APPENDIX E.

OTHER MATTER.

1.

THE SALE OF LAND AT SEKONDI.

The Aborigines' Rights Protection Society Petition the Governor.

Important Correspondence.[1]

AXIM,
September 23rd, 1901.

MAY it please your Excellency and the members of the Legislative Council,

The humble petition of the Axim Branch of the Aborigines' Rights Protection Society showeth:

1. That the attention of your Excellency's petitioners has been drawn to Government Notification No. 355, published in the Government Gazette for July 27th, 1901, in regard to the sale of land by public auction at Sekondi, in the Gold Coast.

---

[1] Reproduced from *West Africa* of July 5th, 1902, p. 702.

2. Your Excellency's petitioners take it that the said sale of land by public auction at Sekondi by the Colonial Government is authorised by the Towns (Amendment) Ordinance of 1901, under which the Colonial Secretary may acquire any land within the area of a town under the Public Lands Ordinance, 1876, as though it were land required for the service of the Colony. The said Ordinance incorporates sections 1 and 2 of clause 16 of the Towns Ordinance of 1892, which relates, among other things, to the declaring of open spaces by the Government with a view to the promotion of the public health.

3. The Towns (Amendment) Ordinance of 1901, therefore, would seem merely to contemplate the acquisition of land for the public service and the regulation of open spaces.

4. While your Excellency's petitioners are in full sympathy with the Colonial Government as regards the proper laying out of the several towns of the Gold Coast, and the promotion of the public health in general, they cannot shut their eyes to the course taken by the Government in disposing of lands so acquired for the use of the public at a profit to persons who may simply happen to have more means than the original owners.

5. It is obvious, your Excellency's petitioners would humbly point out, that if the intention of the Government be merely the promotion of the public

health, the same end might be secured by either directing the owners of the freehold areas in a given town to build substantial houses thereupon under proper regulations, failing which they might be directed to grant the same on lease to others able to raise such substantial buildings on suitable terms as to consideration and annual rental. Thus, the original owners would, as they are entitled to, be allowed to reap the benefit of their ancient heritage, which, under the working of the present Ordinance, they cannot do. As it is, the public, under the impression that they are giving up their lands for the public service, simply alienate them to third persons at nominal rates, the whole advantage or profit of the bargain going to the Government.

6. It may also be respectfully submitted that your Excellency's humble petitioners have always understood that one of the main principles guiding the administration of the Gold Coast is the protection of the rights of the people to their ancestral lands. It is clear that the operation of the Ordinance under discussion absolutely violates that principle.

7. In support of the foregoing submission, your Excellency may be respectfully referred to the Report of the Proceedings of the Deputation of the Kings and Chiefs of the Western Province to the Colonial Secretary *re* the Lands Bill of 1897. At page 3 of the report of the interview, Mr. Chamberlain

is reported to have said, in answer to Mr. Grant:
"I should like the chiefs to know what the object
of the Government at any rate has been in proposing any legislation. The main object, almost
the sole object, is to protect the chiefs against the
action of speculators, who, in many cases, get hold
of their land for insufficient consideration and without regard to the various interests in the land. For
instance, a chief sells his land for a perfectly insufficient consideration: the interests of the tribe are
not considered at all in that case, and the Government desires that the interests of the whole population
—the whole of the tribe as well as of the chief and
of the Government—should be taken into account
whenever a concession is arranged; that a speculator
from this country should not be able, trading upon
the weakness of a chief, to get his land for a mere
nothing, and to oust from it those to whom really it
in right belongs."

8. Two or three reflections occur to your
Excellency's humble petitioners upon reading the
above extracts from Mr. Chamberlain's reply to Mr.
Grant:—

(*a*) It is obvious that in the acquisition of land by
the Government under any Ordinances, past
or present, the native chief or, for that matter,
any other native from whom land is sought
to be acquired, deals with the Government

at a disadvantage. As a matter of general experience, under the Public Lands Ordinance, the Government has practically the right of saying how much it would give as consideration for the land in question. Therefore, it is clear that the Government, consciously or unconsciously, takes advantage of the weakness of the native with whom it deals, thus going diametrically against the principle enunciated by Mr. Chamberlain in his answer just quoted.

(b) It is equally obvious that the native who thus deals with the Government sells his lands for a perfectly insufficient consideration, and it is a well-known fact that few natives would ever part with their lands to the Government were it not for the fear that the same might be forfeited if they held out. Thus, again, it is clear that the interests of the natives are-not at all considered in such a case, and, therefore, the colonial Government directly goes against the desire of Mr. Chamberlain expressed in the foregoing answer.

9. Your Excellency's petitioners may be permitted humbly to enquire in what way the native is supposed to be protected in his rights under the Ordinance, when it is quite clear that, if he were allowed to make a fair bargain in granting leaseholds

of lands he may hold in a town area, the "tribe," or the successors of such grantor, would draw substantial rents for, say, a period of fifty years, the tenement raised upon his land falling to the reversion after the lapse of the lease.

10. It occurs, therefore, to the Aborigines of the country, whom we have the honour of representing, that while they in good faith, and with all due loyalty to the Government, freely give up their land for a nominal consideration for the use of the public, the protectors of the Aborigines directly turn such lands to uses which were not contemplated by the Aborigines in so parting with their lands. This, your Excellency's humble petitioners would point out, is a great hardship.

11. Your Excellency's attention may respectfully be drawn to the fact that the operation of the Towns (Amendment) Ordinance of 1901 practically introduces the principle of vesting the lands of the country in the Crown, which your Excellency's petitioners were made to understand in the case of the proposed Lands Bill was not the intention of the Government. As such, your Excellency's petitioners view with grave apprehension the existence of the said Ordinance upon the Statute Book of the country.

12. Therefore, your Excellency's petitioners pray that the Governor in Council may be pleased to

repeal the Towns (Amendment) Ordinance of 1901, or amend it in such a way as to give the native landowner the opportunity and the right of granting leaseholds for the purpose of erecting houses or buildings thereupon, and, as in duty bound, your Excellency's humble petitioners will ever pray.

We have the honour to be,
Your Excellency's most obedient humble Servants,

(*Signed*) S. Sacoom, *President*.
,, A. Bissoe, *Secretary*.

To His Excellency,
　　the Governor in Council, Accra.

Sekondi,
October 9th, 1901.

Sir,—The communication dated September 23rd, signed by yourself and Mr. Bissoe, purporting to be a petition on behalf of the Axim branch of the Aborigines' Rights Protection Society in connection with the acquisition of certain lands at Sekondi by the Government of the Gold Coast, was received by the Governor at Tarkwa this morning. Before replying to it, His Excellency would be obliged by your informing him as to when this body you state that you represent was formed, who are its members, the dates on which they joined the body, and the authority under which they claim to represent the Aborigines of this country.

I have the honour to be, Sir,
Your most obedient Servant,
STUART M. VINES,
Private Secretary.

S. SACOOM, ESQ.,
AXIM.

AXIM,
October 14*th*, 1901.

May it please your Excellency,—We beg leave respectfully to acknowledge the receipt of your Excellency's letter, bearing date October 9th, 1901, written at Sekondi, and signed by Stuart M. Vines, Private Secretary, and addressed to S. Sacoom, Esq., in reply to the communication dated September 23rd, 1901, signed by us on behalf of the Executive Committee of the Axim Branch of the Gold Coast Aborigines' Rights Protection Society, which said communication was humbly addressed to your Excellency and the honourable members of the Legislative Council. We unfortunately omitted to send a copy of the letter of September 23rd, 1901, to the Clerk of the Legislative Council. We have supplied that omission by transmitting to that officer a duplicate original of the said letter, with copies of the present correspondence.

2. We note that your Excellency, before considering the various vital questions raised in our said communication of September 23rd last, with the honourable members of the Legislative Council, is desirous of being informed upon the following points :—
1. When the body we represent was formed.
2. Who are its members.
3. The dates on which they joined the body.
4. The authority under which they claim to represent the Aborigines of the country.

3. Dealing first with the last matter upon which your Excellency seeks information, we may state that the Aborigines' Rights Protection Society of the Gold Coast had its birth in the stirring events of the year 1897, in connection with the Lands Bill of the late Governor Maxwell, which resulted in the Concessions Bill, now in force in the country.

4. In the constitution of the body all the native kings and chiefs had a voice, in accordance with native custom, in the election of the different members of which it is composed.

5. It was the Aborigines' Rights Protection Society whose senior President, Mr. J. W. Sey, of Cape Coast, with other two prominent members, formed the deputation which waited upon the Secretary of State for the Colonies in the year 1898.

6. Your Excellency cannot be unaware of the

fact that Mr. Chamberlain, the present Secretary for the Colonies, fully recognised the deputation, discussing matters with it through counsel, with the happy result referred to in paragraph three of this communication.

7. Since the return of the deputation from England, your Excellency's predecessor, Sir F. M. Hodgson, over and over again granted members of the Executive Committee of the Society interviews, whereat important issues affecting the welfare of the country were discussed. Your Excellency will no doubt find the minutes of the proceedings at such interviews in the Government archives at Accra.

8. Moreover, on various occasions correspondence has passed between the Society and the colonial Government upon different matters of public importance.

9. These things being so, we have only now to inform your Excellency that the Axim branch of the Aborigines' Rights Protection Society of the Gold Coast is a duly recognised section of the parent Society, which has its headquarters at Cape Coast, the said section being duly constituted in accordance with native custom, and we would respectfully ask that paragraph ten of our letter of September 23rd, 1901, be read with that qualification.

10. This section has, since the year 1897, regularly corresponded with the Colonial Government

upon matters of public importance. To illustrate this we may refer your Excellency to a communication of Acting Colonial Secretary the Honourable G. B. Hadding-Smith, dated June 10th, 1897, numbered Conf. 135/97, and addressed to A. Bissoe, Axim, which ran thus: "Mr. A. Bissoe is informed by the direction of the Secretary of State for the Colonies, with reference to the telegrams transmitted to England by him on behalf of the kings, chiefs, and people of Axim and Appolonia, that all representations of this kind must be forwarded through the Governor of the Gold Coast Colony, and not otherwise."

11. The foregoing returns an answer to the first point upon which your Excellency asks to be informed; and as to who are the members comprising this section, and the dates upon which they joined the body, these are matters regulated entirely by native custom.

12. At the same time we hope that your Excellency does not lose sight of the fact that, apart from the Gold Coast Aborigines' Rights Protection Society having the right to address your Excellency in Council upon matters of public importance, and of criticising any Government measure calculated to be detrimental to the interests of the community or any portion of it, or any member or members thereof, that same right is inherent in every individual member of the community being an Aborigine.

13. While dealing with the various points raised in your Excellency's communication, we may be allowed, on behalf of the Aborigines of the Gold Coast, to point out respectfully that there is, as the Colonial Government is at present constituted, no means for the people to express their sentiments and opinions in relation to any course pursued by the Government that may be detrimental to their inherent rights; and to express the hope that during your Excellency's administration the ventilation of native opinion through recognised channels will be encouraged than otherwise.

14. To return to the subject-matter of our letter of September 23rd last, we need hardly urge that it is a matter affecting the vital interest of the Aborigines of this country, and that your Excellency in Council may be pleased to give it full and careful consideration, and thereby restore the confidence of the people in the intention of the Government in this connection.

We have the honour to be,
Your Excellency's humble Servants,
S. SACOOM, *President*.
A. BISSOE, *Secretary*.
On behalf of the Executive
Committee of the Axim Branch.

To His Excellency, the Governor.

GOVERNMENT HOUSE,
ACCRA,
November 15*th*, 1901.

No. 230.

SIR,—I have the honour to acknowledge the receipt of the letter dated October 15th, 1901, signed by Mr. A. Bissoe and yourself, enclosing a petition which you desire should be placed before the Legislative Council at their next meeting, and to suggest that you should take the steps for its presentation laid down in No. 8 of the Standing Rules and Orders of the Legislative Council, which is as follows:—

"Petitions shall be presented and laid on the table by some member of the Council, whose duty it will be to inform the Council, if required, that in his opinion the petition is properly and respectfully worded."

2. I return the petition in order to enable you to act on the above suggestion.

I have the honour to be, Sir,
Your most obedient Servant,
STUART M. VINES.
Clerk of the Legislative Council.

S. SACOOM, ESQ.,
AXIM.

Axim,
October 15*th*, 1901.

Dear Sir,—We have the honour to transmit herewith, to be placed before His Excellency the Governor and the Honourable Members of the Legislative Council, at the next meeting of the Legislative Council, the following documents :—

1. Duplicate original petition of the Axim Branch of the Gold Coast Aborigines' Rights Protection Society, dated September 23rd, 1901, signed by S. Sacoom, as President and A. Bissoe, as Secretary, relating to the sale of lands by the Government at Sekondi, addressed to His Excellency the Governor in Council.

2. His Excellency's letter acknowledging the receipt of such petition, dated October 9th, 1901, signed by Stuart M. Vines, Private Secretary, and addressed to S. Sacoom, Esq., Axim.

3. The reply of the Axim branch of the Gold Coast Aborigines' Rights Protection Society to His Excellency's letter above referred to, dated October 14th, 1901, and signed by S. Sacoom, as President, and A. Bissoe, as Secretary, on behalf of the Executive Committee.

In transmitting the original petition we omitted to forward the same through you. We now supply that omission by transmitting the duplicate original of the petition referred to above.

    We have the honour to be, Sir,
        Your obedient, humble Servants,
          S. S<small>ACOOM</small>, *President*.
          A. B<small>ISSOE</small>, *Secretary*.

To the Clerk of the Legislative Council, Accra.

        G<small>OVERNMENT</small> H<small>OUSE</small>,
         A<small>CCRA</small>,
          November 15*th*, 1901.

No. 229.

S<small>IR</small>,—I am directed by the Governor to acknowledge the receipt of your letter dated October 14th, 1901, signed by Mr. A. Bissoe and yourself, and written in reply to mine dated at Sekondi on October 9th.

    I have the honour to be, Sir,
      Your most obedient Servant,
        S<small>TUART</small> M. V<small>INES</small>,
          Private Secretary.

S. S<small>ACOOM</small>, E<small>SQ</small>.,
 A<small>XIM</small>.

2.

Some Principal Native States of the Gold Coast, with the Names of the Paramount Kings.

State.	Paramount King.
Mankessim	Okra Kwa (Regent).
Gomua	Kojo Inkum.
Egimaku	Kwamin Hama.
Ekumfi	Kofi Akini.
Anamaboe	Amonoo V.
Abura	Otu V.
Cape Coast	Kojo Imbra.
Denkera	Inkwantabisa.
Western Akim	Kofi Ahinkura.
Eastern Akim	Akwasi Duma.
Akuapim	Kwami Fori.
Lower Wassaw	Kwamina Enimil.
Upper Wassaw	Kwesi Wereku.[1]

[1] The above list is based upon information principally to be found in Anaman's "Gold Coast Guide" for 1902, pp. 29–31.

INDEX.

ABONU, 57.
Aborigines, *query*, whether benefited by the presence of the British, 4.
Abrah, 187.
Abura, Fanti King of, 156. Native state of Gold Coast, 397. King of, = Otu V., 397.
Abusa = a one-third share, 48. When and in respect of what payable, 48, 49.
Accra, ordinance applied, 111. Fort James at, 136. English fort at, 136.
Ackinie, King of Akumfie, 208, 273. Arrested Oppon, for default in payment of award, 208. Sued by Oppon, 208. Judgment against, 208. Appealed, successfully, 209.
Acquah, Quamina, present at palaver, 380.
Adai, a custom, 96.
Adankum, 105.
Adansi, federal state of Kumasi, 31.
Adansis, the, subordinate community of Ashanti, 19.
Adayi, a custom occurring every fortieth day, 28. National festival, 28. When king distributed money to chiefs, etc., in trust for trading, 28.
Administrator, appointment of, 377.
Aduasi tried for wilful murder, 146.

Adziwa, 105.
"African Company of Merchants," 318.
African (West) Exploitation and Development Syndicate, Ltd. v. *Sir Alfred Kirby and others* cited, 41.
Agambra, township of, referred to, 253.
Aggery, King of Cape Coast, 162. Claimed jurisdiction over ground within a few yards of British forts, 162. Resisted by Governor; Governor refused to recognise him, 162.
Aggrey, an interpreter, 291.
Aggrey, Joe, signed Bond, 1844, 368.
Agimaku, King of, 57.
Akuapim, King of, = Quamin Fori, 279.
Ahanta, a native state of Gold Coast, 21, 253. King of, = Baidoe Bonso, 32.
Ahuba = yam festival in Fanti States, 85.
Ahuba Kakraba, 85.
Ahuba Kesi = great festival, 90. Real harvest festival, 90. Celebrated separately by each province, 90.
Ahuma, Rev. Attoh, 178. Editor of *Gold Coast Methodist Times*, 178, 311.

AIK

Aikunfie, King of, =Ackinie, 274.
Ajiman, King of Jaman, 13. Desire to recover gold stool, 13.
Akataki people = the Commendas, 52. Originally came from *Akatakiwa*, 52. *Akataki* = masculine form, 52. *Akatakiwa* = feminine form, 52. Query exact order of descent, 52. Branches of *Inkusukum* people, 52. Own allegiance to Essandor, 53.
Akem country, 57.
Akempims. *See* Inkidoms.
Akempon, 154.
Akim, Eastern. *See* Eastern Akim.
Akim, Western. *See* Western Akim.
Akropong Manasu, federal state of Kumasi, 31.
Akuapim, native state of Gold Coast, 397. King of, = Kwami Fori, 397.
Akwasi Duma, King of Eastern Akim, 397.
Akwuamus = the aristocrats of Kumasi, 27. Furnished the king, 27. Consulted in all internal matters, 27. Assafubuaki, their head, 27.
Allegiance, shown by payment of occasional contribution by subordinate chief to a paramount chief, 48. Fee, 49. An incident of paramountcy, 49. = *Personal* relationship between occupants of stools, 51, 52. Acknowledged by military or other service, or fee, 52. Has nothing to do with lands, 52. Essential features of, 55. Penalty and result of transfer of, 55. Received at stool celebrations, 87.
Amankwatsia, General, referred to, 26. Chief of the Kwaintsirs, 26.

ASH

Amba Danquah, Regent of Southern Assin, 53.
Amissah, Mr. J. F., 173.
Ammah tried for wilful murder, 146.
Amonoo IV., King Anamabu, 316, 397. Signed Bond, 1844...368.
Amonoo Ekroful, 57.
Anamaboe, referred to, 56, 57, 156. Native state of Gold Coast, 397. King of, = Amonoo V., 397.
Anaman, "Gold Coast Guide," referred to, 223, 397.
Anansu Mensah, 34.
Ankraku, a village, 22. Chief town of, = Ayenasi, 23.
Ansah. *See* Osoo Ansah.
Antrobus, Mr., 171.
Apafram, festival of stool celebration in Ashanti, 90.
Apenquah, his case cited, 53. Subject of the stool of King Chibbo, 53.
Appeals, provided for by draft proclamation, 365.
Appolonia, State of, referred to, 23. Handed to Dutch, 154.
Aquamoo country, referred to, 359.
Arrest, power of, exerciseable by native kings, 274. Illegal, damages as compensation for, 279.
Arsafu, or Company System, 252. A corruption of *Insefu*, = friends, *i.e.*, friends in arms, 252.
Arthur, Sir Geo., 230.
Asanti Akim, federal state of Kumasi, 31.
Ashanti, rising in, referred to, 11. Communities owned allegiance to the paramount stool of, 19. Subordinate communities of, were Manpons, Juabins, Kokofus, Beckwas, Adansis, etc., 19. Stool

INDEX.

ASH

of Kumasi paramount stool of, 19. Attained zenith of power first quarter of 19th century, 20. Occupation of, 21. War and expedition, 21, 140; burden of, placed on the Fantis, 183. Union, premier state of, was Kumasi, 26.

Ashantis, speak same language as Fantis, 24. Probably the original type, 25. Not a barbarous, blood-thirsty people, 25. Fought with Fantis over coast-trading, 29. To sell real-born Ashantis, punished by death, 30. Did not war in order to immolate captives, 30. Desired to act as middlemen for distributing goods to hinterland, 98. *Query*, should they be treated as a conquered people, or as allies? 241. Fusion of, with Fantis desirable, 241. King of, claimed right to direct trade relations with Europe, 242. Began to trade directly with Assinee after the war, 243.

Assankra Breman, 41.

Assembly, representative legislative, advocated, 164. And greatly required, 165.

Assessors, judicial. *See also* Jurisdiction. Kings and chiefs sat with, 71. Their jurisdiction explained, etc., 165, 349. How powers to be exercised when assessors away, 350. Powers not derived from statute, 352. Founded on assent and concurrence of sovereign power of state, and long and general acquiescence, and treaty, 352.

Assikamba = picked men of company to guard its flag, 91.

BLA

Assin, referred to, 98, 187, 239. Chief of, referred to, 153.

Ateni chief = chief of the lamplighters, 26.

Atta, head of Province of Axim, 32.

Attuabu, capital of a province, 23.

Awiku, federal state of Kumasi, 31.

Awoossie, signed the Bond, 1844, 368.

Axim, province of, in State of Ahanta, 32, 253. Head of, is Atta, 32.

Ayan, 186, 187.

Ayanmain, 186.

Ayenasi, district of, referred to, 23.

BAIDOE BONSO, King of Ahanta, 32.

Bailey, Chief Justice, 275.

Bannerman, Mr. Ch., of Accra, lawyer, wit, and publicist, 175.

Bannerman, Mr. Edmund, 175.

Bannerman, Hon. Jas., 95.

Bannerman, Mr. S., signed Bond 1844...368

Bantuma Chief = chief of the Royal Burial Grove, 26.

Barracoons, formerly forts served as, 136.

Bat, mammiferous, representative of the departed spirit, 102.

Beckwa, federal state of Kumasi, 31.

Beckwas, the, subordinate community of Ashanti, 19.

Beyin, King of, referred to, 59.

Bingham, Hon. Major, 121.

Bissoe, Mr. A., secretary of Aborigines' Society, 388.

Blacks, the, have had no chance in America, Hayti, Liberia, or Sierra Leone, 247. But may and can have in Gold Coast, 248.

BLA

"Blacks and Whites" quoted, 21, 177, 264.
Blankson, Hon. G., mentioned, 95.
Blankson, George, 175, 185.
Blyden, Dr., quoted, 3.
Boatsin, linguist of King of Ashanti, 70.
Bond, the, 1844, referred to, 159, 314, 356. No longer truly expresses extent, etc., of Great Britain's power, 356. The only document purporting to define extent of Queen's jurisdiction, 356. Grants rights to try and punish crimes, 356; to repress human sacrifices, 356; to repress panyarring, etc., 356. Silent as to collection of customs, 356; administration of civil justice, 356; legislation for public health, 356; provision for education, 356; construction of roads, etc., 356: which matters are only justified on assumption of usage, sufferance, and tacit assent, 357. Referred to as obsolete, 357. Printed in full, 367.
Bonso. See Sai Bonso.
Bosman, referred to, 136. His great work reproduced in modern journals, 177.
Boundaries. British, in Gold Coast, none, 162. Of land, naturally fixed by trees, rivers Prah and Volta, lagoon at Quittah, etc., 195, 359. Maintenance of, 310.
Bourne, Mr. Fox: his book, "Blacks and Whites," referred to, 20, 21, 177, etc.
Brackenbury, Capt., 138. "Fanti

CAP

and Ashanti" quoted, 138, 158, etc.
Brempon = civil chief, 64.
Brew, Prince, arrested, 173.
Brew, Hon. S. C., mentioned, 95.
British Charter, constituting Gold Coast and Lagos Settlements into a separate colony, 369. Constitution of Legislative Council, its powers and jurisdiction, 372. Establishment of courts and officers, 373.
British possessions on Gold Coast = actually only forts, 319.
Brofoo, 187.
Brown, Mr. J. P.; 179.
Bruce, query, illegally arrested, 279.
Burnett, Hon. Ch. W., 121. His question, 123.
Busua (near Dixcove), capital of Ahanta, 32.
Busumchie Abosso, Enimil Koomah II. and Quasie Ankuma, chiefs of, 290.
Butlers. See Royal Butlers.

"CABBOCEER," term once used to distinguish chiefs of first importance, 33, 147.
Calicali, King of Ashanti, 172.
Cane-bearer of King, 204.
Cape Coast, native state of Gold Coast, 397. King of, = Kojo Imbra, 397. Leading town of Gold Coast, 260. Castle, formerly harbour of foreign kidnappers, 261.
Capital Punishment, how to be carried out, 353.
Captains in King's household—of the swordbearers, stoolbearers,

INDEX.

CAR

elephant's tail bearers, court-criers; of the Royal butlers, huntsmen, farmers, physicians, 26, etc.
Cardwell, Rt. Hon. Edw., 147.
Carnarvon, Earl of, letter to Governor Strahan, 315, 354.
Carnegie, Mr. Andrew, quoted, 4.
Cases cited — *African (West) Exploitation and Development Syndicate, Ltd.* v. *Sir Alfred Kirby and others*, 41. *Chidda Concession*, 289. *Le Neve* v. *Le Neve*, 301. *Punchard* v. *Tomkins*, 301. *Yates and Shattuck* v. *Garshong*, 301. *Oppon* v. *Ackinie*, 208, 273. *Regina, on the prosecution of Donovan*, v. *Kudjoe Imbrah*, 281. *Donovan* v. *Cudjoe Imbrah*, 260. *Enima* v. *Pai*, 41. *Hima Diki* v. *Agiman and others*, 34. *Homia* v. *Huma*, 22. *Hutton* v. *Kuta*, 202. *Impatassi*, 49. *Quamina Fori's Case*, 209.
Cedar, 238.
Certificate of validity, 305. Form and substance of, 306 *et seq.*
Chalmers, Mr., opinion etc. on proclamation, to be obtained, 361.
Chalmers, Sir David, Chief Magistrate of Gold Coast, 71.
Chamberlain, Mr., 171. Speech of, 11. Reply to Aborigines' Society, 385.
Charter. *See* British Charter.
Chibbo, King of Assin, 53.
Chibboe Coomah, signed Bond, 1844, 368.
Chidda, village of, 290.
Chidda Concession, 289, etc.
Chief = strictly, subordinate ruler under the paramount king, 32. Used indiscriminately for king,

COM

chief, or headman, 63. Tendency to describe kings as, 316. Properly so-called is person next to a king in a native state, 63. Head chief = principal chief of a king, 63. Vary in rank according to local importance, 63. Originally selected by king for valour, intelligence, etc., 63. War chief = *sarfuhim*, 64. Civil chief = *brepmon*, 64. Generally captain of a company, 64. Duty to hold judicial Court and decide disputes, 66. *Tufu Hin* (which see). Minor chiefs accompany their head chiefs to palaver, 66. Shares in palaver, 66. Deliberates with king in time of war, 66. Takes oath of allegiance to king on king's enstoolment, 67. Succession to his stool regulated by same principles as those governing succession to king's stool, 67. Judicial power of, 274.
Christian Commonwealth, The, quoted, 230.
Cinnamon Bippo Range, 290.
Classes, 81. Freemen, 81. Slaves, 81. Pawns, 81.
Cochrane, Hon. J., 171.
Colonial Minister, course of conduct, 10.
Colonial Office, its policy, 9. Discourages national spirit, 130. Effect of influence with, 218.
Colonial Secretary of Gold Coast, 225.
Colonial Treasurer, 225.
Colony — or Protectorate ? — 311. Definitions of, 312.
Commenda, handed to the Dutch, 154.
Committee, Select, 139. To ascertain relation between Gold Coast

COM

and Great Britain, 139. Report of, 139.

Community. *See* Native Community.

Company, system = *arsafu* or *insefu* (which see), constituted in ward, 85. With captains and subordinate officers, 85. Captain-general = *Tufu Hin*, 85. Had its own flags and banners, 85. Annual review before king, 85. Its system described, 85 *et seq.*

Compulsory Labour Ordinance, 260. See also Ordinance.

Concessions Ordinance, 198 *et seq.* Greatly abused by those ignorant of facts, 198. Analysed and explained, 199 *et seq.* Concessions Court, 200. Has its rules and precedents, 200. Who may grant a concession? 201. All natives legally entitled by customary law to make valid grants, 201. Concession means not land, but the "writing" by which the right is acquired, 202. Must be signed by "grantor, or some person duly authorised by him," 203. Procedure of, described, 203 *et seq.* Customary rights of grantors to be considered, 206. *See also* Ordinance.

Confederation of Fanti tribes,149,173

Conran, Col., 147.

Consideration, must be earnest money plus rent (?), 296. Must be adequate and valuable, 305.

Conspiracy, charge of, against members of Mankessim Constitution, 173.

Constitution of Fantee Confederacy, 327 to 344. 'Objects of—to promote friendly intercourse between

CON

kings, chiefs, etc., 328 ; to improve the country, 329 ; to make good roads, 329 ; to erect school-houses, etc., 329 ; to promote agricultural and industrial pursuits, 329 ; to develop, etc., working of minerals, etc., 329. Formation of executive council, 329. Conduct of its business, 329. Exercise by, of all legislative functions, 330. Its national assembly, 331. Its annual gatherings, 331. Establishment of national and normal schools, 332. Training of female students, 332. How expenses to be borne, 332, 333. Provincial assessors, how appointed, their judicial functions, 333. Management of provinces, 333. Secretary, his duties defined, 333, 334. Treasurer, his duties defined, 334, 335. Under-Secretary, his duties defined, 335, 336. Assistant treasurer, his duties defined, 336. Provincial assessors, their duties defined, 336, 337. Executive Council and Ministry, duties of, 337 ; to advise king-president, to see laws, etc., carried out ; to examine financial condition of confederacy, 337 ; to try appeals, 338 ; to try all disputes between native kings, chiefs, etc., 338 ; to determine by votes the succession to stools, 338 ; to consider all applications for alliances by tribes, 338. National Assembly, duties of — to elect president for year, to consider all programmes, to place on stool elected person, 339. Its education scheme set forth, 340—344 ;

subjects to be taught, 342; kinds of schools, 342; scholarships, 343.
Contribution, an occasional—when, and in respect of what, payable, 48 et seq.
Correspondence. *See* Official Correspondence.
Cotton Trees, 238.
Council, the, is ruling voice in all matters political and judicial, 74. Right to approve or disapprove all acts done by a chief or headman affecting interests of community, 74.
Councillors, introduce legislation, 42. = Intelligent men selected by head of community to assist in affairs of community, 73. Chiefs are *ex-officio*, 73. Hold office for life, 73; or during good behaviour, 73. Succeeded by heir of mature age and experience, 73; or by heir's guardian during immaturity and inexperience, 73. Represent sovereignty of the people, 74. Pay homage to king as their head, 74. Must legalise every step by tradition and custom, 74. Entitled to a portion of public revenues, 75; which they in turn sub-divide among their dependents, 75. Cannot exercise rights capriciously, 74.
Court-criers, captain of, 26.
Court, full, 279, Judgment of, 279.
Crimes, etc., to be tried by British Government, 367.
Croboe country, referred to, 359.
"Crown Colonies of Great Britain" quoted, 118, etc.
Cudjoe Ammoo, opposed Chidda Concession, 289.

Cudjoe Buaful, 289. Opposed Chidda Concession, 289.
Cudjoe Chibboe, signed the Bond, 1844...368
Cudjoe Chibbo, an Assin chief, 153.
Cudjoe Imbrah, 260. His people desired to enstool him as king, 177. Had nothing to do with Compulsory Labour Ordinance, 260. Treated as felon, 262.
Cultivation, shifting, 307.
Customary rights, 307. Shifting cultivation, 307. Collecting firewood, 307. Hunting, snaring game, 307.

DAMAGES, action for, 299.
Datum point to be observed, 310.
Dawuna, King of Christiansborg, 316.
Death, offences punished by, included murder, stealing, rape, treason, kidnapping, etc., 29, 30.
Decided Cases. *See* Cases Cited.
Denkara, King of, — Tutim Cackidi, 155. Referred to, 187.
Denkera, native state of Gold Coast, 397. King of, = Inkwantabisa, 397.
Department of War, formed at Kumasi, of Kwaintsirs, 26. To command respect of federal states, 28.
Deportation of natives as slaves to West Indies and America, 318.
District Commissioner, 273.
District Commissioner of Cape Coast, 281. Case stated by, 281.
Divisional Court, Cape Coast, 273.
Dixcove (near Busua), 32. King of, was Hima Diki, 34. English fort

DON

at, 136. Handed over to Dutch, 154.
Donovan—*Regina* v., 281.
Donovan v. *Cudjoe Imbrah*, referred to, 260.
Downing Street patronage, 218.
Duben trees, 238.
Dutch naval officers captured by Commendas, 185.

EARNEST MONEY, custom of giving, 296. *Query*, synonymous with consideration, 296.
Eastern Akim, native state of Gold Coast, 397. King of, = Akwasi Duma, 397.
Eckumfi, 187.
Edginacoe, 186, 187.
Education, Governor to promote, 170. Of all children, 186. Of females, 187. To be provided for, 366.
Edum, a herbal preparation, drunk in ordeal, 94.
Egimaku, native state of Gold Coast, 397. King of, = Kwamin Hama, 397.
Ejectment, action of, 299.
Ekumfi, native state of Gold Coast. King of, = Kofi Akini, 397.
" Elements of Law," 118.
Elephant's tail-bearers, captain of, 26.
Elmina, French fort at, 135. Dutch fort at, 135. Founded by French Company at Dieppe and Rouen, 317.
Emancipation Ordinance, 81.
Enima v. *Pai* cited, 41.
Enimil. *See* Kwamina.
Eshroa, 57.
Esiama, referred to, 56. In the

FLA

State of Elmina, 56. Own allegiance to State of Anamaboe, 56.
Essandor, King of the *Inkusukums*, 56.
Esubankassa, 58.
Evidence, mis-reception of, 285. Satisfactory, as to *status* of a party, 286.
Execution, stay of, pending appeal, 284.

FAMILY, the : the unit for the purpose of ownership, 47. = The entire lineal descendants of a head *materfamilias*, 76.
Fanti, natives of native states of Gold Coast, 21. Petty traders, 96. Probably an offshoot from Ashantis, 25. Fought with Ashantis over coast-trading, 29. Pioneers and developers of the mahogany, gold, and rubber industries of Gold Coast, 75. Confederation of, 149, 182 ; its constitution, 327 ; meetings at Mankessim, 327.
" Fanti Customary Laws " quoted, 60, 165, 315.
" Fanti and Ashanti " quoted, 138, 148, 158, 162.
Farmers. *See* Royal Farmers.
Farms, ancient, lie neglected and unattended, 237.
Fetishism, system of faith and worship described, 101 *et seq.*
Firewood, collection of, a customary right, 307.
Fitzgerald, Mr., of *African Times*, 174. Supported the " Confederation " movement, 174.
Flags of a company held as sacred trust, 91. Guard of honour attached to each company to guard

INDEX.

its flag, 91. This guard called *Assikamba*, 91; and are picked men of the company, 91.
Fomina, 57.
Fortnightly Review quoted, 258.
Forts, = British settlements, 135; governed by Governor, 350. French, at Elmina, 135. English, at Elmina, cession of, 156. St. George del Mina, 135. Fredensberg, or Ningo, 135. Cabo Corsa, or Cape Coast Castle, 135. Nassau, or Mori, 135. Conradsburg, or St. Jago, at Elmina, 135. Kramantine, 136. James at Accra, 136. Vanderpurgh at Commenda, 136. Dixcove, 136. Anamaboe, 136. Formerly served as barracoons for human cargo, 136. Practically the sole British possessions in Gold Coast, 137 *et seq.*
Fraud, charge of, against claimants of Chidda Concession, 289.
Freeman, Dr., "Travels and Life in Ashanti and Jaman" quoted, 13, 14.
Freemen = *dihi*, 81. Long ancestry, 82. Eligible for office, 82.
Freetown, 97.
Fynn, prosecution of, 192.

GA, native state of Gold Coast, 21.
Gapee, Quacoe, present at palaver, 380.
Gebre, signed Bond, 1844...368.
Ghartey, King of Winnebah, 173, 185, 316. Ratified treaty with British Government, 185.
Ghartey, charged Otchafoo with bribery, 274.
Gibraltar, referred to, 314.

Gold Coast, contains native states of Fanti, Ahanta, Insima, Ga, Wassa, etc., 21. Legislated for by Governor in Council, 119.
Gold Coast Aborigines' Rights Protection Society, 171. Deputation of, received by Mr. Chamberlain, 171. Correspondence with Governor, 382—396.
Gold Coast Amalgamated Mines, Ltd., 289.
Gold Coast Chronicle, 175, 178.
Gold Coast Colony, or Settlement: history establishes that this has no reference to natives of soil, but exclusively to European merchants, 319. British possessions in = forts only, 319. Proposal and petition to divide into four provinces, 267.
Gold Coast Echo, 121, 177. Advocated cause of Cudjo Imbrah, 177, and a scheme of municipal government on native lines, 177.
Gold Coast Government Gazette quoted, 141.
"Gold Coast Guide" quoted, 135, 223, 397.
Gold Coast Independent, 178.
Gold Coast Methodist Times, 178, 311.
Gold Coast People, 177.
Golden stool, debate on, in House of Commons, 11. "Moral and intellectual value," 11. "Gives supremacy," 12. "Emblem of possession," 13. Ill-advised hunt for, 268.
Gomey, 105.
Gomua, native state of Gold Coast, 397. King of, = Kojo Inkum, 397.
Goomowah, 187.
Gong-gong, for what used, 42, 253.

GOT

Gothic House at Cape Coast, 261.
Gowans, a mining engineer, 293.
Government, support of British, dependent on feelings entertained for local administration, 161. Municipal, 109 *et seq*. Representative, idea of, among the people, 126; perfect and efficient, 128.
Governor to have a negative voice in passing of all ordinances, 373; power to suspend any person from exercising powers, 376. To be resident in Settlement, 376. Appointment of Lieutenant-Governor, 377. May appoint a deputy, 378. Tenure of office uncertain, 11. Not generally well acquainted with Native Institutions, 11.
Grant, Mr. Corrie, represented Aborigines' Society before Colonial Secretary, 171, 385.
Grant, Mr. F. C., 191.
Grey, Lord, first attempted to impose poll tax, 163.
Griffith, Sir W. B., Governor of Gold Coast, 115, 120, 138, 258, 261, 320.

H

HACKETT, Mr. Wm., 140.

Hanno, the Carthaginian, of the Gold Coast, 326.
Hansen, Mr. Robert, 175.
Hansens, the, 95.
Hayford, Mr. J. D., arrested, 173.
Headman = head of a village community, or ward in a township, or of a family, 76. Must properly train members of family, 76; in matters political and traditional, 76. Responsible for general conduct of those in his charge, 76.

HUY

Must insist on their conforming with customs, laws, etc., 76. Formerly could exile by sale a troublesome relative, 76. Assisted by female members, 77. Judge of family or ward, 77. Entitled to hearing fee, 77. Important member of his "company," 77; often its captain, 77. Always succeeded by uterine brother, cousin, or nephew, 78.
Head *Panin*, or Chief Elder, = head of the ward, 251.
Hennessy, Mr. Pope, 184, 189, 191.
Hill, H. W., Lieut.-Governor, signed Bond, 1844...368.
Hill, S. J., Governor, 170.
Hima Diki, King of Dixcove, 34. Deposed by the people, 34. Replaced by Anansu Mensah, his uncle, 34. Sought to recover stool, etc., 34. Brought action to test legality of his destoolment, 34.
Hima Diki v. *Agiman and others* cited, 34.
Hindle, Hon. E. Bruce, Queen's Advocate, 120.
Hodgson, Sir F. M., despatches of, etc., 12, 120, 141.
Holmes, Mr. J. K., 112.
Homia v. *Huma* cited, 22, 23.
Hughes, Mr. Geo., 171.
Human sacrifices to be abolished, 365.
Huni River, 290.
Hunt, Mr. E. F., 171.
Huntsmen. *See* Royal Huntsmen.
Hutchinson, J. T., Chief Justice, 120.
Hutton v. *Kuta* quoted, 202.
Huyshe, Captain, 138. "Fanti and Ashanti" quoted, 138, 158.

IMM

IMMORALITY punished by death, 30.
Impatassi case cited, 49, 50.
Imperegus, 57. Of Abura, 57. Acknowledge stool of Anamaboe, 57.
Imperial West Africa, how to be achieved, and built up, 259.
Imprisonment, power of, exerciseable by native kings, 274.
Indemnity, war, 50,000 ozs. of gold, 265.
Indumsuasu, 58.
Inheritance, native law of, 249.
Inkee, referred to, 54.
Inkertsia, a huntsman, 22. Founded Inkertsia Krom, 22.
Inkidoms, or Akempins, were king's bodyguard, 28, 87. Chief of, = Subir, 28.
Inkwantabisa, King of Denkera, 397.
Insima, native state of Gold Coast, 21.
Insuta, federal state of Kumasi, 31.

JAMAN, Ajiman, King of, 13.
Johnson, Mr. J. W. de, 179.
Jones, Mr. T. F. E., 171.
Juabins, the, subordinate community of Ashanti, 19. Federal state of Ashanti, 31.
Judges, power to constitute and appoint, 375.
Judicial powers of, native chiefs, etc., 275; in no way impaired, 209. Of assessors. *See* Assessors and Jurisdiction.
Jurisdiction—of Great Britain: originated in a desire to mitigate the effect of cruel and barbarous customs by influence of Christianity and civilisation, 353; attempt

KIN

to define, 355 *et seq.*; should be made subject to distinct agreement with native chiefs, 356; fully defined by draft proclamation, 364—367; acknowledged by the Bond, 1844...367. *Query* extent of British, in Gold Coast, 149. Assessors', 165, 166. Natives', 166. Civil and criminal, exerciseable by Great Britain, concurrent with that of native kings and chiefs, 277. "Inherent," *query* meaning, and whether Governor has power to take away, 280.

KIDNAPPING punished by death, 30.
Kimberley, Lord, 190. Despatch to Governor Keate, 360.
King, the, is paramount, 19. Arbiter in disputes between provinces within his state, 23. Does not interfere in internal government of a province, 23. Is chief magistrate, 32. Is chief military leader, 32. Is first executive officer of the state, 32; but not of the executive council of the state, 41. Influence measured by character, 32. Office of, elective, 33. Does not acquire indefeasible title to the stool, 33. May be removed for just cause, 33. Generally holds position for life, 33. Generally succeeded by uterine brother, cousin, or nephew, 33. Often indicates his own successor, 33. Fountain of justice, 37. His linguist opens all proceedings, 38. Probably chosen originally for personal valour, intelligence, and

KLA

warlike capability, 38. Mode of choosing, 40, 41. Acts done by, without concurrence of executive council of state, liable to be set aside, 41. Is President of Legislative Board, 42. Seldom initiates legislation, 42. Presides over judicial proceedings, 43. *Qua* King, does not own land, 44. Owns ancestral lands, 44. Ratifies subjects' grant of land, 45. Spiritual Head of his people, 106. Early jurisdiction of, 143 *et seq.* His person and stool are sacred, 259. Judicial powers of, 275. Of Ashanti, his household controlled by captains, *e.g.*, of the sword-bearers, etc., 26 ; his sons have distinct rank in the nobility, and known by title of " Sai " or "Osoo," 27 ; his bodyguard were Inkidoms, 28 ; minor bodies, *e.g.*, scouts, and keepers of royal arsenals, 28.

Klanamonoos, the, referred to, 57.

Knowledge, pleaded, as to possession of another, 302.

Knutsford, Lord, 149.

Koffee Kalkalli, King of Ashanti, 141.

Kofi Ainibah, referred to, 41.

Kofi Ahinkura, King of Western Akim, 397.

Kofi Akini, King of Ekumfi, 397.

Kofi Nyam, 57.

Kojo Buaful, guardian of King Kwamina Enimil of Eastern Wassaw, 25. An Ashanti, 25.

Kojo Inkum, King of Gomua, 397.

Kokofu, federal state of Kumasi, 31.

Kokofus, the, subordinate community of Ashanti, 19.

KWE

Kong Mountains, former habitat of Ashantis and Fantis, 24.

Kudjoe Enimil Kooma II. opposed Chidda Concession, 289.

Kumasi, stool of, paramount stool of Ashanti, 19. Seat of golden stool, 20. State of, was premier state of Ashanti, 26. Seventy-seven stools in, 26. Local government of, in hands of Kwaintsirs, keepers of the golden stool, 26. Centre of state system of trade between the coast and hinterland, 28. Centre of convict establishment, 29. Federal states of, were Mampon, Beckwa, etc., 31. Occupation of, 151 ; alleged to have enlarged the field of commerce and industry, 151.

Kuntum = yam festival in Wassaw and Ahanta, 85.

Kwaintsirs, controlled local government of Kumasi, 26. Keepers of the golden stool, 26.

Kwami Fori, King of Akuapim, 397.

Kwamina Enimil, King of Eastern Wassaw, 25, 397. Guardian of, is Kojo Buaful, 25. Charge against Kweku Inkruma, with acts unbecoming kingly office, brought before him, 35. Opposed Chidda Concession, 289.

Kwamin Hama, King of Egimaku, 397.

Kwantabissa, King of Denkira, 39. Claimed right to lease certain land, 39.

Kweku Atta, 261. King of Axim, 34. Called as expert witness, 34, 50.

Kweku Dua, King, father of Sai Bonso, 27.

INDEX. 411

KWE

Kweku Inkruma, ex-King of Peppissa district, 35. Destooled by King Kwamina Enimil's Court, 35.

Kwesi Wereku, King of Upper Wassaw, 397.

Kwinbontu, 41.

Kwofi Kara Kari, King, dominion of, broken down, 21.

LACHES, pleaded, 302.

Lagos. *See* Protectorate of.

Land, king's ancestral, 44. General, over which king exercises paramountcy, 45. Nature of king's paramountcy over, 45. How originally acquired and apportioned, 45. Acquired by individual becomes practically ancestral, 47. Natives asked to make grant of, to Great Britain, 140. Legislation, 172. No right by British to administer, 172. Public—no such thing in Gold Coast, 194. All—either stool land, private land, or family land, 194. Tribe, country, town, company, family or individual, 195. Ownership of, carefully preserved by natives, 195. Boundaries of, fixed by natural features, 195. None "unoccupied," 195. Of Cape Coast *apparently* acknowledged by some native chiefs and people to belong to Great Britain, 381. Power to dispose of, 374.

"Lands Bill," 112, 194, 223, 320.

Law, how promulgated, 42. To be enacted with due regard to native law and custom, 365.

MAC

Legislation, to be effectual must be result of native representation, 164.

Legislative Council, laws passed by, 125. Not consulted when Governor Hodgson went to Kumasi for the golden stool, 268.

Lemaire, clerk of Chief of Busumchie, 292.

Libations offered to departed spirits, 86.

Linguist, king's, 38. Opens all proceedings, 38. Announces decision of Council to the people, 38. Promulgates laws, 42. Not a person skilled in tongues, 68. = "Spokesman," 68. All superiors have their linguist, 68. Is a confidential officer, 68. = King's or chief's mouthpiece in every public function, 69. His place not filled by the successor to his ancestral stool, 69. But probably by his son, 69. Generally a walking encyclopædia, 69. Acquainted with court etiquette, 69; functions, history, and traditions, 69—70. When speaking leans on king's gold cane, 70. Represents master where latter cannot be present, 71. Represents master at public enquiries, 71.

Lucas, Mr., 138. "Historical Geography of British Colonies," quoted, 138.

MACARTHY, Sir Ch., 147. His aggressive policy, 244.

MacGregor, Sir Wm., 197.

Maclean, Governor, referred to, 24. His policy of "open market," etc.,

MAC

between coast and hinterland, 243.
Maclean, Mr. Geo., 165. Signed Bond, 1844...368.
Macleod, Mr. Justice, 94, 209.
Manpon, federal state of Kumasi, 31.
Manpons, the, subordinate community of Ashanti, 19.
Mamponsu, federal state of Kumasi, 31.
Mankessim, 186. Native state of Gold Coast, 397. King of, = Okra Kwa, 23, 397.
Mankessim Constitution, 149 ; its members arrested, 173 ; its provisions studied, 182 et seq. Objects of, set out in Article 8, 185 et seq.
Markby's "Elements of Law" quoted, 118.
Maxwell, Sir Wm. E., 142, 151, 178. His preconceived notions, etc., 321.
Mayan, Quamina, present at palaver, 380.
McCarthy, M.P., Mr. A., 149.
McDowell, Dr. D. K., District Commissioner of Cape Coast, 281.
Meade, Mr. R. H., 149.
Members of Council, non-official, not to criticise but advise, 123.
Mensa, King, succeeded to stool, 265.
Military forces of native rulers in alliance with Queen, to be organised, 366.
Minstrels proclaim glory of king and his house, 87.
Misrepresentation, charge of, against Chidda Concession, 289.
Missionary, his mistakes, 104 et seq. Ignorance of local customs, beliefs, worship, etc., 105.

NAT

Monasteries, Roman Catholic, in Africa, have crumbled to dust, 239.
Mpredwi, 57.
Mulattoes, included in "natives," 202. If able to trace a clear descent through or from a pure native *materfamilias*, 202.
Municipal government, 109. Each township has Sanitary Board arrangements for public works, and other necessary provisions for local government, 109. Supervised by headman, 110.
Municipalities, to be established, 366.
Murder, punished by death, 29.

NATGLASS, Governor, 185. Represented Netherlands Government, 185.
Native, the, consent and co-operation necessary for progress and development in right direction, 222. His confidence in Bench and Bar, 221. Of Gold Coast, may have been immigrant from Timbuctoo, 325.
Native Community, is a composite whole, 32. Each has form and method of government the same in all essentials, 33.
Native Courts, full powers and authority of, always been fully recognised by Great Britain, 274—280. Recognised and provided for, by draft proclamation, 365.
Native Jurisdiction Bill, 320.
Native Jurisdiction Ordinance, 166. Making it possible for British authorities to remove a native

INDEX. 413

sovereign from his stool, cited and explained, 209 et seq.
Native prisons to be supervised, 365.
Native State—found where many communities combine and own allegiance to paramount authority, 19. Federated under same laws, customs, faith and worship, and language, 19. Disorganised by British aggression, 27. Its system summarised, 250 et seq. Principal states of Gold Coast enumerated, together with their kings, 397.
Nephew, succession of king's nephew gradually became an institution, 39.
Netherlands, King of, 154.
Nineteenth Century Magazine referred to, 4.

O DUM, the, 238.

Offerings of food and drink to departed spirits, 102.
Office, of Governor, 315. Of Commander-in-chief, 315; constituted by letters patent, 315.
Official Correspondence, 345 et seq. Lord Stanley to Lieut.-Governor Hill on Assessors' Jurisdiction, 348 et seq. Earl of Carnarvon to Governor Strahan on Great Britain's power and jurisdiction in Gold Coast, 354 et seq. Aborigines' Rights Protection Society to the Governor, 382 et seq. The Governor to Aborigines, etc., Society, 388. The Society to the Governor, 389 et seq. The Governor to the Society, 394. The Society to the Governor, 395. The Governor to the Society, 396.

Offin River, 39.
Ohin = the king, 32. = Head of any considerable community of aborigines, 32.
Okra Kwa, King of Mankessim, 23, 397.
Oppon, became surety, 208. Refused to meet award, 208. Arrested by King of Akumfie, 208. Sued king for damages, succeeded, 208. Lost upon appeal to full court, 209. Referred to, 273.
Oppon v. Ackinie cited, 208.
Option, 298. Granted to Bridges, 298. Assignment of, 300. Priority of, 300, 301, 304. Registration of, 301. Lease higher than, 301.
Ord, Colonel, 139, 146, 149.
Ordeal, practised and described, 94. Consists of drinking *edum*, a herbal preparation, 94; practice of eating a handful of rice in other parts of West Africa, 94.
Order of Queen in Council, 1874, set forth, 345.
Ordinance: Supreme Court, 1876, 276; how to be construed, 276 et seq.; does not say that jurisdiction other than Her Majesty's is to cease, 277; on contrary, implies jurisdiction of native kings, etc., to be co-existent, 277; has in no way impaired the judicial powers of native kings, etc., 280. Compulsory Labour, 1895...281, 283, 286, 320; case stated under, 281; effect and construction of explained, 283 et seq., 287 et seq. Criminal Procedure, 1876, referred to, 283. Emancipation, 81; recognises jurisdiction of kings and chiefs in judicial rites, 94; and

treats native tribunals as existing, 276. Native Jurisdiction Ordinance—cited, 166; and explained, 209; made it possible for British authorities to remove native sovereigns from their stools, 166. Assessors, 165, 166. Public Lands, 1876...383. Towns (Amendment), 1901...383; introduces principle of vesting lands of the country in the Crown, 387. Poll Tax, 160, 163. Local Native Courts, 277. " To facilitate and regulate exercise of powers, etc., by native authorities," 1878...278.

Osai Tutu I., 155.

Osoo Ansah, 27, 243. Father of Prince John Osoo Ansah, and Prince Albert Osoo Ansah, 27.

Otchafoo, David, charged with bribery, 274.

" Owl " column in *Western Echo*, 176.

"PALAVER " = a suit before the court in which king and councillors sit, 93. Described, 93 *et seq*. Record of, 380. Some chiefs and people assembled at, *apparently* acknowledge lands in Cape Coast belong to the Queen, 381.

Panins, or Elders, = heads of the families, 251.

Panyarring to be abolished, 365.

Paramountcy of king, 46. Distinguished from ownership, 47—62.

Paramount Kings of Gold Coast. names and states of, enumerated, 397.

Par hi, 42.

Pawns, 81. = A human pledge as security for an advance, 83. Proviso for redemption, 83. Disgrace of not redeeming, 83. Uncle pledged nephew, 83. Generally to persons well known, 83. Pledgee trained the pawn, 83.

People, the, take interest in politics, 79. Mothers educate their sons in traditional history, 79. Their characteristics, 80.

Peregwans, 28.

Peynins, 147.

Physicians. *See* Royal Physicians.

Pike, Mr. Chas., 120.

Pine, Governor, 139, 146, 153. Refused to restore runaway slave boy, 153.

Plebiscite, how obtained, 254. Binding on all the people, 254.

Pogson, Mr. F., signed Bond, 1844, 368.

Police force, armed, to be organised for internal order, etc., 366.

Political ethics animadverted upon, 231 *et seq*.

Poll Tax Ordinance, 160. Imposition of, 163. Rapidly fell off, 163.

Poor Law, none in Gold Coast, 249.

Ports, French and German, 98.

Prah, river = natural boundary, 359.

Prempeh, King, 265. His degradation, 265.

Priests—work the spiritual system, 106. Cure disease, 106. Are good doctors, skilled in herb remedies, 106. Invest their practice with secrecy, 106. Training begins in early life, 107. Sent to seminary

INDEX.   415

PRO

in another district, 107. Apprenticeship for three years, 107. Clever in dancing, 107. In frenzy of excitement the "fetish" comes upon them, 107. In time of war go forth with army, 107. Supposed to be bullet proof, 108. Give aid in dressing the wounded, 108.

Proclamation, draft of, 363. Defining nature and extent of Queen's jurisdiction on Gold Coast, 363.

Province, is the district of a head chief, 22. Consists of a number of towns and villages, 22. Constitution of, same as that of federal state, 22.

Protected Malay States analogous to Gold Coast, 323.

Protectorate, definitions of, 320. Rightful name for Gold Coast, 323. Of Lagos, 360.

Public Health, to be promoted with assent of natives, 366.

QUAMINA ANNOBIL, principal linguist of King of Lower Wassaw, 58.

Quamin Fori, 279. King of Aguapim, 279. His case cited, 209.

Quamina Imnuama opposed Chidda Concession, 289.

Quamina Mayan present at palaver, 380.

Quantamissa, Prince, 243.

Quashie Ankah signed Bond, 1844, 368.

Quashie Ottoo signed Bond 1844, 368.

Quasie Ankuma opposed Chidda Concession, 289.

SAL

RAPE punished by death, 29.

Railways, doubtful whether they affect the position of native trade, 98.

Regina v. *Kudjoe Imbra*, 281.

Religion, Governor to promote, 170.

Rents, importance of paying, in respect of, and before applying for, concession, 297. Kinds of—retaining, 309 ; working, 309.

Revenue to be raised by licences and customs, with assent of native rulers, etc., 366.

Rice, eaten in trial by ordeal, 94.

Rights, of aborigines, inalienable, 320. Customary, 307.

Roads, width of, to be fifteen feet, 186.

Robertson, Mr. Isaac, present at palaver, 380.

Rooke, Sir G., 314.

Royal African Company, 318.

Royal Butlers, captain of, 26.

Royal Farmers, captain of, 26.

Royal Huntsmen, captain of, 26.

Royal Physicians, captain of, 26.

SACOOM, Mr. S., President of Aborigines' Society, 388.

Sacrifice offered, 88.

Sacrifices, human, contrary to law 159.

"Sai" = "Osoo" = prince, 27.

Sai Bonso, son of King Kweku Dua, 27. Father of Osoo Ansah, 27.

Salmon, C. S., ex-Administrator of the Gold Coast, wrote "Crown Colonies of Great Britain," 118, 134, 155, 216, 230. Quoted, 2 *et passim*. Disapproved of Fanti Confederation, 189. Arrested its

SAL

members, 173. His inconsistent attitude criticised, 174.
Saltpond, 273.
Sam, Mr. W. E., 290.
Sarbah, Hon. John M., 121. Wrote "Fanti Customary Laws," quoted, 146, 165, 196, etc.
Sarfuhim = war chief, 64.
School, High, 81.
School-houses, to be erected, 186.
Scott, Sir Francis, expedition of, 26.
Seal, public, to be provided, 374.
Sekondi, lands at, 125 ; sale of, 382. Handed to Dutch, 154.
Sekondi and Tarkwa Company opposed Chidda Concession, 289.
Selborne, Lord, 171.
Selling real-born Ashanti punished by death, 30.
Service of notice, 282.
Settlement, definitions of, 313 *et seq.*
Settlements, British, comprise number of forts, enumerated and located, 135 *et seq.*
Settler, definition of, 312.
Sey, Mr. J. W., 171.
Shifting cultivation, 307. A customary right, 307.
Simpson, Governor, 185.
Slaves, 81. Masters of, humane, 82. Members of master's family, 82. Adopted by masters, 82. Sometimes named heir, 82. Never forgot position, 82. Trading in, to be abolished, 366.
Slavery, 362. Existence of, 362. Domestic, 366. Pawning, 366.
Smith, Mr. Justice Francis, 94, 209.
Smith, Mr. Justice Smallman, 94, 209.
Smiths, the, 95.

SUC

Society, Aborigines' Rights Protection, etc. *See* Gold Coast Aborigines, etc.
Spanish Succession War, 314.
"Solvent influence" of British Administration, is curtailing the freedom of the natives, 226.
Spirits, sale of, prohibited without licence, 163. Departed, 86. Libations offered to, 86.
St. Andrew's cross, 204.
Stanley, Lord, letter to Governor Hill, 315.
State, native. *See* Native State. Principal, or premier, 22. Federal takes rank in order of importance, 22.
Stead, Mr. W. T., 181.
Stealing, punished by death, 29.
Stool. *See also* Golden Stool. Sprinkled with sacred water, 88. Celebration described, 86. Bearers, captain of, 26. Procedure of destoolment, 34—36. Bringing together of stools at a "palaver," 37. Represents an ancient house in the community, 37. Lands attached to, 44. Whether a subject chief can rid himself of allegiance to a superior stool, 53, 54. Is sacred, 259.
Stormonth's English Dictionary quoted, 312.
Straits Settlements, comprise Singapore, Penang, Province of Wellesley, the Dindings, Malacca, Malay, etc., 322 *et seq.*
Stream, sacred, 88. Waters of, sprinkled on stools, 88.
Subir, Chief of Inkidoms, 28.
Succession, to kingly office, 40 ; sought through female line, 40. To land, 47, 48.

Surety, custom of finding in certain suits, 274.
Swanzy, Messrs., 290. Estate and Company, 290.
Swearing an oath on king's life punished by death, 29.
Swordbearers, captain of, 26.
System of administration, at fault, 193. How to be righted, 193.

TACKIE, King of Accra, 113, 316.
Takieman, immigrants from, 241, 325.
Tarkwa, where Chidda lease signed, 291.
Tarkwa and Sekondi Company opposed Chidda Concession, 289.
Tavievies, small tribe in Krepi district, 177. Atrocities upon, 177.
Tax, poll, 160. Right to, never been acquired by British Government, 164. Right to, can only be by consent and co-operation of the people, 164. Query, whether native authority to be allowed to levy, = crux of contention between "confederators" and local administration, 189.
Technical instruction, 187. To be given in schools, 187.
Territory, British, whether forts are, 147. Protected, 275.
Thompson, Mr. J. R., present at palaver, 380.
Timber, rights as to, in connection with mining, 307.
Timbuctoo, immigrants from, 325.
Times newspaper quoted, 12, 13, 264.

G.C.

Tolstoy, Count, quoted, 18.
Trade encouraged by state system of Ashanti, 96. King took active part in promotion of, 96. Disorganised by British diplomacy and aggrandisement, 98. Primary object of Great Britain in settling in the country, 145.
Traditions, natives carefully preserve and hand down, 195.
Transportation of convicts, 351. Not without special instructions of Secretary of State, 351.
Treason, transferring allegiance from one chief, prince, or king to another is, 54.
Treaty, relations between Great Britain and Gold Coast, 163.
Treaty of Utrecht, 314.
Tribute, payment of, made to a superior chief, 47. Payable to the licensor of land, 47. Distinguished from "allegiance fee," 49. An incident of ownership, 49.
Tuafus, referred to, 87.
Tufu Hin = captain-general of forces, 43. An officer of the king, 43. Exercises judicial functions, 65. Next in rank to the king, 65. Holds regular courts, 65. Receives court fees and fines, 65. Hears appeals from minor chief's court, 65. Head of military system of the community, 65. Regulates the seven companies of the community, 65. Present at annual general drill, 65. Leads van of army in time of war, 65. Is *ex officio* principal civil councillor of the king, 66.
Tutim Gackidi, King of Denkara, 155.

INDEX.

USSHER, Governor, 184, 191.
Utrecht, Treaty of, 314.

VASSAL, obligation of, to render allegiance fee, 51.
Victoriaburg, 268.
Villars, a native king's secretary, 292.
Vines, Mr. S. M., secretary to Governor, 389.
Volta, river, 239, 359.

WARD : every adult = member of ward, 85. Ward constitutes a company, 85.
Wassaw, Eastern, or Lower : Kwamina Enimil = King of, 25, 397. Native state of Gold Coast, 21, 397.
Wassaw, Upper, native state of Gold Coast, 397. King of, = Kwesi Wereku, 397.
Webster's International Dictionary quoted, 313, 320.
Werempims = councillors, 41. Right of selecting king, 41.
West Africa quoted, 125, 203.
Western Akim, native state of Gold Coast, 397. King of, = Kofi Ahinkura, 397.
Western Echo, 176. Edited by Prince Brew, 176.
West African Herald, 175. Edited by C. Bannerman, 175.
Willcocks, Sir James, expedition of, 24.
Wines, sale of, prohibited, without licence, 163.
Wingfield, Mr., 171.
Women, as mothers, teach children traditions and customs of the district, etc., 77. Dance before king at " stool celebrations," 89. Propitiate the gods in time of war, 92 ; and act as commissariat department to their own company, 92. Chant war-songs, 92. Are bedaubed with white clay and dressed in white calico in time of war, singing dirges, 92. Sweep out whole ward in townships, 110. Brush up and burn all waste vegetable matter, 110.
Wolseley, Lord, 141. At Prahsue, 141, 172.
" *Wontsey, wontsey* " = " hear hear," 94.

YAM, its festival, 85, 238.